TRADITIONAL RELIGION AND GUERRILLA WARFARE IN MODERN AFRICA

Traditional Religion and Guerrilla Warfare in Modern Africa

Stephen L. Weigert
Bureau of Intelligence and Research, Department of State
Washington, D. C.

First published in Great Britain 1996 by
MACMILLAN PRESS LTD
Houndmills, Basingstoke, Hampshire RG21 6XS
and London
Companies and representatives
throughout the world

A catalogue record for this book is available
from the British Library.

ISBN 0–333–63798–4

First published in the United States of America 1996 by
ST. MARTIN'S PRESS, INC.,
Scholarly and Reference Division,
175 Fifth Avenue,
New York, N.Y. 10010

ISBN 0–312–12715–4

Library of Congress Cataloging-in-Publication Data
Weigert, Stephen L.
Traditional religion and guerrilla warfare in modern Africa /
Stephen L. Weigert.
p. cm.
Includes bibliographical references and index.
ISBN 0–312–12715–4 (cloth)
1. Africa, Sub-Saharan—Religion. 2. Africa, Sub-Saharan–
-History—20th century. 3. Guerrilla warfare. Africa, Sub
-Saharan—History, Military—Religious aspects. I. Title.
BR1430.W45 1996
960.3'2—dc20   95–20245
                                                    CIP

© Stephen L. Weigert 1996

10 9 8 7 6 5 4 3 2 1
05 04 03 02 01 00 99 98 97 96

Printed in Great Britain by
Ipswich Book Co Ltd, Ipswich, Suffolk

For my wife, Susan

What is not possible is to have many friends whom we love for their own sake and for their goodness. Enough if we have even a few of that quality.

Aristotle, *Nichomachean Ethics* (IX:10:19–20)

Contents

Acknowledgments   ix

1   Introduction   1

2   Madagascar: The 1947–48 Rebellion   9

3   Kenya: The Mau Mau Insurgency (1952–60)   22

4   Cameroon: The UPC Insurrection (1956–70)   36

5   Congo/Zaire: The Kwilu Rebellion (1963–68)   49

6   Mozambique: From the NRM to Renamo (1977–92)   67

7   Conclusion   96

Notes   107

Bibliography   138

Index   147

Acknowledgments

Many old and new friends made it possible to bring the seed of a six year old idea to fruition. Barry Schutz read a very rough-hewn draft and directed me to literature which provided a more stable foundation on which to build this analytic undertaking. Thomas Ofcansky patiently and painstakingly read through several additional drafts, generously sharing his knowledge of Kenyan history as well as providing many helpful suggestions throughout the text. Roger Glickson carefully screened a penultimate draft and brought my attention to factual as well as analytic finepoints in need of further elaboration or modification. John Peterson reviewed a final draft with his usual eye for detail and precision.

Martin Lowenkopf and Professors Chester Crocker, Rom Harré, Richard Sklar read early drafts of this study and offered valuable constructive criticism and insight. Professor Colin Newbury provided critical advice regarding the world of academic publications.

I am also grateful for the assistance offered by John Berntsen, Gary Bohl, William Eaton, Joseph Fenrick, Professor John Marcum, Nancy McCabe, Craig McKee, and Don Zimmer for sharing books and articles from their personal collections or directing my attention to literature I would otherwise not have found. finally, a word of gratitude is due to my wife Susan whose response to far greater challenges as well as constant support inspired and encouraged me to continue this project at times when it was tempting to abandon it altogether.

'Africa is not just about power. Africa is about culture and traditional values before colonialism set in.'

UNITA General Altino Bango Sapalalo
Huambo, Angola, 8 July 1994

1 Introduction

Wars fought for religious purposes often are characterized by apparently irrational and impractical behavior. Combatants frequently make an emotional and fanatic commitment to using violent means for the achievement of sacred ends. With the exception of the Middle East, theologically inspired struggles generally are considered a phenomenon of greater interest to historians than to analysts of current political and military affairs. Crusades or Holy Wars have not typically been associated with contemporary sub-Saharan Africa. Imperialism, colonialism and competing secular ideologies associated with the Cold War usually were more pertinent reference points during the past fifty years of African history. The post-World War II transition from colony to independent nation-state presumably represented a commitment to a secular, rational-legal, form of government. Many analysts expected this phase to foster an even further break with the political, religious and cultural traditions of Africa's pre-colonial past. In many respects, however, the volatile character of sub-Saharan Africa's relatively young nation-states has occasionally reflected the extent to which pre-colonial African religious perspectives remain a vital influence in military and political affairs.

The end of the Cold War era of competing secular ideologies promised to shift the focus of competition in Africa and elsewhere in the world to a peaceful debate over more enduring philosophical and moral issues. The persistent impact of traditional religious views on domestic and foreign affairs in many areas of the world underscores the fact that the 'age of ideology' has not yet ended. 'Church and State' have not been thoroughly or conclusively separated and the relationship between 'magic' and science is still a subject of lively debate. In the context of contemporary sub-Saharan African nationalism, this debate has endured in the polling place as well as on the battlefield.

Although contemporary governments in sub-Saharan Africa may have taken on the political and military form of modern nation-states, the history of the last few decades makes it abundantly clear that many have yet to acquire either the financial or military substance necessary to resist a determined insurgent challenge. Armed dissident forces continue to represent a potentially serious threat to many governments. A reassessment of recent African history suggests that successful insurgencies can be inspired by a wider ideological spectrum than that which seemed relevant during the apex of the Cold War. A revisionist interpretation of guerrilla

1

warfare in various corners of Africa supports the view that insurgents motivated by traditional religious or revivalist ideals represented a force whose prospects for military success frequently were underestimated. Some of the most skeptical analysts were those who insisted that only 'progressive' or 'revolutionary' ideologies guaranteed true liberation, independence and the ability to wage an effective military campaign.

The prognosis for insurgent challenges to independent African governments has shifted considerably in the past twenty years. In the early 1970s, many observers expected effective, rurally based guerrilla warfare to occur with increasing frequency throughout sub-Saharan Africa. Ten years later, the prospects for such insurgencies were considered bleak. This changing outlook, in part, reflected an assumption about the comparative vulnerability of independent African governments and earlier colonial administrations. Those who had sought to oust colonial rulers presumably found it easier to create a nationwide coalition on which to base an insurgency. Moreover, in the aftermath of independence, many African governments had made explicit or tacit arrangements with the former colonial power which assured them of support against internal military threats. Indeed, by the late 1970s, *coups d'état* led by disgruntled military officers appeared to be a much greater threat to the status quo in sub-Saharan Africa than insurgencies.[1] More importantly, however, contemporary skepticism about rural rebellions has often been based on what are seen as insurmountable sociological and ideological weaknesses. Twenty years ago, those who had anticipated more frequent outbursts of guerrilla warfare in Africa believed that such campaigns would fail if they did not mobilize support from among urban dwellers and intellectuals. Without such broad support, the causes which peasant insurgents espoused, such as land reform, would not draw enough dissidents to their ranks to pose a serious threat to the government. A related view held that peasant leaders were not sophisticated enough to couch their political aspirations in terms that would elicit support in larger cities or gain the sympathy of other countries. Furthermore, in the African context, rural insurgents often have had to face ethno-linguistic constraints as well as geographic and demographic barriers to the organization of a larger insurgency.

Narrowly defined political views, or what some observers regard as antiquated religious beliefs, were frequently seen as evidence of the limitations of a primarily rural insurgency. The familiar example of guerrillas who expected ointments and/or rituals to make them bulletproof is one of the most glaring manifestations of such a world view. An even more critical flaw than a reliance on potions to become bulletproof is the reactionary or revivalist political program which characterized some agrarian rebellions and presumably condemned them to inevitable defeat. Although they varied from country to country, these programs usually called for the restoration of traditional tribal and religious leaders or social and cultural values and institutions.

Historians of guerrilla war in modern and post-colonial Africa generally have shared a skeptical view of the prospects for insurgencies whose leadership was largely rural or whose political program was essentially reactionary.[2] In the latter years of the colonial era, the Mau Mau uprising in Kenya usually is regarded as a prime example of such an insurgency. The 1947 rebellion in Madagascar also seems to be a relevant, if less well known, case. In post-colonial Africa, the failure of the 1964 Kwilu rebellion in the Congo/Zaire is often attributed to its predominantly rural base and its excessive reliance on a magico-religious world view. It is also readily apparent, however, that in each of these uprisings, rurally based radicals were already far more influential and decisive than Westernized urban leaders. The former often took the lead in formulating demands for change in the existing order and in determining the strategy and tactics pursued by guerrilla forces when the insurgency finally started. The characterization of these uprisings as reactionary or revivalist is also one that overly simplifies what is more accurately described as an unstable blend of contemporary and traditional outlooks.

The role of military veterans is an interesting sub-theme that appears in each of these rebellions. African conscripts who served in metropolitan armies during World War II, or later fought for conventionally trained government forces, often transformed what might have been little more than short-lived riots into organized insurgencies. While the rebellions in Madagascar, Kenya, and Congo/Zaire may have sought the restoration of traditional values and institutions, their participants were not so naive or anarchistic as to call for the dissolution of contemporary structures such as the nation-state, much less the organizational principles necessary for the functioning of large armed forces.

The uprising which spanned the last years of colonialism and the first years of independence in Cameroon provides a useful analytic counterpoint to the questionable conclusions that historians have drawn from the defeat of guerrillas in Madagascar, Kenya, and the Congo. In Cameroon, a war against a colonial power, led by educated urban elites and a Marxist-Leninist inspired ideology, nonetheless failed miserably. Moreover, the availability of rear area bases in neighboring countries and military aid from sympathetic states outside Africa did not suffice to avert this failure. The leaders of the insurgency may, in fact, have crippled their cause fatally by an explicit arrogance in their attitude towards critical population groups in the countryside. The guerrilla defeat in Cameroon demonstrated that an undervaluation of peasants and their loyalty to traditional institutions could be equally as dangerous as an excessive dependence on such factors in planning and executing an insurgency.

By the mid-1960s, analysts of contemporary African politics and modern guerrilla warfare were nevertheless increasingly convinced that a successful insurgency had to be led by an urban, educated elite which espoused a progressive ideology. The failed rebellions in Madagascar, Kenya, and the Congo were regarded as examples of insurgencies whose shortcomings should be avoided. At best, they were seen as manifestations of primitive or underdeveloped nationalism, or at worst, atavistic xenophobia. Their rural leaders had spoken with the voices of a culture and a way of life which was on its way to extinction and could not delay the inevitable imposition of a European concept of the modern nation-state.

The certainty with which this view was held later merged with an equally assertive doctrine of guerrilla warfare as practiced by Mao Tsetung in China, Ho Chi Minh in Vietnam, and Ben Bella in Algeria. For the next fifteen years, the idea of guerrilla war was almost automatically linked with terms such as 'liberation', 'progressive', 'socialist', Marxist-Leninist, and others indicating sympathy and support from China, Russia, and states in the former Soviet bloc. In the early 1980s, however, incumbent governments in Nicaragua, Afghanistan, and Angola described insurgent opponents as 'bandits', 'reactionaries', and 'terrorists'. These and a host of other terms were intended to denigrate their leaders and demoralize their supporters. Those who sympathized with their struggles referred to the members of these movements as 'freedom fighters', 'anti-Communists' and 'would-be democrats'. In general, however, such labels often reflected political motives rather than a considered, dispassionate, analytic assessment of the aims pursued by the insurgents and their military capability.

Similar semantic traps also entangled those who sought to understand the nature of Mozambique's transition from a five hundred year history as a Portuguese colony to that of a newly established nation-state. In the late 1970s, independent Mozambique began to experience a growing number of hit-and-run attacks along its border with white-ruled Rhodesia. These raids were viewed as the latest efforts of an embattled white-settler regime in Southern Africa to use covert operations to destabilize a hostile neighbor. An examination of the fifteen-year war waged by what eventually became known as the National Resistance of Mozambique (Renamo), however, indicates that this insurgency has more in common with the uprisings in Madagascar, Kenya, and Congo/Zaire than with any of the numerous guerrilla wars waged throughout Southern Africa during the past three decades.

While many recent assessments of Renamo differentiate it from other Southern African insurgencies, they generally have based this distinction on assertions that its members were essentially a mercenary force operating, initially, at the behest of the white-ruled Rhodesian army and, subsequently, the South African Defense Force (SADF). A related characterization of Renamo portrayed it as a criminal phenomenon comprised of loosely aligned rural bandits whose leadership exercised, at best, a limited degree of command and control over far-flung members. Although there are factual bases for these characterizations, they distort or minimize significant historical considerations which must be addressed to account for Renamo's persistence and politico-military success.

A brief review of the Malgache, Kenyan, and Congolese insurgencies readily illustrates the kind of politico-military tradition which has survived in contemporary Mozambique. This historical foundation also supports a more extensive discussion of Renamo, highlighting features which distinguish it from its predecessors. Two of the most salient factors are the extent of external support provided to Renamo and the degree to which the ruling Front for the Liberation of Mozambique (Frelimo) government had failed to consolidate its own control over the countryside. These two variables were probably far more decisive than sociological or ideological issues in accounting for the persistence and impact of the war on Mozambique. Indeed, they must be considered necessary, if not sufficient, conditions for a successful guerrilla war, regardless of its sociological foundation or ideological orientation. Conversely, it can readily be shown that a lack of outside support and the overwhelmingly favorable military advantage enjoyed by their government opponents were the most crucial factors in determining the outcome of the wars in Madagascar, Kenya, and Congo.

A lack of outside support and safe havens in neighboring countries deprived Malgache, Kenyan, and Congolese insurgents of more than arms and ammunition. All three guerrilla forces lost a critical amount of time necessary to develop a political infrastucture because they could not prevent government forces from rapidly regaining tactical political and military initiatives. Consequently the insurgents were unable to consolidate the rapid military gains they made in the initial months of their campaigns. The forerunners of the Renamo war all began their struggles with poorly developed political networks. Mass arrests of their leaders by the colonial or incumbent government crippled the insurgents' administrative support systems as well as blunting the elaboration and articulation of an ideology and political program. As a result, the guerrillas were forced to rely on supporters galvanized by their opposition to government institutions and authorities. They opposed the status quo but they did not propose a fully developed alternative. A concomitant emphasis on traditional religious beliefs and institutions has therefore been viewed by skeptics as nothing more than a pragmatic and simplistic effort to legitimize insurgent movements which had failed to design a modern alternative to the regimes they sought to replace. Analysts who questioned Renamo's claim to represent traditional religious values were convinced that this assertion was nothing more than a callous attempt to manipulate and exploit an inchoate mood of dissatisfaction. Government supporters argue that this dissent eventually would have been dampened by a government program of gradual political and economic reforms if Renamo and its foreign supporters had not exacerbated an already fragile social and economic system.

Like their Malgache, Kenyan, and Congolese forerunners, Renamo members also were accused of hiding their pursuit of narrow ethnic or regional interests behind the mask of a commitment to an allegedly nation-wide 'tradition'. There were undoubtedly manipulative as well as parochial features in all four insurgencies. Guerrilla campaigns inspired by Marxism-Leninism or other secular ideologies appear to have been equally as prone to such distorting influences. An appreciation of these factors may help to determine whether a guerrilla movement 'emphasized' or was 'inspired' by a particular ideology. This kind of understanding can help an analyst anticipate the extent to which a particular political theory might have been put into practice if an insurgency had been militarily successful. Renamo and its predecessors appear to have emphasized religious values and revivalist aims rather than insisting on a fanatic restoration of local tradition. A study of the manner in which they combined a traditional world view and modern principles of warfare provides a basis for an alternative interpretation of recent African military and political history.

There are several conclusions to be drawn from an analysis of the Renamo insurgency which places it on a historical continuum reaching back at least as far as the late 1940s. In some respects, the course of the war in Mozambique, and the debate that it engendered in academic as well as policy-making circles, revealed an interesting metamorphosis of the concept of 'nationalism' and its place in explanations of contemporary African politics. Nearly forty years ago, in his seminal book on the subject of modern African nationalism, Thomas Hodgkin highlighted the role of movements led by 'prophets and priests' in colonial Africa. Hodgkin acknowledged that '... these movements represent a relatively primitive phase in the development of nationalism, in which political and social reconstruction is envisaged as a new world order, and rejection of European authority is expressed through the characteristic forms of "enthusiasm". But at least the prophets have awakened men's minds to the fact that change can occur and the ablest of them, like their European prototypes, have shown themselves wholly capable of constructing a myth, a literature and an organization.'[3]

The idea that 'priests and prophets' could contribute to African struggles for independence and the emergence of modern nation-states gradually fell out of favor. Thirteen years after Hodgkin's assessment, Gerard Chaliand discussed the 'Objective Conditions of the Armed Struggle' facing guerrillas in Africa and concluded it was '… necessary that political work directed toward breaking down magico-religious superstructures be carried out with the greatest tact and delicacy. If this job is well done, the people's war of liberation can by its very development reduce the hold of magico-religious beliefs. On the other hand, if sufficient attention is not paid to these beliefs, they may become a considerable hindrance to the organization of the struggle.'[4] Chaliand's conclusions concerning the necessary suppression of traditional religious belief in the service of secular nationalism was elaborated on by Basil Davidson in 1978. Davidson suggested that 'progressive' African nationalist movements which had conducted a 'dual revolution' against colonial rule and 'traditional strictures which can no longer serve them' had taken a critical step forward into the 'politics of liberation'.[5]

With the enunciation of a theoretical perspective which gradually gained wider acceptance among African political and military leaders, European notions of a secular nation-state and Maoist-Leninist precepts of 'revolutionary' guerrilla warfare had achieved the apex of their influence in modern Africa. 'Prophets and priests' of traditional religion were considered irrelevant to the evolution of African nation-states and the struggle against racist and colonial bastions which still dominated Southern Africa in the 1970s. The ideological revolution of the past decade, however, has revealed that the 'false gods' of pre-colonial Africa, which were so easily denounced two decades ago, have proven to be more durable than the idols of Marx, Mao, and Lenin. The Renamo insurgency is merely the latest in a series of uprisings which underscores the fact that rural civilians can still be mobilized to support rebellion across a much larger ideological spectrum. Moreover, such rebellions can successfully implement the principles of modern guerrilla warfare espoused by strategists such as Mao and Ho Chi Minh without necessarily adopting a Marxist or other secular ideology.

Despite the political leanings often associated with this twentieth century military heritage, the application of the principles and related tactics of modern guerrilla warfare is ideologically neutral. These principles may as readily be used by 'reactionaries' as they have been by 'revolutionaries'. Such an assertion seems almost a truism in light of similarly successful insurgencies elsewhere in the world such as the war waged by Afghanistan's *mujahedin* against the former Soviet Union. In the context of the past twenty years of African history, however, most observers had concluded that Mao Tse-tung's guerrilla 'fish' could only swim in civilian 'waters' whose ideological currents had been inspired by the thoughts of Marx and Lenin.

The idea that peasants might fight for their own, locally determined, political and religious values, while still serving a larger nationalist cause was considered hopelessly outdated by the early 1970s. As far as most historians were concerned, the inevitable failure of such rebellions had been foreshadowed in numerous contexts ranging from the Vendée in eighteenth century France to the Boxer Rebellion in turn of the century China. By 1980, the idea of a successful 'conservative' or 'revivalist' guerrilla war was almost unthinkable.

A reassessment of the Renamo insurgency and previous insurgencies which emphasized traditional religious and cultural themes suggests a persistent willingness on the part of those who cherish such values to 'think the unthinkable' and fight for it. Military victory may not ensure that these movements will survive the transition from war to peace. Nevertheless, their influence and the ideas which inspired them evidently represent a vital and vibrant tradition which continues to shape the character of modern African nationalism and the manner in which guerrilla war is waged. While contemporary African governments are determined to adopt the form of the Western nation-state, it appears that traditional African religion and cosmology will continue to play a lasting role in shaping its political and military substance.

2 Madagascar: The 1947–48 Rebellion

The 1947 Malgache uprising is often described as the first genuine nationalist insurgency in post-World War II African history. This characterization usually stems from an assumption that the Democratic Movement for the Malagasy Renovation (MDRM), was solely responsible for persuading its adherents to use force to gain the island's independence. The MDRM was an organization whose structure resembled that of many modern political parties which were gradually emerging throughout sub-Saharan Africa in the 1940s. Many Malgaches who made the transition from party member to guerrilla in early 1947 did in fact proclaim their loyalty to the MDRM. Nonetheless, comprehensive studies of the uprising make it amply clear that two underground movements, which had been in existence for several years prior to the outbreak of the rebellion, played far more decisive roles in providing leadership to the insurgency and shaping its ideological dimensions. Moreover, the island's pre-colonial religious and political traditions proved to be a powerful source of inspiration for a rebellion whose reliance on 'sorcery' was as surprising as its early military success.

LOOKING TO THE FUTURE, RECALLING THE PAST

The MDRM was established on 22 February 1946 and several of its founding members and initial leaders were drawn from an intellectual, generally urban-based, elite. Within a year the party was reported to have as many as 300 000 members.[1] Many of the MDRM's earliest and most ardent supporters, however, already had participated in two clandestine organizations – the Parti Nationaliste Malgache (Panama), secretly created in 1941, and the Jeunesse Nationaliste Malgache (Jina) established in 1943. Both organizations opposed the colonial regime which had chosen to ally itself with the Vichy government of Nazi-occupied France.[2]

In the aftermath of the British invasion and liberation of Madagascar in late 1942, the island's administration was turned over to the Free French forces under General Charles de Gaulle. During the next two years, Jina successfully enlarged its membership in the southern reaches of the island.

9

Panama likewise gained additional supporters in the north. Both movements sought to revive nationalist, pro-independence sentiments that had flourished briefly in the late 1920s. In 1946 the two parties merged, having already mobilized a sizeable number of Malgaches, many of whom subsequently joined the MDRM a year later.[3]

At its most fundamental level, the MDRM easily could be considered what one author has called a pan-Malagasy nationalist movement. The party's primary goal was to end French colonial rule and obtain the island's independence.[4] However, the party also fostered the creation of a network of rural cooperatives, employment bureaus, and centers for technical and social assistance to its members. In some instances, businesses run by French settlers sought out local MDRM leaders to help them formulate labor contracts with farmers and mine workers.[5]

These progressive programs were supplemented by several equally important and emotionally held views which reflected the vibrant influence of traditional Malgache values and beliefs. Many of these principles ultimately motivated the MDRM's rank and file members in a much more immediate sense than notions of a modern nation-state. The movement's cause was widely regarded as a struggle to restore what had been lost in 1896 when France abolished the Malgache monarchy and added the island-nation to its colonial holdings.[6] Unlike most African colonies, Madagascar already had a history of previous independence as a sovereign nation. The restoration of religious and cultural values, suppressed by the imposition of fifty years of French colonialism and an even longer presence of Christian missionaries, reappeared as a compelling motivation for those who had grown increasingly impatient to regain the island's independence. Many MDRM members who anticipated Madagascar's future as an independent country also yearned for the revival of a national past free of French culture and Western religious teachings.

RESTLESS REFORMERS, CONSPIRING RADICALS

While the MDRM temporarily combined progressive and traditional perspectives in its political platform, the organization's leadership ultimately enjoyed much less success in creating a consensus regarding the proper strategy and tactics to pursue toward France. Joseph Raseta, Jacques Rabemanenjara and Joseph Ravoahangy, founding members of the MDRM, were also elected as Malgache representatives to the National Assembly of the Fourth French Republic. Shortly after their arrival in Paris in 1946, the three Malgache parliamentarians introduced a bill calling for the island's independence. Although the proposal had the sympathy of some French legislators, it soon became apparent that this support would not be sufficient to convince a majority of representatives. As the parliamentary debate dragged on, splits in the ranks of the MDRM's leadership soon fostered a polarizing process which eventually pitted urban intellectuals against rurally based, and more traditionally oriented, mid-level leaders as well as rank and file members.

In mid-1946 the urban, intellectual elites represented by Raseta, Rabemananjara, and Ravoahangy, who had established the MDRM, still anticipated an eventual legal breakthrough in Paris. All three of the MDRM's principal leaders had socio-economic backgrounds which predisposed them to a non-violent approach to changing the colonial status quo. Joseph Raseta's father had been a high-ranking official under the Merina monarchy in the years immediately prior to the French annexation of the island in 1896. Raseta received a university education and subsequently trained to become a doctor. Joseph Ravoahangy was born in 1893, to parents who were members of the uppermost levels of the Merina aristocracy. His father was a landowner. After interrupting his studies to engage in political activities, Ravoahangy completed his medical degree in 1923. Jacques Rabemananjara, Secretary General of the MDRM, was the son of a land-owning member of the Merina aristocracy. His mother was a Betsimisaraka, and the daughter of one of that tribes' most prominent families. After an education in several seminaries, Rabemananjara became a functionary in the French colonial administration and later became active in a union of Malgache bureaucrats. He eventually received French citizenship and subsequently pursued literary studies at the Sorbonne.[7] Their backgrounds clearly did not preclude the MDRM's founding leaders from espousing a revolutionary path. Nevertheless their previous commitment to work within the prevailing French political system and their apparent interest in simply replacing those who directed the administrative infrastructure rather than overturning the entire colonial establishment made it difficult for men like Raseta and his colleagues to opt for a radical approach.

In the regional centers established by the MDRM, however, local leaders were already making contingency plans for a violent campaign against French colonial rule. Large demonstrations were organized in Tananarive and elsewhere on the island where participants called for immediate independence, resulting in the arrest of numerous mid-level MDRM leaders. Provocations by French settlers and the arbitrary arrest of MDRM members by conservative colonial authorities exacerbated an increasingly tense political climate. French support for the establishment of a conservative opposition movement, the Parti des Désherités de Madagascar (Party of the Disinherited or PADESM) was widely viewed as an effort to undermine the MDRM by dividing Malgache nationalists along traditional fault lines separating *côtiers* (coastal residents) from highlanders who lived on the island's central plateau.[8]

As the demonstrations and protest marches grew, the MDRM's urban elite felt compelled to denounce these outbursts as the expression of a xenophobic and racist nationalist minority, especially as they occasionally included denunciations of French culture as well as French colonialism. By early 1947, it was increasingly apparent that rural radical elements of the MDRM were preparing to launch an uprising. This placed the MDRM's parliamentarians and other urban leaders in an even more difficult position. In the weeks before the first shot was fired, the MDRM's urban elite repeatedly issued statements denouncing the trend toward violence.

Nonetheless, it has been suggested that Raseta and his colleagues may secretly have hoped that the threat of violence would compel France to act more expeditiously on their proposal to the French parliament for Malgache independence.[9] On 27 March 1947 the three parliamentarians sent a telegram to all regional MDRM branches urging local leaders to maintain calm in the face of provocations by the colonial regime. This appeal failed to delay a plan of action whose commencement was only days away.

SPONTANEOUS COMBUSTION AND NEW LEADERSHIP

On 29 March 1947 a series of well-organized attacks occurred across a wide area of the island. Several large towns were assaulted. Probably the largest initial engagement involved an attack by an estimated 2000 insurgents, armed mainly with spears and 'slashing hooks', against a French garrison at Moromanga, 100 miles east of Tananarive. The attack succeeded and the insurgents seized a substantial amount of weapons. Several small towns in the vicinity of Farafangana and Manakara were also overrun. A raid on a naval armory at Diego Suarez in the north failed and a planned assault on the capital by some 200–300 guerrillas was called off at the last minute because they mistakenly believed that French security forces had been forewarned and had therefore brought additional troops to Tananarive.[10] The insurgents soon dominated major portions of the island's east-central coast. Shortly thereafter, Tananarive was cut off from the coast, forcing the French to rely on an armored train on the rail line leading to Tamatave, the island's main port. The insurgents nevertheless managed to cut the line several times during the following months. In the early weeks of the rebellion, the insurgents' weapons were principally spears, axes and a paltry arsenal of shotguns. A modest amount of modern weapons were captured when some small French garrisons were occupied. A month after the uprising began, the rebels possessed only 27 rifles, 70 muskets, three machine guns, nine revolvers, one machine pistol, four anti-tank recoilless rifles, and an indeterminate, but probably limited, quantity of weapons that had been lost during the course of hostilities on the island in World War II.[11] Throughout the next 21 months of the uprising, the insurgent forces may have grown to some 15 000–20 000 armed members. An unknown number of the island's civilian population who sympathized with the guerrillas probably also served as part-time combatants.[12]

Within months after the start of the insurgency, it was clear that a rurally based leadership cadre had arisen to command the guerrilla forces. All three of the MDRM's parliamentary representatives had been arrested shortly after the first attacks and were incarcerated for the duration of the rebellion. Commanders such as Victorien Razafindrabe, Michel Radaoroson and Samuel Rakotondrabe, all of whom came from far more humble socio-economic origins and had links to Jina, quickly emerged as key figures in the rebellion. Razafindrabe was born to a Merina family whose members belonged to a servile caste on the lowest rung of the Merina social hierarchy in the waning years of the monarchy. After receiving a limited education, he abandoned a brief career as a provincial functionary in the colonial administration. Radaoroson was born into a peasant family of the Betsileo tribe and had only a very brief mission school education. Rakotondrabe, married and the father of six children when the insurrection began, was a manager in a tobacco processing plant.[13]

Radaoroson initially commanded central and southern zones in the insurgents' area of operations while Razafindrabe led combatants in the north. In mid-July 1947, following Rakotondrabe's capture and trial as the so-called 'Commander in Chief' of the insurgent forces, Razafindrabe assumed the title of 'Marshal of the Malgache Army'. The insurgents also created a command structure which included headquarters elements for a northern and southern sector as well as creating a position for an 'Inspector General'. There were also about ten secondary headquarters, each led by a 'president', 'vice-president', and assorted special branches such as 'civil-military affairs', 'logistics', 'justice', and 'gendarmerie'.[14]

VETERANS AND VISIONARIES

The insurgents' inclination to establish a fairly extensive politico-military structure reflected a variety of modern influences. While their reliance on mobility, hit-and-run tactics, remote bases, and other features may have been influenced by the tenets of modern guerrilla warfare, the impact of French military standards was probably much more pronounced on many of the senior and mid-level Malgache guerrilla commanders. Although the insurgents were drawn from a fairly diverse spectrum including members of Jina, Panama, port and rail workers, and local villages, probably some of the most influential figures were those Malgache *anciens combattants* (veterans) who had fought for the French Army in World War II. Between 1939 and 1945, about 15 000 Malgaches served as civilians (7000) or soldiers (8000) in France until 1940 and during subsequent campaigns in Africa, Italy, France, and Germany between 1942 and 1945. Of these, possibly as many as 1000 had also participated in the underground French resistance to Nazi occupation.[15]

Many of these veterans evidently thought they would return to Madagascar as liberators or at least as messengers of an imminent independence. Instead, after numerous delays during which they were sometimes used as manual laborers in French camps, government officials made what was probably an ill-timed decision to demobilize some 8000 veterans en masse on 7 August 1946, one day after the fiftieth anniversary of the French annexation of the island. A stagnant economy, widespread unemployment, and France's refusal to grant immediate independence to Madagascar eventually prompted many of these veterans to join the 1947 uprising.

Weeks after the rebellion began, an estimated 2000–5000 veterans reportedly rallied to the insurgents' cause. In a taunting communiqué mailed to French colonial officials in May 1947, an insurgent commander recalled that 'for us, soldiers of the great war, who acquired experience and modern technique ... and then, having done all the campaigns of Europe for five years ... and not forgetting the Maquis ... now we are Home, and we free our dear country which our ancestors and our illustrious king Andrianampoinimerina left to our safekeeping.'[16] The insurgents' subsequent preference for an extensive structure of rank, command and control, logistics, and other factors clearly reflected the perpetuation of a modern military organization undoubtedly influenced by the experience of French-trained veterans.

However, just as the MDRM's political platform initially melded a modern, progressive outlook with a worldview influenced by a longing to renew a link with the island's nineteenth century status as a sovereign nation, the insurgents' ideology, as well as their strategy and tactics, likewise reflected an occasionally problematic blend of modern and archaic methods. As one historian of the era noted, the cult of the ancestors became equated with patriotism for many Malgaches in the late 1940s. Moreover the 'politico-religious' vocabulary which had prevailed during the late nineteenth century monarchy reemerged in the insurgency's early phases. It was therefore no accident that the uprising started on 29 March, a day which marked the beginning of the ancestral year – during the month of Alahamady in the traditional calendar. Numerous insurgents favored a hymn, composed in the mid-nineteenth century, which emphasized traditional influences in its references to rituals of purification and communion.[17]

The historical inspiration of the rebellion also was reflected in the flag the insurgents chose. Their banner contained the red and white colors of the monarchy that had been deposed by the French in 1896, ending an uninterrupted reign of kings and queens chosen from the Merina tribe since the late eighteenth century. The insurgents of 1947 added 18 stars to their flag to represent the eighteen Malgache tribes. It has been suggested that the ideological inspiration of many Jina and Panama members who joined the MDRM harkened back to the *menalamba* (red shawl) revolt of 1895. The nineteenth-century insurgents had insisted that the French imposition of a protectorate over the Merina monarchy was a direct result of the royal family's adoption of Western cultural and religious values that had been introduced by French and British missionaries earlier in the century. The *menalamba*, so called because of the red shawls they wore, advocated a return to previous religious practice and the worship of the island's original gods and ancestors, as well as the expulsion of the French.[18]

The significance of the island's pre-colonial history also manifested itself in other features of the ideology which eventually inspired the 1947 rebellion. According to one of the guerrilla commanders, the insurgents sought independence in order, eventually, to rule by the methods of 'our ancestors'. The principal idea behind this aspiration was embodied in the *fokonolona* (village council) concept which can be traced back to at least the eighteenth century.[19] The institution of the *fokonolona* was the manifestation of what one historian has described as a decentralized communal ideology. In the days of the Merina monarchy, the *fokonolona* was based on the rural village as the key demographic unit. Serving as a form of local legislature, the *fokonolona* theoretically gave each of its members the same rights, regardless of age, gender, or economic status. All decisions were taken on the basis of unanimity. Representatives, chosen by the consent of all residents, played specific communal roles – military, religious, judicial, and others – in the name of the entire community. As part of a larger territorial unit, the *fanjakana*, the *fokonolona* collectively were seen as the source of pre-colonial Malgache sovereignty.[20]

The insurgents' commitment to ancestral political and social institutions was supplemented by a variety of traditional rituals and practices. Early participants in the uprising took an initiation oath which has been described as a 'quasi-religious' act requiring the initiate to swear allegiance before God and the ancestors. Their oath also included accompanying rituals involving the use of fetishes, holy water, sacred stones, and the invocation of the ancestors.[21] Captured documents revealed the insurgents' belief in 'sorcerers' who could turn bullets into water and other rituals which could magically trap or kill enemy troops.

Some guerrillas reportedly charged into battle shouting 'Rano! Rano!' (Water! Water!) expecting bullets fired at them to be turned into water. Insurgent members of the Manende tribe believed that the sacrifice of a bull, a black ram, and a red cock would persuade the deity Ratsimalah to cause their enemy to flee. Combatants from another tribe were confident that if they held up a particular idol in the direction of the enemy, the latter would be struck by lightning and made insane. As in the case of similar practices noted elsewhere in sub-Saharan Africa, the efficacy of these beliefs was dependent on the observation of a variety of dietary and other rituals. In order for their talismans to be effective, the insurgents were required to abstain from the consumption of certain kinds of fruits, meats, and vegetables. Some of the guerrillas wore amulets made of crocodile teeth mounted in silver or the tips of bull's horns decorated with woven patterns of glass beads and filled with various potions thought to provide some form of magical benefit to the wearer.[22] Many of these traits clearly reflected a religious perspective which dated back to at least the late nineteenth century and which achieved a certain degree of notoriety in the early twentieth century 'Maji Maji' rebellion in German East Africa, or Tanganyika as it was later known.

PARIS GRADUALLY REGAINS THE INITIATIVE

In the early stages of the Malgache uprising, the insurgents appeared to be managing a campaign which effectively blended modern and traditional concepts. From May until October of 1947, the insurgents conducted a sustained level of operations, forcing the colonial administration to declare a 'state of siege' in ten districts representing nearly one-eighth of the island.[23] France had an estimated 6500 troops available at the time but their limitations were readily apparent. Of these, about 4000 were Malgache conscripts, 1000 were Senegalese troops and another 1500 were French officers and non-commissioned officers. The initial response of the Malgache conscripts, organized into four battalions, undoubtedly shocked their French commanders and underscored the security threat which confronted colonial authorities. Two of the battalions mutinied. Many of the troops in these battalions were from the central plateau and the eastern coastal areas where the insurgency soon posed the greatest challenge to colonial forces. Members of one rebellious battalion killed all their French officers and escaped, taking many sub-machine guns with them. The other dissident battalion was less successful. A third battalion conducted anti-French demonstrations in Majunga on the northwest coast.[24]

By late April, French and Senegalese units arrived to bolster the island's shaken defenses. In June 1947 Paris sent two additional Senegalese battalions and a battalion of Foreign Legionnaires to stem the growing insurgent threat. Air assets available to French commanders grew from one operational military aircraft and fourteen commercial planes to ten Junkers-52 troop transports, four Anson trainers and ten DC-3 Dakotas. On 27 July, a troop ship arrived in Tamatave with two battalions of Algerian Tirailleurs and two battalions of Moroccan Tirailleurs. Two weeks later, a second ship arrived with an additional 1300 troops including Somali, Senegalese and North African Tirailleurs. In late July, the Legionnaires led the transition from defensive to offensive operations in areas north of the Tananarive–Tamatave railroad. Under the command of Lieutenant General Pellet, French forces launched an intensive counterinsurgency campaign. The guerrillas' northern and southern headquarters were overrun in early August. Insurgent forces were quickly pursued and forced to divide into smaller groups. Six months after they arrived, government troops had established an estimated 200 military outposts with sufficient soldiers to conduct patrols between them. The east coast was rapidly cleared of insurgents, the Tananarive, Tamatave, Fianarantsoa–Manakara rail lines secured, and the guerrilla forces pushed back into more remote, heavily forested zones.[25]

By December 1947, the colonial forces had tripled in size over the number originally stationed there when the uprising began, finally reaching some 18 000 troops. Convinced that he had already attained his primary objectives, General Pellet handed over his command to Brigadier General Garbey on 20 October, and returned to Paris. In late 1947, the onset of the rainy season and the growing number of government reinforcements gradually slowed the pace of insurgent operations. French military engineers had already constructed 700 kilometers of forest roads, significantly improving the mobility of government forces. Colonial officials reported, in mid-November, that the insurgents only had some 150 rifles left and that coordination between isolated groups was minimal; most guerrilla attacks were conducted with less than a dozen rifles.[26] A series of arrests, executions and combat losses further eroded the MDRM's regional leadership.

The rainy season put a halt to major military activity for the first few months of 1948 and French forces were unable to pursue sizeable insurgent groups still roaming forested areas 100 kilometers east of Tananarive. One year after the rebellion began, territory dominated by insurgent forces had shrunk to an area of 11 000 square miles, less than half the area affected in mid-1947. Active insurgent zones had been cordoned off into three distinct northern, central, and southern sectors, denying them access to the coast and pushing the guerrillas back from key lines of communication.

By early 1948, most insurgent attacks generally comprised small groups of 50 to 100 men with only one or two rifles, often targeting villages in an effort to obtain food and other increasingly scarce supplies. In April 1948, French forces resumed counterinsurgency operations. On 20 July, Michel Radaoroson, the southern and central zone commander, was tracked down and killed. Seven weeks later, security forces captured Victorien Razafindrabe, the former 'Marshal of the Malgache Army'. Between July and December, French forces reportedly captured 25 rebel generals and several other high ranking commanders.[27]

During the second half of 1948, guerrilla operations led by local leaders took on a more haphazard quality, suggesting that whatever remained of national or regional leadership was no longer capable of exercising effective command and control over the insurgent forces. Fearing reprisals by colonial forces, thousands of rural Malgache residents had fled into the mountains and forests of the country's central and northern plateau, in an effort to escape being caught up in the hostilities. Eventually, the government's superior firepower, mobility, and logistics wore the insurgents down. By the time the rebellion was declared officially over on 1 December 1948, more than 550 000 people, presumably civilian supporters, sympathizers, and others who had fled into insurgent areas, had 'surrendered' to the colonial authorities.[28]

During the 20 months from 29 March 1947 to December 1948 the insurrection affected a territory which contained an estimated 1.6 million people, roughly one-fourth of the population, and ten of the islands' 18 tribes.[29] Trials of captured insurgents continued until 1954 and the state of siege was not lifted in some coastal areas until 1956. Initial government estimates claimed some 60 000–80 000 Malgaches had died during the course of the uprising. A subsequent official inquiry, conducted between 1950 and 1952, reduced the figure to 11 200.[30] The final casualty count is still disputed and an agreed figure may never be reached. Many Malgaches who died during the insurgency were presumed to have succumbed to famine and disease after fleeing their villages rather than as a result of wounds received during hostilities. By contrast, the losses of the non-Malgache population were estimated at approximately 350 military and 200 civilian casualties, a figure which was less than 1 percent of the resident foreign population on the island in early 1947.[31]

OBITUARY OF A REBELLION

Much of the damage inflicted by the guerrillas, and the targets of their attacks, suggested that the uprising ultimately came to represent an anarchic expression of xenophobia and despair rather than a struggle for independence and the creation of a modern nation-state. Of the estimated 8500 plantations destroyed during the rebellion, only 1500 belonged to French and Creole settlers. The vast majority were owned by Malgaches who had achieved the somewhat privileged status of so-called *evolués* or *assimilés*. Their economic and political position in Madagascar, as well as in other French colonies in Africa, often made them more inclined to support the metropole rather than incipient nationalist movements.[32] In addition to targeting plantation owners, the insurgents also attacked Malgache merchants, teachers, and other representatives of the colonial system.[33]

An unsophisticated rural leadership cadre and the parochial ideological outlook advocated by the insurgents were thought to have preordained the uprising's eventual failure. An eminent historian of the war, Jacques Tronchon, has argued that, while it may have served to inspire the insurgents, the revival of the *fokonolona* was ultimately flawed as an ideological rallying point and gradually lost its vigor and efficacy. Though they often evoked *fokonolona*, the guerrillas rarely explained or elaborated on this concept. As a result, it was never clear if it implied the structure of a decentralized democracy or an egalitarian ideology. More often than not, those who evoked the notion seemed to be seeking a return to some ill-defined 'golden age'. The insurgents' initial resort to primitive weapons was considered symptomatic of the extent to which their goals and means were naive and undeveloped.[34]

In the end, the ideology implied in the concept of *fokonolona* came to be regarded as the reactionary cause of a peasantry whose way of life had been steadily threatened with extinction by the imposition of European political, economic, and religious institutions. As a result, it failed to have any mass appeal to the island's urban population many of whom viewed the insurrection as an ill-considered and impulsive act. Instead, many of the rebels' potential supporters chose a path of evolution toward independence in the framework of a post-colonial French commonwealth rather than independence in the context of traditional Malgache values and ideology.[35] Paris finally granted Madagascar its independence on 27 June 1960. The processes leading up to that transition presumably vindicated leaders such as Raseta and other Westernized, assimilated, and even Francophile elements of the MDRM. Their earlier aversion to violence had already underscored the fact that this MDRM faction did not seek to topple the structures of French colonial rule so much as they wanted to replace the personnel staffing it.[36]

Interpretations which fault the insurgents' ideological proclivities and the socio-economic background of their leaders, however, may be too facile. The logistical as well as geographic obstacles facing the insurgents very likely would have been difficult if not impossible to overcome regardless of the ideological outlook or sociological background of any guerrilla commander. Although they naively expected assistance or sympathy from the United States and Great Britain, the insurgents never received any outside support before or during the uprising.[37] Nevertheless few accounts of the insurrection seem to have acknowledged the degree to which the insurgents' lack of outside support was critical in accounting for their eventual defeat.[38] Geopolitical obstacles were also daunting. The guerrillas were unable to retreat across borders to neighboring countries or find safe haven in the remote districts of nearby states that might have been neutral if not sympathetic. The insular position of the rebels was further reinforced by the fact that the nearest island or mainland territories were all still under British, French or Portuguese colonial rule. Lacking small boats, the insurgents failed to supplement any mobility they might have had by taking advantage of favorable coastal terrain features and constantly shifting bases around the island's shoreline.

While the hilly and, in certain areas, mountainous terrain of the island's central plateau initially provided some advantages to the insurgents, it eventually also proved to be an impediment. Without any radios or modern means of transportation, the rebels had to rely on couriers to relay messages between their northern and southern sectors and various regional commands.[39] As the French gradually regained control of key areas and lines of communications, the amount of time it took to transmit messages between guerrilla forces grew. Eventually communications became impossible as government forces killed or captured more couriers. Under the circumstances, it was only a matter of time before the technical advantages provided by the aircraft, trucks, radios, and superior firepower of French weapons overcame the guerrillas.

Although the rebels' cause may have had the sympathy of some members of the French parliament, neither the personnel and property losses nor the cost of supporting an expeditionary force ever became as contentious an issue as the wars in Algeria and Indochina a decade later. Thus, France's will to persist in maintaining its colonial presence was never seriously challenged by the metropole's population. Though a number of their contemporaries agreed that the insurgents of 1947 bore the torch of anti-imperialist independence and modern Malgache nationalism, they had to acknowledge that the insurgents were also burdened by traditional and in some respects even reactionary ideological components. Its harshest, and perhaps overly facile, critics still insist that 'The Madagascar rising was unplanned, uncoordinated, and unorganized, an anarchic affair, an act of despair against the present rather than a considered effort to create a better future.'[40] The 1947 rebellion in Madagascar has never completely escaped an inherently contradictory portrayal as an expression of admirable idealism and appalling parochialism. As a result, its value as a prototype for subsequent generations of anti-colonial African nationalists never appeared to be as salient as the war in Algeria or even the more distant struggle waged by Ho Chi Minh in Southeast Asia. Nevertheless, the synthesis of traditional values and modern techniques which motivated the MDRM's combatants was far from extinct as a relevant paradigm for subsequent generations of African nationalists. Several years later, events in Kenya revealed a persistent but uneasy coexistence of traditional and modern perspectives strongly reminiscent of the politico-military cyclone which struck Madagascar in 1947.

3 Kenya: The Mau Mau Insurgency, 1952–60

The Mau Mau insurgency sparked a decades-long debate over the appropriate leadership and ideology for a successful nationalist struggle. This controversy is still unresolved in many sub-Saharan African countries. The issues which military historians and students of African nationalism continue to debate use Mau Mau as the starting point for nearly all post-World War II assessments of independence movements and guerrilla forces. Many of the central issues in the Mau Mau uprising were foreshadowed in the Malagasy revolt. An ethnically based solidarity movement sought radical economic and political reforms as well as eventual independence. Denigrated by elements of an intellectual elite and deprived of the leadership of a radical urban-based faction, a rural cadre of insurgents and supporters came to the fore. This obscure vanguard emphasized traditional religious and cultural themes and found them useful as a means of mobilizing and motivating a large number of combatants. Kenyan veterans of England's World War II campaigns were instrumental in forging contemporary military precepts with tactics influenced by religious traditions. Despite their eventual defeat, the Mau Mau insurgency was nevertheless implicitly more successful than its Malgache predecessor if only as measured by the extent to which the former became a reference point, albeit an ambiguous one, for subsequent generations of African politicians and insurgents.

THE METAMORPHOSIS OF AMBITIOUS REFORMERS

The roots of rebellion in Kenya can be traced to earlier efforts at non-violent reform. In Kenya, the organizational origins of the insurgency are linked to the emergence of the Kikuyu Central Association (KCA) in 1924. For the next twenty years, the KCA campaigned for reforms in land tenure, education, labor, and other issues. Members of the KCA frequently denounced European and missionary influences on African culture and also fostered the establishment of independent African churches and schools. In May 1940 British colonial authorities declared the KCA illegal and arrested its leaders. The remaining KCA members went underground and the organization was virtually moribund throughout World War II.

Evidently convinced that they posed no serious threat to England's war effort, British authorities released the arrested leaders from prison in 1944.[1] Between 1944 and 1946 a new political organization, the Kenya African Union (KAU), appeared and soon established a broad base of support. Its membership quickly grew to some 100 000. Although the KCA was still banned by the British colonial administration, its members actively participated in the KAU, which initially functioned as a 'united front' for a Kenya-wide 'congress'. The KAU eventually advocated many of the goals previously espoused by the KCA and ultimately looked forward to African self-rule or outright independence. However, the KAU was initially a moderate, non-violent, reform movement. Radical nationalist sentiments were not a prominent feature in its program during the late 1940s. Like their Malgache counterparts in the MDRM, many of the KAU's leading members were clearly more concerned with eventually replacing Europeans in the existing political and economic infrastructure than with completely overhauling it.

It was generally assumed that former KCA members were the more radical component of the KAU. Former KCA cadres also were thought to be more militant than most of the KAU's prominent leaders, surpassing even the charismatic Jomo Kenyatta who had been the KCA's Secretary General in 1929 before leaving Kenya for a fifteen-year stay in England.[2] In the late 1940s KCA members became more active and influential, although the organization itself was still considered a select and secret movement whose membership was limited to trusted individuals. In the early 1950s, the KCA made a dramatic revision in its membership policies and attempted to become an underground mass movement. The precise reason for this shift was not immediately apparent. Some historians assume that the organization's changing character stemmed from an assessment that British colonial administrators and settlers would not support democratic reforms and that further efforts to realize KCA goals could probably not be achieved by constitutional means. The increasing intransigence of white settlers, the arrests of Kenyan labor leaders, and the suppression of newspapers sympathetic to KAU aims corroborated this pessimism. Alternatively, it has been suggested that the KCA itself underwent a split between elder and generally moderate leaders and younger, more militant, supporters. The latter espoused a more active and aggressive reform campaign on behalf of a restive Kikuyu squatter population faced with a mounting number of oppressive legal and economic constraints imposed by white settlers and the colonial administration.[3]

The KCA's shift in organizational and strategic perspectives was paralleled by the emergence of a movement known to colonial authorities as

'Mau Mau'. The existence of such an organization was first publicized at the 'Naivasha Trial' of 31 May 1950 where it was described as a secret association. At Naivasha, suspected Mau Mau members were charged with the organization of rituals among members of the Kikuyu tribe who swore oaths of allegiance to the movement and were allegedly responsible for numerous incidents of unrest and economic sabotage dating from 1947. While the holding of oathing rituals worried British settlers about the political loyalty and allegiance of what appeared to be a growing number of Kikuyu, the escalation of violence associated with the oaths was even more alarming. Some of these incidents involved the assassination of Kikuyus thought to be loyal to white settlers or collaborating with colonial officials.[4]

Although the colonial administration officially banned an organization known as 'Mau Mau' in August 1950, those Kenyans who swore the initial oaths of allegiance and later took a more militant 'warrior' oath rarely referred to themselves as Mau Mau. A variety of origins and etymological interpretations of the term 'Mau Mau' have been proposed over the years. Nevertheless, it appears that 'no generically accepted meaning of the term exists'.[5] Moreover, 'the term itself and, particularly, its attachment to the underground movement and revolt were fortuitous developments', and, more important, 'the underground movement which most writers refer to as "Mau Mau" was in fact a direct lineal descendant of the banned KCA.'[6] The accuracy of this imputed political genealogy is further supported by the fact that the role of oaths of allegiance in modern Kenyan politics dates from 1926 when they began to be used extensively by the KCA.[7]

IDEOLOGY – NATIONAL OR LOCAL?

As in the case of the Malgache rebellion, the ideology espoused by dissident members of the Kenyan population who supported the KAU or belonged to the growing clandestine network organized by the KCA (Mau Mau) contained an ambiguous mixture of nationalist and parochial elements. Both the KAU and the Mau Mau sought Kenyan independence and land reform. The popular phrase 'Land and Freedom', which became associated with the insurgents and those who sought non-violent reform, simplifies what was a more complex set of aims and principles. It has been suggested that independence was, in fact, a later aspiration of KAU leadership and an even less salient concern of Mau Mau members. In the words of one Mau Mau guerrilla, 'For my part I was only hoping to be given a small piece of land somewhere and to be treated a little more decently by the Kenya government and white settlers.'[8] A recent reassessment of Mau Mau notes that the insurgents named their movement *ithaka na wiathi*, more accurately translated as 'land and moral responsibility' or 'freedom through land'.[9] The ideological aims of those who chose to rebel are even more difficult to pin down in light of the fact that 'unfortunately, the Movement issued no manifesto and all those who address themselves to its ideology are obliged to make inferences from a wide array of songs, prayers, oaths, etc., which in their variety can be used selectively to support any number of generalizations.'[10] While goals such as independence were clearly nationalist and appealed to Kenyans across the entire ethno-linguistic spectrum, land reform had a somewhat more limited audience, primarily members of the Kikuyu and one or two other tribes which had lost large tracts of land to white settlers in the first few decades of British colonial rule.

Parochial dimensions were further underscored by the emphasis on oaths of allegiance and warrior oaths administered to Mau Mau members. By late 1952, when the insurgency began, few non-Kikuyu, with the exception of some Kambas, had taken oaths, although the insurgents were said to have had plans to create an oath which was designed to be acceptable to other tribes.[11] The taking of oaths had the obvious value of emphasizing traditional Kikuyu culture and religion. However, there were elements of the oath taking ritual in which non-Kikuyu members could have participated. A frequently cited clause in the oath required the would-be Mau Mau member to swear: 'I shall never help the missionaries in their Christian faith to ruin our traditional and cultural customs.'[12] As in the case of the Malgache rebels of 1947, it is difficult to establish the extent to which traditional and cultural customs were expected to serve as a model for a post-colonial Kenyan government.

A LEADERSHIP CRISIS

It has been suggested that this emphasis on tradition met a more immediate need for cohesion among those Kenyan peasants who chose to become insurgents in late 1952 and soon found themselves cut off from more educated and urbane leaders.[13] This view, however, reveals only a portion of the sociological and ideological factors involved in shaping the character of Mau Mau commanders. In the aftermath of the 1950 Naivasha trial, at which 19 men were accused of oathing or joining a secret society, British colonial authorities began to infiltrate Mau Mau and acquired increasingly useful information about the movement. By September 1952, more than four hundred people had been imprisoned on charges of taking or administering an oath and several hundred more were still awaiting trial. On 20 October 1952, the colonial government declared a state of emergency; this has generally been regarded as the beginning of the insurgency. Several days later, the authorities arrested nearly two hundred Kenyans and held them for trial or detention under emergency regulations. These arrests, including that of the KAU's Jomo Kenyatta, essentially removed the upper layers of KAU leadership, the clandestine KCA (i.e. Mau Mau), trade union leaders, and other prominent figures in the nationalist movement. This left only a semi-educated leadership cadre with no connection to the detained central leadership element.[14]

Colonial authorities sometimes described Mau Mau as the armed wing of the KAU. By arresting senior KAU members, however, British officials also had detained some of the movements' most moderate leaders. Consequently, the decapitated nationalist movement consisted primarily of an embryonic 'military wing' which also had to fill a 'political' void.[15] As colonial authorities soon discovered, efforts to prevent a rebellion by arresting its presumed leaders or pressuring some of them to denounce violence were at best belated, if not misguided.

Jomo Kenyatta's stature as a spokesman for nationalist aspirations was mistakenly perceived by British officials as an indication that he also exercised complete control over the behavior of the vast majority of the Kikuyu people, particularly those who had enlisted in Mau Mau. Kenyatta's relationship with Mau Mau, however, was much more ambiguous. Thus, at a rally held in July 1952, Kenyatta equated Mau Mau with 'theft and drunkenness'.[16] One month later, at a rally organized by the colonial government to pressure Kenyatta and other KAU leaders to denounce Mau Mau, Kenyatta asserted that 'Mau Mau has spoiled the country. Let Mau Mau perish forever', and 'all people should search for Mau Mau and kill it.'[17]

Like the Malgache parliamentarians' telegram, sent on the eve of the 1947 rebellion, Kenyatta's denunciations of Mau Mau violence were part of a delicate balancing act. On one hand, Kenyatta and other KAU spokesmen tried to keep colonial authorities from pursuing an increasingly repressive policy of arresting nationalist leaders and otherwise stifling the nationalist movement. Alternatively, Kenyatta and his colleagues probably sought to employ the growing threat of violence, by a younger generation of Kenyans, to convince London of the need to implement a more rapid and substantive reform process. Although they were dismayed by his denunciations of Mau Mau, those militant KCA and KAU members who subsequently launched the insurgency continued to use Kenyatta's stature as a rallying point. His heroic image was undoubtedly enhanced by the fact that he was brought to trial in late 1952 and given a seven year sentence in 1953. Kenyatta's imprisonment throughout the course of the war gave him the status of a martyr in the eyes of many insurgents.[18]

The ambivalent relationship between Kenyatta and Mau Mau's rank and file cadres was played out at intermediate levels of Kikuyu society as well. While educated, urban, Kikuyus also opposed colonialism and sympathized with the political objectives sought by Mau Mau members, they were nonetheless put off by those aspects of the oathing rituals and other features of the movement which were seen as demeaning and primitive phenomena. Moreover, the lower middle-class status of many educated Kikuyu meant they had more to lose in rebelling against colonialism. Furthermore, because they had moved from traditional Kikuyu settlement areas, many of them lived in areas outside the districts from which early Mau Mau recruits were drawn.[19] Consequently, 'of the several thousand Kikuyu, Embu and Meru tribesmen to enter the forests during this early period, the educated were notably conspicuous in their absence.'[20] This sociological dimension clearly influenced not only the mixture of modern and traditional ideological components of the insurgency but also its military strategy and tactics.

THE INTERMITTENT ONSET OF REBELLION

Establishing the precise date on which the insurgency actually began is a somewhat controversial process. Several apparently spontaneous attacks on the homes of government loyalists in early 1952 are sometimes considered the opening rounds of the uprising.[21] A 'Central Committee' of Nairobi-based leaders had established a Kikuyu War Council and escalated an ongoing campaign to steal or buy weapons in early 1952.[22] By August, militant KAU members in Nairobi had deployed personnel to rural districts to prepare for a large-scale insurgent campaign.[23] The government's declaration of a state of emergency caught the insurgents off guard, however, and from the last few months of 1952 until March 1953, very little activity occurred beyond an occasional attack on isolated white farms or the assassination of Kikuyu loyalists.[24]

In late 1952, Mau Mau was thought to have some 400–800 modern weapons and about 140 000 rounds of ammunition. During the next twelve months, the insurgents acquired an additional 280 weapons. Kikuyu artisans also manufactured a number of homemade rifles and other weapons.[25] What the insurgents lacked in the way of weaponry was more than compensated for by an initial surge of recruits. By early 1953, there were an estimated 12 000–15 000 insurgents active in four main areas: the Aberdare Mountains, Mount Kenya, Nairobi, and the Kikuyu tribal reserve north of the capital.[26] Additional recruits flocked to insurgent bases in 1953 and eventually may have swelled Mau Mau ranks to as many as 30 000.[27] According to one estimate, between 75 and 90 percent of the Kikuyu population had taken the 'oath of unity' by 1952. Mau Mau influence began to spread in Nairobi as well as among other ethnic groups such as the Kamba, Maasai, Kipsigis, and somewhat among the Luo and Baluhya.[28]

On 26 March 1953, some 80 Mau Mau insurgents attacked a small government outpost in Naivasha. After driving off the small police contingent, the guerrillas seized 47 weapons and a truck-load of ammunition. On the same day, a force estimated at 1000–3000 attacked a Kikuyu farming area at Lari, located only a few miles outside of Nairobi. By the following morning, 97 villagers were dead. The insurgents had burned over 200 huts and maimed some 1000 cattle.[29] Many of the dead included family members of several Kikuyu chiefs and headmen who had sided with the colonial government. Mau Mau forces were thought to have suffered even greater casualties during the course of a running battle and subsequent pursuit operations launched by government reinforcements sent to relieve the local Kikuyu Home Guard militia unit.[30] What subsequently became known as the 'Lari Massacre' ultimately proved to be the largest single battle of the Mau Mau insurgency. During the next twelve months, Mau Mau elements involving several hundred guerrillas managed to stage only a few additional large-scale attacks on isolated police and militia outposts.[31]

For Mau Mau members the attacks at Naivasha and Lari clearly marked the opening rounds of the insurgency. These operations also confirmed that the guerrillas had begun to establish a chain of command and control from among the leadership element which remained after the hundreds of preemptive arrests of suspected Mau Mau members in late 1952. What began as a rudimentary and largely isolated group of base camps, comprised of guerrilla units ranging in size from several hundred to over a thousand insurgents, was finally consolidated by August 1953.[32] Dedan Kimathi was appointed 'Field Marshal' and the bulk of the insurgents were organized into eight 'Armies' or 'Brigades'. These units, some of which had as many as 3000 men, consisted of troops from various districts and were organized under a larger structure known as the Kenya

Defense Council.[33] The various Mau Mau 'armies' were led by 'generals' and subordinate officers with ranks such as 'major' and 'captain'. Some insurgent camps were extensively organized. Routines included an early morning bugle call and a 'parade call' at which troops were assigned daily duties. This was followed by calisthenics, marching, and instruction in preparing ambushes, the use of camouflage, the maintenance of weapons and defensive measures to be taken during air raids.[34]

These organizational preferences bore a stronger resemblance to British military rules and regulations than they did to any contemporary theories or practice of guerrilla warfare of which Mau Mau members might have been aware. As in the case of Madagascar's 1947 rebellion, the influence of Kenyans who had served in the British army during World War II was significant. Some of Mau Mau's early leaders, as well as a considerable number of rank and file insurgents, had had combat experience with British forces in Burma, Europe and Africa. Of the approximately 100 000 Kenyans who volunteered for the British Army, many served outside their country during the course of the war.[35] The insurgents' Field Marshal, Dedan Kimathi, was among those who had served in the British Army.[36]

SEERS AND STRATEGY

While the experience of British military organization and administration gave Mau Mau insurgents a contemporary structural reference point, the *mundo mugo wa ita*, practitioners of traditional religious belief/seers, nonetheless exercised significant political and military influence on guerrilla tactics. These individuals traditionally had played a vital role in support of Kikuyu warriors. They were presumed to be mediums, capable of receiving divine messages in their dreams concerning enemy plans, opportune times to conduct attacks, and taboos to be observed.[37]

As a recent account of the insurgency has pointed out, however, the status of those known as prophets was due to more than just the accuracy of their predictions. These individuals traditionally held esteemed positions as a result of a rigorous process of training, initiation, and the demonstration of a high degree of ability. Thus 'the term "prophet" greatly oversimplifies the role of a *mundo mugo*. In addition to foretelling the future, these men, and – less often – women, treated illness, defended clients against witchcraft and sorcery, and divined the causes of illness and misfortune. Their prophecies were made possible by their special relationship with god.'[38]

The influence of traditional beliefs and practices made itself felt very early in the course of the insurgency. Spirit-mediums were said to have provided magic powders and potions to each armed unit and military operations often would not be undertaken without a prior assessment by the *mundu mugo wa ita.* Many insurgent commanders also believed in omens. In late March 1953, one of the leaders of a successful Mau Mau raid had been a mute who recently had begun to speak and was thought to have supernatural powers. He reportedly had a knife which turned all bullets into water and was also described as a prophet. Such views also adversely affected military operations. One insurgent group called off a planned raid due to the belief that if a deer or gazelle crossed the path of an insurgent group on their way to a target, they were likely to experience bad luck and should therefore modify their plan. Some guerrillas who did so in June 1953 cited an earlier, unsuccessful raid by their comrades who had disregarded the omen.[39] Sometimes, divination also dictated defensive measures. A former insurgent described an instance in which a seer forecasted a government attack against an insurgent camp on a specific night. Only some guerrillas relocated. The attack occurred on the night predicted, greatly enhancing the *mundu mugo*'s stature.[40]

The importance of such traditional religious views was not lost on colonial authorities. Several months prior to the declaration of a state of emergency, the government also sought to counteract the growing influence of the insurgents' unity and warrior oaths by organizing compulsory 'cleansing ceremonies' for detained sympathizers and suspected supporters. These ceremonies were conducted by 'witch doctors' selected by the colonial government, sometimes sarcastically referred to as 'Her Majesty's witch doctors'. The authorities failed to realize, however, that the individuals chosen to conduct these ceremonies often were Mau Mau sympathizers who had persuaded government officials that they were counteracting Mau Mau oaths.[41] Government officials eventually devised a much more aggressive program to 'rehabilitate' Mau Mau prisoners of war. Captured insurgents were subjected to an extensive psychological operation designed to negate their commitment to the nationalist cause. Using techniques which once might have been described as 'brainwashing' or more recently characterized as the 'deprogramming' of religious cult members, prison camp officials sought to strike at the core of the insurgents' principles and ideology. Their captors placed a great emphasis on denigrating Mau Mau oaths and the replacement of their pre-colonial religious perspectives with various forms of politically neutral Christianity.[42]

LONDON SUBJECTS MAU MAU TO THE 'HAMMER' AND 'ANVIL'

British authorities quickly realized the need for an augmented military presence in stemming and finally defeating the Mau Mau threat. In late 1952, three battalions of the Kings African Rifles from Uganda, Tanganyika, and Mauritius deployed to Kenya. London subsequently sent battalions of Buffs and Devons from its 39th Brigade, battalions of Royal Northumberland and Inniskilling Fusiliers from the 49th Brigade, a battalion of Lancashire Fusiliers, an armored car division and a squadron of Lincoln heavy bombers. By 1953, eleven British battalions, numbering roughly 10000 troops, had deployed to Kenya and were placed under the command of Major General Hind. This contingent was reinforced by a 20000 man Kenyan police force which had been augmented by white colonial reservists and slightly more than 20000 Kikuyu Guard militia.[43]

Initial efforts to directly engage Mau Mau insurgents and clear their base camps out of the forests and mountains north of Nairobi were unsuccessful. Inadequate intelligence and a failure to devise a comprehensive counterinsurgency strategy gave Mau Mau members a brief respite and permitted them to organize a rudimentary guerrilla force. Frustrated by the lack of a rapid improvement in the security situation, London replaced Major General Hind with General Sir George Erskine in May 1953. In early 1954 British military commanders began to pursue a modified strategy. The government's initial aim was to cut the insurgents off from their supporters in Nairobi and the rural areas north of the capital where large numbers of sympathetic Kikuyu residents had provided supplies, information, and other assistance to the guerrillas. On 24 April 1954, a force of 25000 soldiers and policemen launched Operation Anvil. Within a month's time, at least 24000 African residents of Nairobi had been arrested and sent to detention camps.[44] The campaign to root out Mau Mau's sympathizers in Nairobi was supplemented by an equally effective rural 'villagization program' which eventually resulted in the resettlement of over one million Kikuyu in fortified 'strategic hamlets' by the end of 1954.[45] This further separated Mau Mau from their network of civilian supporters and set the stage for subsequent counterinsurgency campaigns which again involved more direct assaults on the guerrillas' base camps.

Like their French counterparts in Madagascar six years earlier, the British Thirty-Nine Corps Engineers Regiment built roads leading directly to the Aberdares and Mount Kenya. Travel time for units engaged in counterinsurgency sweeps had been reduced by more than 50 percent by 1954. Government forces quickly exploited their enhanced mobility and access to Mau Mau areas. On 6 January 1955 British commanders launched Operation Hammer. A nine-battalion force, about 10 000 troops, swept through the Aberdare forests to trap and engage a Mau Mau contingent thought to number less than 2000. The operation ended on 11 February, having resulted in only 99 Mau Mau killed and 62 captured. Several weeks later, the government launched Operation First Flute, using the same division-sized force against some 3000 Mau Mau in the Mount Kenya area. When it ended, after two months, 277 insurgents had been killed or taken prisoner. In July, Operation Dante, a four-battalion sweep supported by artillery and aircraft likewise failed to yield substantial results. While colonial authorities viewed these offensives as disappointing they had nevertheless significantly aggravated conditions for the guerrillas. By late 1955, Mau Mau forces faced growing logistics and ammunition shortages. These and other constraints rapidly demoralized many insurgents who became easy prey for the 'pseudo-gangs' which British authorities turned loose in the forests to hunt down remaining guerrilla groups. Comprised of 300–400 captured insurgents who offered to cooperate with colonial authorities, these former Mau Mau members led loyalist and British forces into the countryside to locate and attack guerrilla camps. Eventually, the 'pseudo-gangs' were permitted to operate without European leadership. Renamed as Special Force Teams they subsequently were credited with the capture and death of numerous insurgent commanders.[46]

By mid-1955, Mau Mau's leaders had split into two large factions known as the Kenya Parliament and the Kenya Riigi group. The latter attacked the former as a group whose personal and parochial interests were pursued at the expense of the majority of Mau Mau's illiterate members. Some Kenya Riigi members were prepared to engage in negotiations and a discussion of possible surrender terms with colonial officials.[47] As supplies became scarce and leadership fragmented, a growing number of ill-disciplined insurgent groups engaged in banditry denounced by the colonial authorities as well as Mau Mau guerrillas.[48] The cumulative impact of these trends was quickly reflected in the insurgent force's rapid reduction. In early 1955, there were only 6000 Mau Mau at large in rural areas. At the end of 1955, the government estimated only about 1500 remained in remote areas of the countryside. The last major campaigns in the rebellion were fought in 1956. Less than four years after the insurgency began, responsibility for pursuit of the remaining Mau Mau members was handed over to the Kenyan police as British forces were gradually withdrawn from the colony. In October 1956, government forces captured 'Field Marshal' Dedan Kimathi. Kimathi was subsequently tried and hanged.[49]

MAU MAU POST MORTEM

The final costs of the Mau Mau rebellion were far greater, in human terms, for Kenya's African population than for the white colonialists. According to official British estimates, the war resulted in 13 500 deaths. This total included 11 503 'terrorists' killed, 63 European police or soldiers killed, 32 European and 29 Asian civilians killed, and 1920 African 'loyalists' killed.[50] These grossly imbalanced figures highlight several features of the war. As in the case of the Malgache rebellion, the colonial power manipulated ethnic as well as socio-economic divisions and thereby turned at least a portion of the nationalist struggle into a civil war as well as a struggle for independence. Many of the war's battles pitted loyalist Kikuyu Guard forces rather than the British expeditionary force or mobilized white settlers against Mau Mau members.

More importantly, the estimated 50 000 combatants massed by Britain and the colonial administration had an overwhelming advantage in firepower. During the four years of their participation in the counterinsurgency campaign, British aircraft deployed to Kenya dropped 50 000 tons of bombs and fired more than 2 million machine gun rounds during air to ground attacks on suspected Mau Mau bases.[51] The financial costs of combatting the Mau Mau insurgency were not so high that London felt compelled to end its colonial presence. Nevertheless, the cumulative impact of the efforts Britain had made in various corners of its global empire during the late 1940s and early 1950s convinced many in Parliament that colonialism was no longer an economically viable institution. When Kenya finally became independent in December 1963, it was merely one of several former British African colonies that had done so during the previous five years. The Mau Mau rebellion had not appreciably accelerated the process of Kenya's decolonization.

Mau Mau forces ultimately succumbed to many of the same limitations experienced in Madagascar in the late 1940s. When the insurgency began, Mau Mau members failed to articulate a comprehensive ideological platform, and lacked any kind of strategic master plan for conducting a protracted insurgency. Some historians have suggested that the 1952 imprisonment of political and labor leaders removed a cadre which might have filled the ideological vacuum as well as devising an effective military strategy. England's rapid seizure of the tactical initiative, however, is likely to have kept a few hundred additional insurgent leaders off balance and would have prevented them from addressing a myriad of material shortcomings. Moreover, Mau Mau never managed to train a significant number of their members in the principles and practice of contemporary guerrilla warfare.[52] The command and control network which had emerged in 1953 was not consolidated and the insurgents were unable to conduct a coordinated nationwide military campaign. Even after they had formed large units and bases, Mau Mau principally conducted hit-and-run raids and low-level attacks aimed at capturing weapons and supplies. In 1953, plans for a large-scale offensive against a number of vital economic targets were never implemented. The reasons for Mau Mau's most glaring tactical failure are still a subject of considerable debate and, in this respect, Kenya's insurgents suffer by comparison with their 1947 Malgache predecessors.[53]

The lack of outside support made it even more likely that the inadequate supply of weapons and ammunition available at the start of the insurgency would quickly become a debilitating factor. While a belated, and unsuccessful, effort was made to send a delegation to seek assistance from Ethiopia, Mau Mau leaders did not fully appreciate the need for an outside source of supply or the value of a safe haven across Kenya's borders.[54] Like their Malgache predecessors, however, Mau Mau's geopolitical position made it unlikely that such support could have been arranged. With the exception of Ethiopia, all of Kenya's neighbors were still under British colonial rule. Moreover, Mau Mau's area of operations was landlocked, thereby ruling out the option of seaborne deliveries of *matériel* from any sympathetic suppliers.

Finally, the ambiguous and often quite tense relationship between Mau Mau members and Jomo Kenyatta continuously threatened to undermine and divide the forces of Kenyan nationalism. In the year between his release from prison in 1962 and his first day as independent Kenya's first President in December 1963, Kenyatta still felt compelled to issue occasional denunciations of the insurgency, describing Mau Mau on one occasion as a 'disease'.[55] Nevertheless, at least 800 Mau Mau accepted Kenyatta's subsequent offer of amnesty and loans for the purchase of modest plots of land. These conditions were not considered acceptable by a residual insurgent faction. This remaining militant group felt that the land reforms they had fought for were being compromised by a government which was afraid to alienate white settlers who chose to remain in independent Kenya. In April 1964, Kenyatta ordered a series of police operations against several hundred remaining Mau Mau insurgents. After a second amnesty offer in early 1965 proved unsuccessful, the government launched another major sweep operation. Security forces killed most major Mau Mau leaders during this campaign, leaving only a few small groups of insurgents in the forests north of Nairobi.[56] Unlike the Malgache uprising, the persistence of the Mau Mau insurgency after the transition from colonialism to independence underscored the depth of the commitment made by some of the insurgents. Their struggle for what were presumably more parochial goals such as land reform was one whose appeal was limited principally to the Kikuyu. As in the case of the Malgache rebellion, this commitment diminished Mau Mau's stature in the history of anti-colonial struggles and created an ambivalent legacy for insurgent movements elsewhere in Africa. Once again, the image which survived was that of a rural insurgency whose failures largely were due to a reactionary or revivalist worldview which crippled and ultimately undermined their efforts to forge a nationalist political-military movement. The defeat of the Malgache and Kenyan insurgencies may have convinced some African nationalists that insurgencies inspired by traditional beliefs could not succeed against heavily armed colonial forces. The subsequent outbreak of insurgencies elsewhere in Africa, however, quickly demonstrated that the governments of newly independent states were not necessarily considered as invincible as their colonial predecessors.

4 Cameroon: The UPC Insurrection, 1956–70

The persistence of insurgency beyond a colonial era into the early years of independence was not unique to Kenya. Insurrection in Cameroon during the mid-1950s and early 1960s grew out of an anti-colonial campaign for independence. This struggle gradually evolved into the militant advocacy of a specific ideology nurtured by the Sino-Soviet camp as the Cold War began to spread to Africa in the late 1950s. For some historians, however, the war waged by the Cameroonian Peoples Union (UPC) between 1955 and the mid-1960s represented the first real attempt at implementing the principles of modern guerrilla warfare in sub-Saharan Africa. According to Basil Davidson, the UPC uprising was an example of a movement based on 'mass participation' rather than just 'mass support'.[1] A detailed examination of the insurrection does not necessarily support this conclusion. While Cameroonian insurgents may have espoused a 'progressive' secular variant of nationalism, they failed to appreciate the necessity of mobilizing critical elements of the rural population whose traditional values were neither extinct nor dormant. This failure ultimately condemned the UPC to a defeat as certain as that which guerrillas in Madagascar and Kenya faced due to a lack of outside support or rear base areas.

FROM 'RADICAL' POLITICIANS TO 'REVOLUTIONARY' NATIONALISTS

The Union des Populations du Cameroun (UPC) was established on 10 April 1948. Many of the movement's early leaders, as well as its founding members, such as Ruben Um Nyobe, Ernest Ouandie, and Abel Kingue previously had been active as labor organizers in the Douala port and other large urban centers. Felix Moumie, who later became an influential ideologue, was trained as a doctor in the Dakar School for African Physicians and later worked in the Cameroonian Public Health Service.[2] Cameroon's post-World War I status as a partitioned League of Nations Mandate and, after World War II as a United Nations Trust Territory administered by England and France, shaped the UPC's political program. The UPC called for the reunification of the two small, distinct territories of British Southern and Northern Cameroon with the much larger French Cameroon, as well as the eventual independence of the single territory which Germany originally colonized. The movement's leaders did not initially consider a military strategy to persuade France or the United Kingdom to fulfill the terms of the trusteeship arrangement.

Between 1948 and 1952, the UPC functioned as a political party whose principal aim was to contest territorial elections in French Cameroon and to nominate candidates to represent the territory in the French National Assembly. UPC candidates emphasized a political platform calling for the creation of local and national institutions which would give the territory greater self-government and internal autonomy prior to full independence. In the first two years of its existence, the UPC focused its energy on the creation of a political and administrative structure which included *comités de village*, located in rural areas, and *comités de quartier*, based in larger towns.

At the UPC's first Party Congress in 1950, the delegates reorganized this embryonic network of local committees and added a second tier, comprised of 'Central Committees'. These committees were to function as an intermediary structure, relaying orders from upper levels of the party to the local committees. The UPC's new administrative hierarchy also included 'Regional Committees', responsible for the activity of several Central Committees, and an even more powerful 'Central Executive Committee' (Comité Directeur). At the apex of this system stood the 'Political Bureau', 'Secretariat', and Treasury. The UPC also established several subsidiary organizations including a youth wing, a women's movement, and a cultural branch.[3]

Initial supporters of the UPC were drawn from members of previously established, tribally based, self-help associations such as Ngondo and Kumsze. The former was comprised of Douala tribe participants and the latter was, loosely speaking, a 'traditional' organization which drew its members from the Bamileke tribe. The Bamileke accounted for some 25 percent of Cameroon's total population in the late 1940s. By 1950, the UPC also had gained substantial support in the Sanaga Maritime Region, heavily populated by members of the Bassa tribe, in southwestern Cameroon. Nearly half of the UPC's local committees were initially located in the Sanaga Maritime Region. Although the UPC quickly succeeded in dispersing cadres throughout the country the majority of its members were recruited principally in the southwest.[4]

For two years after its first Party Congress, the UPC functioned as a 'radical' nationalist party contesting, and frequently losing, local and national elections. Between 1952 and 1955, however, the UPC underwent a metamorphosis which changed the organization into a 'revolutionary nationalist party'. Felix Moumie introduced Marxist terminology into UPC pronouncements as well as professing his admiration for Mao Tsetung and making vague calls for 'direct action'. These statements were a response to what the UPC's more radical leaders believed was a concerted French effort to delay Cameroonian independence and force the territory to become a member of the French Community, which included nearly all of Paris's African colonies.

By 1954, the UPC had launched an intense propaganda campaign and party members were implicated in several isolated incidents of violence. In 1955, macabre rumors, attributed to the UPC, led to a significant deterioration of the political climate in French Cameroon. According to UPC leaflets, a public health inoculation campaign in Bamileke areas was part of a plot to depopulate the tribe by killing off its children. Another widely spread rumor claimed that Europeans were abducting local residents in order to decapitate them and use their heads for purposes of witchcraft. In early 1955, Moumie and Um Nyobe reportedly made several public statements accusing the French administration of conducting a violently repressive campaign against the UPC. The two leaders allegedly also promised their supporters a quick and violent end to the local French regime.[5]

FROM RIOT TO REBELLION

On 22 April 1955, the UPC, and several smaller affiliated organizations, issued a 'joint proclamation' unilaterally declaring an end to the territory's trusteeship status and the establishment of a sovereign Cameroonian state. This was followed by several ineffectual UPC-led strikes and demonstrations. Tensions continued to mount and between 22 and 30 May 1955 disturbances occurred in Yaoundé, Douala, and at least seven other southwestern towns. These UPC-inspired incidents resulted in attacks against European settlers, Africans opposed to the UPC, and widespread property damage. In some instances, pro-French groups also sought to provoke the UPC by disrupting rallies and speeches by various party officials. An estimated 3000 rioters, using machetes, clubs, axes, and a limited number of firearms, stormed the radio station in Douala. By 30 May 1955 the casualty count had risen to 26 dead and some 180 wounded. A third of the wounded were police personnel.[6]

The riots and other violent incidents of late May were apparently coordinated. Some members of the UPC may have expected a largely spontaneous mass uprising to follow these attacks. Speaking to a rally of UPC supporters, Felix Moumie proclaimed that Ruben Um Nyobe, much like Mao Tse-tung and Ho Chi Minh, had already gone to the countryside to lead an insurgency. Um Nyobe and other UPC leaders, however, evidently had not made plans or preparations for a protracted insurgency in early 1955. In the months immediately following the riots of that year, the UPC sought to continue operating as a political party rather than an insurgent movement.[7] When it became increasingly clear that France was intent on stifling the UPC's political activity, the movement had to regroup and reassess its options.

At the time of the May 1955 unrest, Um Nyobe was in Nigeria. Fearing arrest, most of the movement's remaining leaders, including Moumie, Kingue, and Ouandie, fled to Kumba in the southern territory of the British Cameroons where they established a headquarters. On 13 July 1955, the Cameroonian Council of Ministers outlawed the UPC and dissolved its youth and women's leagues as well as other subsidiary affiliates. Not long afterwards, Um Nyobe and other UPC cadres infiltrated French Cameroon to lay the foundation for a protracted insurgency whose earliest combatants were drawn primarily from the ranks of the Bassa tribe.

The UPC established several major bases in numerous administrative regions in southwestern Cameroon. Each base was responsible for several 'sectors' which were further subdivided into 'sections'. The latter had 30 man units led by 'top sergeants' who received orders to attack specific economic targets. After a few months of intensive training, UPC guerrillas struck several economic facilities including roads, rail lines, and telegraph links between Douala and Yaounde on 18 December 1955. The insurgents burned polling booths and intimidated voters in an effort to disrupt French-sponsored elections for the Cameroonian National Assembly scheduled for 23 December 1955. UPC attacks and government counterattacks lasted beyond the election and by the end of the year at least 100 people had died, although some estimates place the casualty figure as high as 2000.[8]

FRANCE OFFERS INDEPENDENCE AND WAGES WAR

Although the 1955 election resulted in the selection of Cameroon's first African Premier, André Marie Mbida, and a French promise of eventual independence, Um Nyobe and other UPC leaders chose to continue the insurgency. Logistics problems and government counterinsurgency operations kept the UPC guerrilla campaign at a fairly low level, however.

Throughout 1956 the UPC generally avoided contacts with French troops and other elements of the territory's security forces. In mid-1957 Um Nyobe was still demanding early independence and the unification of French and British Cameroon as well as amnesty for his supporters. While Mbida agreed to offer a partial amnesty, the UPC's other political demands received no response, prompting Um Nyobe to issue an ultimatum threatening further violence. In September 1957 the Catholic bishop of Douala attempted to mediate between Um Nyobe and Mbida. Um Nyobe refused to compromise and issued even more stringent demands, calling for new elections, immediate independence and a general amnesty.

Talks broke down and the rebellion continued into 1958, as the UPC staged attacks against plantations, mission stations, and government offices. Insurgents also murdered loyal chiefs, missionaries, and local officials. By mid-1958, most guerrilla activity focused on the Sanaga Maritime Region, and to a lesser extent, on districts inhabited by the Bamileke and Moungo tribes in the southwest. The UPC's headquarters at Kumba in British Southern Cameroons had directed attacks in the latter area. In June 1957, however, local authorities ordered the UPC to cease military activity or leave the territory. Felix Moumie and eleven other UPC leaders fled to Cairo, Egypt. Ruben Um Nyobe and Theodore Mayi Matip, who had formerly headed the UPC's youth wing, moved back into French Cameroon to lead their Bassa supporters.[9] The insurgents' plans to gradually expand the scope of their campaign were thwarted on 13 September 1958 when Um Nyobe was killed in an ambush by French forces. His body was widely displayed in Bassa inhabited areas. Within months after Um Nyobe's death, his second-in-command, Theodore Mayi Matip, and over 2500 guerrillas chose to avail themselves of the government's amnesty offer. This ended the rebellion in the territory's Bassa districts.[10]

French success in tracking down Um Nyobe and demoralizing his Bassa supporters was largely due to Paris's rapid response to the UPC's early attacks. Shortly after the opening rounds of the revolt in 1955, the approximately 2000-man gendarmerie and police force in Cameroon, comprising largely African recruits and a limited number of French officers, was quickly supplemented by several thousand African troops. The latter were transported from the neighboring French colony of Chad to conduct counterinsurgency sweeps in the southwest. After December 1957, the arrival of additional French forces supplemented an even more aggressive counterinsurgency campaign which included the arrest of suspected UPC supporters and the relocation of rural civilians into fortified villages. Government operations also relied on the creation of a 'pacification zone' which was, in effect, a 'free-fire zone' permitting security forces greater leeway to pursue and engage armed insurgents. This augmented force succeeded in containing the UPC and kept the insurgents from escalating what was otherwise a low intensity conflict. Between mid-1957 and late 1958, casualties included 371 insurgents and 75 civilians killed. The authorities arrested an additional 882 guerrillas during this same period.[11] What appeared to have been a successful French effort to thwart the insurgent threat soon proved to be a limited tactical gain rather than a strategic breakthrough.

HEIRS OF THE UPC

While Um Nyobe's death briefly held out the prospect of a gradual end to the rebellion, French authorities and loyalist Cameroonians were soon disappointed. In 1958, a year after his flight to Cairo, Felix Moumie moved the UPC's exile headquarters to Conakry, Guinea. Guinean President Sékou Touré's refusal to join other Francophone African countries in the French Union and Paris's abrupt withdrawal of aid to the newly independent country made Conakry a sympathetic host to African nationalist movements such as the UPC. Guerrilla activity in Bamileke areas soon began to increase in frequency, confirming the resiliency of the insurgency. Moumie and other UPC leaders issued communiqués claiming that these attacks had been carried out by their Armée de Libération Nationale Kamerunaise (ALNK).

For the next two and a half years, the ALNK and residual Bassa elements who had fought under Um Nyobe's leadership conducted a military campaign which exceeded the level of violence and destruction recorded between 1955 and 1958. Led by Paul Momo and Martin Singap, ALNK attacks affected numerous districts between Douala and Yaoundé. By late 1959, the insurgents operated in about two-thirds of the Bamileke inhabited areas. Historians assert that there are no reliable figures for the number of guerrillas who fought under Um Nyobe and the ALNK, although an 8000–10 000 range may not be an unreasonable estimate. At the start of their campaign, ALNK combatants operated in bands of 300–400 and primarily used small arms.[12] Many ALNK raids consisted of sabotage operations which disrupted the territory's economic infrastructure. In late 1959, commercial travel between large southern towns was cut off. French officials had imposed a strict curfew in large cities and towns. Damage to the economy had resulted in rising unemployment, and the territory experienced persistent incidents of murder, arson, and vandalism directly or indirectly attributed to the insurgency.

Adding to a rising crescendo of military operations, ALNK partisans began to practice a scorched-earth policy which included the burning of crops, and cutting down coffee and banana trees, as well as more routine attacks against small towns and plantation workers' camps. On occasion, whole villages were attacked and burned. While the ALNK did not appear to be on the brink of a decisive military victory against French and African security forces, its ability to conduct a protracted insurgency had prompted some observers to wonder whether the government would survive beyond the transition to independence which Paris had scheduled for 1 January 1960.[13] In 1959, the UPC's exile leadership claimed they intended to establish a 'revolutionary administration in exile', prior to creating internal administrative structures in 'liberated zones'. One year later, when Cameroon gained independence under President Ahmadou Ahidjo, UPC leaders asserted that a lack of adequate guarantees for public and individual liberties as well as excessive centralization of power in the President's office justified the continuation of their rebellion. Insurgent leaders also criticized the fact that the constitution too closely resembled that of the fifth French Republic, and reflected excessive French influence.[14]

On Cameroonian independence day, UPC insurgents detonated bombs in Yaoundé while several hundred guerrillas attacked the Douala airport. The UPC also launched military operations north of the Sanaga River, an area of the Sanaga Maritime Region which authorities believed they previously had pacified.[15] By late 1960, ALNK claims to have 'liberated' all Bamileke districts and most areas inhabited by Moungo tribe members seemed plausible to some observers. The insurgents purportedly had established an administrative infrastructure and were performing civil services throughout these regions. However, it appears that the rebellion's strength had in fact rapidly begun to fade during Cameroon's transition from trusteeship territory to independent nation-state. It is probably more accurate to say that the ALNK briefly dominated certain areas or temporarily denied the Cameroonian government access to them.

CENTRIFUGAL FORCES AND THE DECLINE OF THE ALNK

By 1961, exiled UPC leaders who had relocated to Conakry, Guinea, and Accra, Ghana, no longer exercised effective command and control over many of the guerrilla forces in Bamileke areas. This loss of control and influence was partially exposed by earlier reports of disputes between the ALNK's principal military commanders. In 1960 Martin Singap broke with Paul Momo who sided with other Bamileke forces active inside

Cameroon. Singap remained loyal to the ALNK and exiled UPC leaders. Momo was later openly disavowed by the exiled Felix Moumie. When Moumie was poisoned in Geneva, in October 1960, his death did not leave the UPC with a martyr whose memory could rally his surviving colleagues. Instead, preexisting fissures in the movement were compounded by additional feuds within the ranks of other Bamileke UPC members.[16]

Leadership splits within the ALNK/UPC, Cameroon's achievement of independence, and a 1961 referendum in which residents of southern British Cameroons voted for federation with the former French Cameroon, undoubtedly combined to further weaken the insurgents' commitment to the causes proclaimed by their political spokesmen. Between 1958 and 1961, at least 5000–7000 insurgents accepted the government's offer of amnesty. The number of those amnestied may have been considerably larger.[17] In an attempt to exploit the widening splits within the ALNK, President Ahidjo permitted the reestablishment of the UPC as a legal political party in independent Cameroon. At a 1962 UPC Party Congress, dominated by Bassa and Douala tribe members who had rallied to the government, the exile leadership was denounced and ALNK cadres inside the country were declared 'bandits'. The newly reconstituted UPC called for an end to all foreign support for the rebellion.[18]

By 1961, the number of ALNK insurgents remaining in the forests of southwestern Cameroon was variously reported as possibly only 500 but perhaps as high as 2000 combatants. Nonetheless, President Ahidjo asked Paris to keep two battalions of French paratroopers in Cameroon after independence because the country's new 2000-man security force did not seem adequate to handle the residual Bamileke/ALNK revolt. Estimates of the size of the guerrilla force dwindled considerably in subsequent years, however, and by 1963, one observer suggested that only some 500 Bassa members of the UPC were still active.[19]

In March 1966, after several years of steadily diminishing activity, insurgent operations declined precipitously when government troops killed Ossande Ofana, the insurgent UPC's Secretary General. In 1967, the Cameroonian Army destroyed several UPC bases and captured large quantities of arms. This offensive ended a desperate ALNK attempt to open a 'second front' in the southeast, operating from havens on the Congo (Brazzaville) side of the border. In 1968, Ernest Ouandie, one of the UPC's founders, reportedly was still active inside Cameroon. Two years later, however, Ouandie also was captured, tried, and subsequently sentenced to death in 1971. By the early 1970s, the last known UPC leader still at large, Woungli Massaga, who had long been in exile, was believed to be living in Cuba. During the approximately seven years of the insurgency's most active phase, from 1956 to 1963, some 10 000–20 000 civilians and 1000 military personnel were reportedly killed. Some historians favor a figure of 6000 civilian deaths while others have given a range of 6000–15 000 and intimate that 10 000 may be a more reasonable total. Property and other damage sustained during the course of the insurgency was, by some accounts, approximately $8 million.[20]

THE ANATOMY OF FAILURE

Unlike its Malgache predecessor or its Kenyan contemporary, the UPC rebellion did not fail for lack of external aid and assistance. Inadequate planning and a lack of foresight on the part of its leaders, however, probably crippled the insurgency because outside aid was not acquired in a timely manner. In its earliest stages, the UPC insurgency had had little if any foreign support. Bassa tribe members who fought for Ruben Um Nyobe between 1955 and 1958 were forced to operate in small groups of less than 50 men, often with less than twelve weapons between them. Many of their original firearms were homemade. The insurgents' primary sources of supplies were captured from local garrisons or provided by sympathizers in the territorial government.[21]

The rebellions' most intense phase, between 1959 and 1961, coincided with the insurgents' receipt of extensive overseas support. The foundation for this new level of operations had been laid when the UPC's exile leadership fled from Kumba in British Southern Cameroons to Cairo. Gamal Nasser allowed the UPC to open an information bureau and broadcast communiqués over Radio Cairo. After 1958, when the UPC opened offices in Conakry, President Sékou Touré provided financial aid. Touré also offered the UPC his government's political support in the United Nations and other international fora. Guinea and other sympathetic states subsequently endorsed UPC claims that Cameroonian governments elected in 1956 and 1958 did not truly represent the territory's population.

Moreover, the UPC's decision to adopt Marxist rhetoric as well as controversial French colonial policy elsewhere in Africa, particularly in Algeria, also persuaded the USSR, the Soviet bloc, and China to support the rebellion. After 1959, Guinea became a conduit for weapons which were variously reported to have originated in China, Czechoslovakia, or elsewhere in Eastern Europe. In 1960, the People's Republic of China's embassy in Conakry opened a special liaison office with the UPC. The North Vietnamese government is likewise said to have contacted the Cameroonian insurgents in Conakry. The subsequent interrogation of captured UPC personnel revealed that the PRC had trained an unspecified number of Cameroonians in the strategy and tactics of guerrilla warfare as well as providing the insurgents financial assistance.[22]

By 1963, however, as it became increasingly apparent that the insurgency would fail, outside support for the UPC ended. Guinea, Ghana, Mali, and other newly independent African states decided to recognize the Ahidjo government. By the mid-1960s, the UPC's exile leadership was further divided by the impact of the Sino-Soviet split. Pro-Soviet UPC leaders went into exile in Algeria, while pro-PRC members moved to Congo (Brazzaville). By 1968, Cameroon's improved relationship with Algiers and Brazzaville prompted both governments to expel UPC exiles.

The UPC's inability to capitalize on the benefits of outside aid and its contentious relationship with potentially supportive elements of Cameroon's rural population ultimately doomed the insurrection. The stage for this defeat had been set in the movement's earliest days. Within a year after its establishment, in 1948, the UPC's ties to the French Communist Party had alienated traditional tribal organizations, such as Kumsze and Ngondo, which had initially supported Ruben Um Nyobe and his colleagues. This rift widened when local leaders from among the Bassa, Bamileke, and Ewondo-Maka tribes established anti-UPC organizations.[23]

The UPC had been forced to make a policy choice, early in its developmental phase, which diluted the party's appeal to a significant segment of the influential Bamileke. By the late 1940s, thousands of young Bamileke had moved from their tribe's traditional areas into Cameroon's larger cities. During the previous two decades, a rapid growth in the Bamileke population had resulted in a serious overcrowding of Bamileke lands. As a result, the prospects for inheriting or otherwise acquiring land for cultivation was diminishing rapidly. Autocratic traditional Bamileke chiefs whose power to resolve disputes, particularly with respect to land tenure claims, had alienated a growing number of younger Bamileke. Driven into urban areas in search of alternative sources of income, these landless and increasingly detribalized individuals were ready recruits for a UPC which espoused programs calling for land reform as well as independence. As the membership of young, landless Bamileke in the UPC grew, the UPC issued policy statements which threatened the power of traditional leaders. These pronouncements forced many of the rural Bamileke elite into an antagonistic relationship with the UPC and made them more inclined to accept French promises of an eventual independence which did not threaten their customary powers.

The UPC's Marxist-inspired rhetoric also alienated potential supporters in rural areas of northern Cameroon. The largely Muslim population in this area opted for the formation of political parties and lobbying campaigns aimed at peacefully pressuring France to grant the territory its independence. UPC leaders denounced this strategy in the harshest terms. In 1962, a UPC/ALNK tract characterized President Ahidjo's northern-based Union Camerounaise as the party of the 'reactionary social classes, the party of the feudalists, and of the bureaucratic bourgeoisie who remain loyal to medieval conceptions.'[24] Clearly, ideologically driven analyses of Cameroonian society had made the UPC/ALNK's leadership inflexible and caused them to alienate potentially significant allies. This flaw ultimately proved as crippling as a dogmatic adherence to magico-religious precepts had been in Madagascar and Kenya.

MARXISM AND MAGIC

Despite its alienation of tribal leaders in the southwest and its subsequent denunciation of local northern authorities, the UPC did not entirely eschew Cameroon's rural traditions. Prior to his death in September 1958, some supporters portrayed Ruben Um Nyobe as having supernatural powers which made him invisible and bulletproof. Um Nyobe was also said to be the son of a spirit medium and some UPC sympathizers allegedly were told he was in direct contact with traditional spirits. The UPC leader's death purportedly was due to the fact that he had forgotten to wear an amulet just prior to being ambushed. Thus he was attacked at a moment when he could be seen and was not protected against bullets.[25] Whether other Bassa tribe insurgents shared a belief in their own imperviousness to bullets is uncertain. Bamileke guerrillas who staged some of the 1960 independence day attacks in Douala and Yaoundé reportedly bore scars on their chests which they had received in rituals designed to make them bulletproof.[26]

Like some Marxist or Maoist-inspired guerrilla leaders who later appeared elsewhere in Africa, Um Nyobe's main interest in traditional institutions and practices was guided largely by a manipulative and opportunistic impulse. This was particularly apparent in Um Nyobe's interest in traditional Cameroonian 'secret societies', many of which already were moribund by the late 1940s. Um Nyobe relied on the influential relationships of colleagues who were members of several Bassa secret societies and managed to purchase membership in one of the Abo societies which was no longer secret. Contacts with Abo society members who also belonged to other, lesser, societies gave Um Nyobe connections which enabled him to acquire recruits and supplies for his early guerrilla camps. Theodore Mayi Matip, who was the grandson of a prominent Bassa chief, gave Um Nyobe access to one of the most powerful secret societies – Um Nkoda Nton. There is little evidence in these contacts, however, that Um Nyobe or his Bassa supporters intended to revive secret societies or other traditional elements of the culture out of which they had developed.[27]

In many ways, the failure of the UPC insurrection should have been as instructive as the defeats suffered by the insurgents of 1940s Madagascar and Kenya during the following decade. An insurgency led by an educated urban elite, espousing a 'progressive' ideology, and backed by outside powers nevertheless had gone down to defeat. The UPC/ALNK had proven to be as ineffective as rebellions led by less educated rural commanders, inspired by revivalist or reactionary ideals, and lacking external sources of support. One of the UPC's critical failures was its inability to develop a broad, nationwide alliance of rural supporters. This coalition might have been forged by a political program which included an appeal to traditional institutions, particularly the economically endangered Bamileke chiefs of the southwest as well as the theologically sensitive Muslim leaders in the north.

Zealous African Marxists or Maoists who aspired to leadership of an insurgent movement had to accommodate the power and influence of the traditional peasantry. Likewise, rural guerrilla leaders favoring a revivalist ideology had to appreciate the importance of acquiring modern weapons from external sources. The need for a pragmatic and eclectic attitude which could blend traditional and modern elements in an African context was ignored by many insurgents during the next twenty years, however. The lessons that might have been learned from the wars in Madagascar, Kenya, and Cameroon were lost in the 1960s glare of publicity and acclaim accorded Mao Tse-tung's precepts of guerrilla warfare as a generic, universally applicable, strategy which could guide any well meaning 'progressive' leader to victory. Subsequent insurgencies in Angola, Mozambique, Portuguese Guinea, Zimbabwe, Namibia, and South Africa were launched on the assumption that a 'progressive' ideology, educated middle-class leaders, and adequate external sources of modern weapons were the only combination of necessary and sufficient conditions for a successful campaign.

The manipulation of peasants, however, is not an adequate substitute for the mobilization and lasting participation of rural civilians in a protracted insurgency. This realization was probably a more important lesson to be learned from the UPC insurgency than any inferences about the applicability of Marxist or Maoist jargon in an African context. By the late 1970s, only a few insurgent leaders had come to appreciate the importance of synthesizing the strongly held values of Africa's past with the contemporary strategy and tactics of guerrilla warfare. In some respects, the UPC insurgency is a forerunner of the kind of failure experienced by the Kwilu rebellion in the Congo rather than some of the relatively successful insurgencies waged in the former Portuguese colonies or Southern Rhodesia/Zimbabwe.

5 Congo/Zaire: The Kwilu Rebellion, 1963–68

The Kwilu Rebellion, which ravaged large areas of western Congo (Leopoldville) in the mid-1960s, reflected the complex synthesis of a political party, a charismatic personality and religiously inspired rural movements. Within weeks of its beginning, the insurgency appeared to have produced a potent mixture of 'bulletproof' combatants led by an equally invulnerable Maoist commander, Pierre Mulele. The aura surrounding Mulele and his supporters soon inspired insurgent Congolese nationalists far beyond the boundaries of Kwilu Province. Although the insurrection eventually met the same fate as its Kenyan and Malgache predecessors, the Kwilu uprising demonstrated that the influence of traditional African religious beliefs had survived colonialism and the transition to independence.

URBAN REFORMERS AND RURAL RADICALS

In 1959, Belgium responded to increasingly strident Congolese demands for independence by embarking on a rapid decolonization process. This decision accelerated an already vibrant and widespread process of political mobilization which had led to the formation of numerous parties. As a result, a large field of contenders prepared to compete in the national elections due to be held shortly before independence in 1960. One of the most prominent of these new parties emerged on 1 February 1959, when a group of Kwango and Kwilu district residents living in Leopoldville established the Parti Solidaire Africain (PSA). Antoine Gizenga and Pierre Mulele served as the PSA's President and Vice President, respectively. Both leaders were to figure prominently in the tumultuous events of the following decade.

Many of the first PSA members had belonged to the Federation Kwango Kwilu, originally established as a cultural and self-help organization. The PSA also attracted supporters from the Action Socialiste, a socialist study group previously active in Leopoldville. In 1957, the Action Socialiste had become the colony's first officially recognized political party. Some members of Catholic and socialist-inspired labor unions in the capital also joined the PSA. The PSA's initial administrative structure included a

49

National Political Bureau, a National Central Committee in charge of administrative functions, and Provincial Committees in Kikwit and Kinge, the district capitals of Kwilu and Kwango.[1]

As in the case of Madagascar and Kenya, urban-based, intellectual political leaders soon found themselves overtaken by a rural population which was more willing to initiate drastic action against the status quo. Several months after the party was established, PSA leaders moved out from their headquarters in Leopoldville and Kikwit to mobilize support from among residents of the surrounding rural areas. Some early PSA leaders 'reported encountering quite a few instances in which the rural population manifested far greater militancy than they themselves desired or thought to be appropriate.'[2]

Many of the peasants which the PSA sought to recruit were not only more militant in favoring civil disobedience but also more radical in their attitude toward Belgian colonial authority.[3] As one account of the PSA's early activity points out, 'Largely spontaneous rural protest triggered by repatriated city youths existed in the Kwango Kwilu prior to the emergence of political parties in this environment. This protest was harnessed or channeled by the modern elite leaders of the PSA. The goals of the leaders and the masses were never really the same – the leaders wished to Africanize the existing system while the masses appeared to wish its destruction.'[4]

Initial frictions between urban PSA leaders and potential rural supporters were overcome, however. The PSA's advocacy of a political program that seemed progressive and radical facilitated the emergence of a rurally based PSA constituency which was willing, at least temporarily, to put aside its early differences with urban members of the party. Nevertheless, the radical impulses expressed by the peasantry had had a significant effect on some PSA leaders. In late 1959, the PSA and its affiliated Alliance des Bakongo (Abako) party had drawn up secret contingency plans to create a 'government in exile' and launch what presumably would have been a guerrilla campaign for independence in the event that Belgium delayed plans to end colonial rule. Several PSA leaders also traveled to Congo (Brazzaville) and on to Guinea possibly to acquire support for their contingency plan.[5]

Within a year after its establishment, the PSA's potential ability to mobilize a significant dissident force was underscored by claims that the party 'controlled' 1 450 000 people. This constituency was drawn from members of 27 different ethnic groups residing in Kwango and Kwilu districts, located approximately 200 miles east of Leopoldville.[6] The Belgian Congo had a total population of 14 million in 1960. What PSA 'control' meant is unclear but this assertion probably indicated that the party could count on their vote in an election and perhaps a substantial amount of assistance in a pre-election campaign. In the meantime, the PSA's campaign platform hinted at a populist program designed to appeal to a rural and urban electorate. Prior to the 1960 national and provincial elections, the PSA promised to end unemployment, provide more schools and free education in rural areas, increase all salaries, improve housing in rural areas, and make free medical care available for all non-salaried citizens.[7] The PSA also espoused a policy of non-alignment *vis-à-vis* the European powers as well as a socialist program based on peasant collectives or traditional communal farms.[8]

INDEPENDENCE AND THE COLLAPSE OF CENTRAL AUTHORITY

The PSA's campaign proved reasonably successful and at independence in mid-1960 the PSA was the country's third most popular party, outpolling at least nine other parties in the country's first national elections. Because none of the parties gained a clear majority, a coalition was formed. Antoine Gizenga became Deputy Prime Minister and Pierre Mulele was named the Minister of National Education and Fine Arts in the newly independent Congolese government led by President Kasavubu. The coalition rapidly disintegrated, however. Less than two weeks after independence, a nationwide army mutiny pitted enlisted personnel against the largely Belgian officer corps. The mutiny was sparked by a realization that independence would not lead to rapid promotions or the Africanization of an army still dominated by seconded Belgian general officers. Shortly after the outbreak of the military mutiny, Katanga Province, acting on threats made by local representatives prior to independence, declared its secession. One month later, the province of South Kasai also seceded.

Disagreements over an appropriate response to these crises led to mutually ineffective efforts by President Kasavubu and Prime Minister Lumumba to revoke each other's powers. Lumumba had appealed to the former Soviet Union and nations of the Soviet bloc as well as radical African states for assistance. Kasavubu sought and finally acquired the support of Western powers and the United Nations for a peacekeeping force. Kasavubu gained the upper hand after several months and Lumumba was subsequently placed under house arrest in Leopoldville. Vice Prime Minister Gizenga fled to Stanleyville in eastern Congo to establish a pro-Lumumba opposition government. Lumumba was later murdered after attempting to escape from Leopoldville and join his supporters in the east. By late 1962, command and control of the Congolese Army had been reestablished and the new government of President Kasavubu and Prime Minister Cyril Adoula successfully negotiated an end to secession in Katanga and Kasai. Nevertheless, radical nationalist elements, represented in part by unreconciled dissidents in eastern Congo, as well as disgruntled factions in the west, chose to launch new insurgencies in late 1963.

RURAL ROOTS OF REBELLION IN WESTERN CONGO

In many respects, the story of the Kwilu rebellion is a tale of at least two leadership elements as well as a tale of two ideologies. In late 1960, a small group of Kwilu district residents established the 'Savoir Vivre' (Art of Living) movement. Like many other Congolese, the members of this movement voiced their disappointment with the lack of the 'good life' which they had anticipated after independence from Belgium. By 1962, Savoir Vivre members expressed the view, at meetings held in Kwilu, that their lives had become even more difficult, economically, than before independence.[9] Savoir Vivre members eventually formulated the ideology of an agrarian development movement which espoused the view that 'Happiness is in the village and not in great centers. Happiness in the cities is an illusion. True "freedom" is to be found in the village not in the city... Manual work is happiness. Agriculture is the most direct form of collaboration with the creative work of God. It provides all men with what they need to live and be happy... .'[10] For the Catholic-inspired Savoir Vivre, 'In effect, the new society [was] conceived as a gigantic village made up of thousands of small villages in which the people find their own authenticity; all that they need materially; justice; creativity and happiness working in the soil together.'[11]

An equally important role in fomenting a climate of rebellion in Kwilu, however, must be attributed to the members of the Mpeve ('Spirit') sect, also known as the Bene Simon ('People of Simon'). The sect was an offshoot of the Kimbanguists, a syncretic religious movement founded by the charismatic preacher, Simon Kimbangu, in 1921. Kimbanguist teachings were based largely on the Old Testament. Kimbangu's sermons also included excerpts that were chosen to provoke anti-Western emotions and, like the later doctrine of Negritude, feelings of pride in being black and part of the pre-colonial African kingdom of the Kongo. Kimbanguist prophecies also anticipated the ouster of foreign rulers, a 'new way of life' for Africans, and other apocalyptic developments. By 1945, Kimbanguism had spread to the Kwilu district. Alarmed by its popularity Belgian colonial authorities outlawed the movement in the early 1950s and its members probably went underground.[12]

In 1959, the Mpeve sect appeared in Kwilu district and quickly filled the void left by the banned Kimbanguists. Like their predecessors, Mpeve members combined Christian and traditional animist beliefs. Its adherents believed in their ability to convoke good and evil spirits. Mpeve leaders also told their supporters that independence would result in a 'new life' in which the vestiges of European rule would disappear. Moreover, the 'ancestors', particularly the former chiefs who had been pushed aside or suppressed by colonial authorities, would be revived or resurrected on the day of independence and would drive out the bad chiefs and all those who had collaborated with the Europeans. With independence and the return of the ancestors, the population would become wealthy and the Europeans would disappear. The failure of these prophecies and the absence of millennial developments, in the months after the Congo's 30 June 1960 independence, did not diminish the faith or fervor of many Mpeve members. Historians have suggested that the commitment to a struggle for a 'second independence' – a phrase which later became associated with the Kwilu rebellion – traces its roots to the Mpeve sect's response to what should have been a profound political and theological crisis.[13]

FANNING THE FLAMES OF RESENTMENT

While the numerous political and economic crises which followed Congolese independence evoked the Savoir Vivre ideology and contributed to the Mpeve sect's alienation, the methods whereby Kwilu Province administrators attempted to exercise their power further provoked province residents who were already inclined to launch an active rebellion. In the early 1960s, the local PSA branch, led by Cleophas Kamitatu, dominated the Kwilu Province Assembly and local administration. Kamitatu and other like-minded officials sought to initiate an ambitious economic program which included the modification of traditional agricultural methods as well as more stringent and efficient tax collection. However, in the view of a contemporary analyst, 'the people of the villages apparently resented the degree and kind of control exercised over them by government officials whom they regarded as not having a traditional village mentality, or a sense of identification with the plight of the population living and working in rural areas.'[14] The implementation, after 1962, of forced cultivation in Kwilu convinced some local peasants that the newly independent government was resorting to the type of bureau-cratic rule and autocratic techniques which had been associated with its colonial predecessor.[15]

Members of the Mpeve sect resisted local Kwilu administrators. Sect leaders advocated the non-payment of taxes and a general opposition to the state. By 1962, at which time Kwilu district had become a province, Mpeve members had set up several camps where they imprisoned and occasionally tortured some of their opponents. In April 1962 Mpeve members captured and held a local Kwilu administrator hostage at one of their camps. Subsequent negotiations with local officials failed, gunfire was exchanged, and the camp was overrun by provincial security forces, resulting in the death of several sect members. Shortly thereafter, the Kwilu Province Assembly banned the Mpeve sect.[16] The Kwilu province leadership continued to press ahead with its agrarian reform program. Between September 1962 and March 1963 the police arrested several traditional chiefs who had resisted local administrators. Subsequent reports asserted these chiefs were mistreated while in detention.[17] By early 1963, despite indications that Mpeve members, dissident traditional chiefs and the supporters of Savoir Vivre had been suppressed, Kwilu Province administrators confronted yet another threat. Local residents who favored the Gizengist faction of the PSA established a 'jeunesse' or youth move-ment which soon set up camps and recruited additional members. In May 1963 some 2000 policemen in Leopoldville mutinied and were subse-quently arrested. A large number of these policemen were from the Kwilu area and were later forced to return to the province after their release. Many of these former policemen are thought to have joined the ranks of the PSA/Gizengist 'jeunesse'.[18]

In July 1963 the 'jeunesse' and other pro-Gizenga PSA elements actively contested local elections in Kwilu Province. The election cam-paign was marred by reports of police intimidation of voters during the registration and polling phases. Moreover, the provincial government annulled the outcome in two districts after the results revealed totals which favored the Gizenga supporters instead of candidates supported by the moderate, Kamitatu-led, PSA branch.[19] In the midst of this persistent atmosphere of repression and imminent rebellion, the PSA's former Vice President Mulele returned to Kwilu Province in late July 1963.

By early August 1963 Mulele and several colleagues had formally decided to organize a rebellion. They contacted members of several dis-sident camps, probably those of the 'jeunesse'. It is noteworthy, however, that Mulele's name was never mentioned in the mounting provincial tensions of late 1962 and early 1963. Leopoldville-based intellectual elements such as Mulele, as well as the Kamitatu-led PSA provincial branch, had evidently alienated rural radicals in the province during the early years of Congolese independence. Between February 1962, when Mulele resigned his cabinet position in Kasavubu's government, and August 1963, when he returned to Kwilu to recruit sympathizers and set up initial base camps, his name was never associated with those opposed to the Kwilu Province administration.[20] Evidently, Mulele also did not send advance word of his aims and intentions to prospective supporters in Kwilu Province.[21] The pre-existing camps with which Mulele came in contact in July–August 1963 were likely those established by local pro-Gizenga PSA members, not Mulele himself or his immediate friends.[22] By September 1963, pro-Gizenga PSA members in Leopoldville who were unwilling to oppose the Kasavubu government forcefully, denounced Mulele and dismissed him from the party.

In a matter of a few months however, Mulele had essentially transformed himself from a political exile without a cause into a rebel leader in search of a party. An inclination to revolt and the existence of sentiments sympathetic to a rebellion obviously had predated Mulele's return to Kwilu Province. Nevertheless, Mulele and a radical nationalist fringe of the PSA ultimately defined the rebellion's objectives, organized its forces, and outlined its strategy. Mulele quickly shaped the insurgency's contemporary organizational features and manipulated its traditional or revivalist dimensions. Like their Malgache and Kenyan predecessors, rebels in Kwilu Province eventually forged a fragile politico-military synthesis of traditional and modern viewpoints.

A POLITICAL AND IDEOLOGICAL ODYSSEY

Three years prior to his return to Kwilu Province, Pierre Mulele, who had initially sided with Premier Patrice Lumumba against President Joseph Kasavubu in the initial post-independence crises, embarked on a two-year global odyssey. In December 1960, Mulele departed for Cairo as an 'ambassador' of the Lumumba faction of the divided Congolese government. In March 1961 he arrived in Accra, Ghana, where he sought Kwame Nkrumah's assistance. By 1962, Mulele had resigned his old cabinet post in the Kasavubu government and made his way to the People's Republic of China, after stops in Prague and Moscow. While in China, he received training in Maoist precepts of guerrilla warfare. When he returned to

Kwilu Province in mid-1963, Mulele found dissatisfied and dissident residents eager to hear the ideological and strategic insights he had gleaned during his travels.[23]

Mulele never published a manifesto or program, however. According to statements from supporters who participated in the insurrection and listened to his speeches, Mulele perceived two main classes in society – 'capitalists' and 'the impoverished masses'. In the Congo, the former category implied foreigners and functionaries of the independent government. Mulele also spoke of two kinds of struggle – 'reformist', which was not desirable, and 'revolutionary' which gave power to the masses. Reflecting his experiences in Maoist China, Mulele also asserted that revolution had to be conducted by insurgents supported by local villagers 'as fish in water'.[24]

According to notebooks subsequently taken from captured Mulele supporters, the insurgency was waged for a radical but nonetheless ill-defined future. Thus, the guerrillas were told: 'when the government is overthrown, we will establish a new regime in which all must and will work in order to eat, in which foreigners cannot come to take the wealth of the country, and in which we cannot steal the wealth of others either. A beautiful house, complete with furniture, will be built for each person by the new government.'[25] Mulele also purportedly made occasional, and fairly general, references to China as a 'country of happiness' and some of the notes which his supporters made during the course of his speeches hint that post-'revolutionary' Congo would seek help from 'another country' for assistance in the establishment of a manufacturing and industrial sector.[26] This agenda evoked an immediate response from Kwilu residents whose previous political and religious interests already had primed them to move from theory to practice.

THE RUSH TO REBELLION

By late August 1963, using recruiting tactics which strongly resembled those employed by Savoir Vivre leaders, Mulele had attracted a growing number of supporters. Mulele maintained three camps in different areas of Kwilu Province and the movement had over 550 members.[27] An increasingly nervous Kwilu Province Assembly put a price on Mulele's head and in September 1963 the authorities arrested more than thirty unarmed supporters. More arrests followed in the next few weeks. Local government security forces searched for Mulele's headquarters and had launched two attacks on his main base by the end of October. Mulele quickly relocated his camps to more remote, heavily forested, areas of the province.[28]

The initial success of their preemptive strikes did not reassure Kwilu Province administrators. Prior to 1964, only four platoons of Congolese National Army (ANC) troops, approximately 160 soldiers, defended the entire province. Mulele's determination to recruit additional members and mobilize civilian supporters, along with the late 1963 searches for his camps, delayed the start of insurgent operations until January 1964. The insurgents then launched widespread attacks against government outposts, missionary stations, palm oil mills, bridges, ferries, and telephone lines. By late January, Mulele's guerrillas had isolated an area of about 350 kilometers by 150 kilometers, roughly the size of Belgium.[29]

The scale and coordination evident in the attacks staged by Mulele's combatants reflected the formation of a fairly elaborate guerrilla force which drew its inspiration from modern military principles. Between September and December 1963, Mulele and his commanders had established a table of organization which included 'zones', 'sub-directions', 'brigades' and 'équipes' or cells. Each of the five 'zones' which Mulele originally designated 'east', 'west', 'north', 'south', and 'central', contained 3–4 'sub-directions'. Each 'sub-direction' had four companies, with the latter being further subdivided into two or three 'équipes'. Captured documents later revealed references to a 'military academy', 'department of archives', 'paracommando department', 'military affairs department', 'medical affairs', 'social affairs', and 'popular masses'.[30]

These subdivisions responded to orders from 'Central', Mulele's headquarters, which was linked to its subordinate units by a 'Direction' or 'major' who moved from one group to another to pass orders, oversee operations and perform other liaison functions.[31] A 'corporal of war', a platoon chief, and a section chief assisted those who led the 'équipes'. Cells also included political commissars and assistants such as a secretary who prepared regular reports, a chief of the camp, a man and a woman to attend to domestic chores at each camp, and a 'chief of the posts'.[32] The average strength of a 'company' was approximately 180 combatants. 'Equipes' normally operated in groups of 20–100 insurgents and were sometimes subdivided into 'sections'(squads) of 13–26 insurgents. These forces were supplemented by local 'comités de village' which, in addition to administering to the needs of the movement's civilian supporters, also raised their own militia and police units.[33]

While Maoist influences on Mulele's ideology and his organizational preferences were readily apparent, it is also clear that the guerrillas utilized conventional military principles which Belgium had introduced in the colonial era. Members of the 2000-man police force who returned to Kwilu Province after their March 1963 mutiny in Leopoldville and subsequently joined Mulele's camps probably transferred some of their organizational and administrative experience to the insurgency. Moreover, many guerrillas, including Mulele himself, had served in the colonial Force Publique under Belgian military officers during the 1950s. Some of Mulele's most able commanders were also ANC deserters.[34] Like the Malgache and Kenyan veterans of the 1940s, Congolese insurgents most likely applied at least a portion of their former military experience as members of a Belgian-trained conventional army to their operations as a guerrilla force.

MAGIC, CHARISMA, AND MORALE

The Kwilu insurgents' traditional religious world view had a much greater impact on their military tactics. These beliefs soon overshadowed the conventional, European-inspired organizational structures or Maoist guidelines for the conduct of guerrilla war which appeared in captured documents. Indeed, Mulele quickly acquired a reputation for being bulletproof, a notion he reportedly fostered by staging occasional demonstrations in which he would point a revolver (loaded with blanks) at his head, pull the trigger, and then walk away. Before long, many supporters claimed that Mulele had supernatural powers which enabled him to move through government lines by making himself invisible as well as the ability to turn arrows into bullets in flight. Additionally, many people thought Mulele had the power to turn himself into a bird or snake and that he could transport himself through the forest by using an airplane the size of his hand, leading some supporters to believe he could be omnipresent.[35]

Mulele's willingness to encourage, or at least tolerate, the myth of his invincibility by relying on traditional magico-religious perspectives stemmed from more than just a need to impress new or potential recruits or to intimidate opponents. Mulele was, in fact, benefitting from the persistence of a local millennial theme, associated with the 'talking serpent' or 'snake man' sect which initially appeared in 1932. According to this sect's teachings, a special serpent's appearance would bring forth prophets and messiahs to fight European masters and expel them. A variety of apocalyptic portents, including a collective resurrection of the dead, the eclipse of the sun, the ubiquitous appearance of a black talking dog, and the arrival of a man who would be part white and part black, were expected to accompany this event. Cult followers also expected to acquire invincibility by drinking a magic potion from special cups.[36]

In addition to attributing special powers to Mulele, sympathetic traditional religious leaders also established numerous taboos for his forces to observe. Prior to combat, the guerrillas were ordered (1) not to eat certain foods, such as the liver, heart, or head of animals, (2) to avoid using or touching objects belonging to Europeans, (3) to avoid washing or cutting hair until final victory, (4) to enter battle bare chested, (5) never to retreat or stop advancing in battle, (6) never to pronounce Mulele's name. Moreover, French was prohibited in Mulele's camps; the insurgents spoke Lingala instead.[37] In battle, the insurgents were to advance shouting 'Mai, Mai' (Water, Water) which was expected to turn their enemies' bullets into balls of mud. The guerrillas also rubbed their torsos with red clay and adorned themselves with amulets containing human fingernails, to facilitate their becoming bulletproof.[38]

Each insurgent camp had its own *sorcier* or traditional medicine man (*nganga*) and a *soigneur* or medic who applied European drugs which usually had been captured in attacks on missionary dispensaries. By the time the insurgency had spread throughout much of Kwilu Province, some insurgents and local civilians believed that Mulele's powers were such that a failure to support or sympathize with his movement would make them infertile or cause their children to be more susceptible to illness and death. Those insurgents who later died in combat were thought to have lost the powers they derived from Mulele because they had violated certain rules and practices or did not believe sufficiently in victory.[39] Alternatively, Mulele allegedly assured his supporters that those who died in combat would be resurrected after four months.[40]

Ultimately, it was Mulele's association with traditional magico-religious precepts and their application to military operations that elevated him to the status of a national leader. During the late 1950s, and in the immediate aftermath of Congolese independence, Mulele had played a relatively minor role in the PSA and in the cabinet of the Lumumba government. Even after his 1963 return to Kwilu Province, reports that he was organizing a Maoist-Chinese inspired insurgency did not have nearly the same impact as his subsequent reputation as a charismatic guerrilla leader with 'prophetic-superhuman qualities'. Moreover, his reputation, and that of his 'bulletproof' troops soon spread to supporters of the National Liberation Council (CNL) insurgency. In early 1964 the CNL rebellion had advanced rapidly through Congo's eastern provinces where rebel groups reportedly were chanting 'Mulele mai' as they charged into battle. This occurred despite their leaders' efforts to change the chant to 'Lumumba mai' to reflect local loyalties to the murdered Prime Minister.[41]

FUTILE ATTACKS AND LOST MOMENTUM

Mulele's partisans were undoubtedly heartened by the rapid gains they had made in early January 1964. Aside from prominent roles which members of the Bambunda and Bapende tribes played as early Mulele supporters, the insurgency also had begun to draw recruits from elements of at least seven other tribes, including the BaDinga, BaLori, BaNkutshu, BashiLele, BaSuku, BaWongo, and BaYanzi – all located in Kwilu Province.[42] Encouraged by their initial success, the guerrillas launched several ill-conceived large attacks on some of the principal towns in Kwilu Province, such as Gungu and Idiofa. Thwarted by the superior firepower of the defenders, these assaults were unsuccessful and proved costly to Mulele's forces which suffered more than 1000 killed by early February 1964. Government forces had sustained only eight ANC fatalities.

In March 1964, ANC General Mobutu told journalists that the number of insurgents in Kwilu had risen to 10 000 but that their morale had declined. Mobutu said that he expected to have the situation under control in about two weeks. While the accuracy of Mobutu's assessment of Kwilu guerrilla strength has been questioned, historians of the rebellion generally eschew a precise estimate of the number of insurgents involved. Although Mulele's commanders assigned numbers to their 'équipes' which ranged in the thousands, the number of men in an 'équipe' also appeared to have varied considerably. In mid-1964, there may well have been some 20 000 insurgents active in Kwilu Province. If unarmed but active supporters are inferred from the incomplete membership lists which were later captured, a proposed figure of as many as 90 000–100 000 partisans is not implausible. In any event, Mobutu's assessment was, at best, an imprecise estimate of the size of the insurgent force and certainly overstated his expected success against it.[43]

Undeterred by their previous losses, Mulele's forces staged several additional large, but unsuccessful, attacks against the government-held towns of Kikwit and Idiofa. The last major assault occurred in May 1965. During the first 17 months of the war, the insurgent's largest and only successful major engagement was a 30 June 1964 attack by a force of several thousand guerrillas against a small ANC outpost at Kimpata Eku on the road between Idiofa and Kikwit. This engagement was, in some respects, the military high water mark of the rebellion. Weakened by the cumulative impact of the disastrous major attacks on Gungu in February 1964 and Idiofa four months later, the insurgents gradually began to avoid major engagements with large ANC units.[44] This probably reflected a reluctance to risk high casualties as well as an inability to capture or otherwise acquire a reliable supply of weapons and ammunition.

The Congolese military lost little time in responding to the insurgent threat. In February 1964 helicopters carried additional troops to the province. Within several months, the government had deployed three companies of gendarmes, a commando battalion brought in from Katanga Province and an ANC infantry battalion. After April 1964 the ANC slowly regained the tactical initiative. Government forces launched a 'pacification' program in June but did not begin to register any significant progress until December 1964. In the program's initial phase, government delegations entered the forests and attempted to negotiate terms under which civilians who had fled their villages in the early months of the rebellion could return to villages that were now under ANC control. Villagers were offered better food and medical care than they were receiving at or near Mulele's camps. By February 1965 the ANC had reopened many major roads and secured numerous strong-points in Kwilu Province. Efforts to entice villagers out of the forests became more successful as the ANC began to demonstrate that it could protect them against insurgent reprisals.[45]

REBELS ON THE RUN

In March 1965 there were an estimated 2000 guerrillas remaining at Mulele's headquarters. The territory affected by the insurgents, however, had grown much smaller. On 9 June 1965, ANC troops found and destroyed Mulele's headquarters camp. The insurgents barely had time to flee with their weapons. Numerous documents were captured. Within a month after this operation the ANC had reoccupied a large area east of Idiofa with almost no rebel resistance. On 7 September 1965, ANC troops again found, attacked, and wrecked Mulele's relocated headquarters. Six months later, Mulele's main base camp held no more than 600 combatants. In mid-March 1966, the ANC once again ferreted out the insurgents' headquarters. Attacking government troops forced Mulele and his dwindling number of supporters to scatter. The ANC's counterinsurgency offensive dispersed many of the insurgent's principal commanders. Mulele made a long retreat into northern Kwilu Province to avoid further ANC encirclements. In mid-1966 he had managed to regroup some 700 insurgents at a new base. By August of that year, however, the ANC was again in pursuit of Mulele's forces.[46]

Many of Mulele's early advances had occurred in a military vacuum. The Kwilu insurgents never had the firepower necessary to mount an effective direct challenge to government forces. Throughout the insurgency the ANC never conducted more than battalion-sized sweep operations. Despite their rapid territorial gains and crippling acts of sabotage in the early months of the insurgency, by 1966 the guerrillas had killed only 10–20 soldiers, wounded a few dozen and captured three. Two ANC officers were among the fatalities, including the ANC Chief of Staff who was killed by a poisoned arrow. In early 1964, Mulele's forces probably also assassinated more than 100 government sympathizers. Several hundred additional civilians may have died in clashes between the ANC and insurgent elements. These and other statistics graphically reflect the insurgents' limited military capability. Mulele's combatants probably never had more than 100 modern rifles; the rest of their armory consisted of bows, poisoned arrows, clubs, machetes, homemade rifles, and Molotov cocktails. By 1966 this armory had shrunk to 19 rifles, six sten guns and six revolvers.[47]

The guerrillas' rapid loss of the initiative, their abandonment of large-scale offensive operations, and their self-imposed geographic isolation had severely limited the number of weapons they were able to capture.[48] Their inferior firepower became a mounting and ultimately irreversible disadvantage as their ANC pursuers pushed them further into remote areas of the province. Tribally based splits and desertions also began to dissipate Mulele's forces after mid-1965. In March of that year, guerrillas loyal to Bapenda leader Damien Kandaka challenged Mulele's authority and that of his fellow Bambunda commanders. This dispute worsened, and the factions eventually engaged in armed clashes.[49] As the ANC regained the tactical initiative and the insurgency imploded, Mulele lost the sympathy of ethnic groups whose support for the guerrillas had not been consolidated in the first year of the rebellion. Likewise, ethnic groups whose initial response to the insurgents was ambivalent gradually shifted their support to the government.[50]

Finally, Mulele's inability to reestablish command and control irreparably exacerbated the guerrillas' shortcomings. According to an account published in late 1965, 'as time went on, the Kwilu rebellion seemed to become more destructive and less subject to the influence and control of the values, beliefs and norms of Mulelism, or to the authority of its chiefs. Burning, pillaging, attacking women, murdering became more and more widespread. This was especially true once the majority of the Europeans had been evacuated from the Kwilu and the Congolese Army arrived.'[51] The burning of villages and the execution of their chiefs convinced members of some ethnic groups, such as the Bambala, that the guerrillas did not deserve their support. Despite indications that Mulele and his cohorts deplored and denounced the rebellion's vindictive tendencies, they repeatedly failed to prevent reprisals against villages and local leaders who did not rally to their cause.[52]

MULELE'S FLICKERING FLAME

The ANC's relentless pursuit forced Mulele to change camps several times between January and October 1967. Their frequent retreats demoralized the guerrillas and led to a growing number of defections. Illness also began to take a mounting toll on the insurgents. In November, government units again threatened to encircle Mulele's camp. The ANC attacked and pursued Mulele for six days. The insurgents had to divide into even more dispersed groups. Many of the movement's weakened leaders were subsequently killed or captured. By the end of the year, the Kwilu rebellion had been reduced to the activities of two small guerrilla bands. Pierre Mulele and a limited number of supporters had relocated their base from Mulele's Bambunda area to a Bading tribal area north of Idiofa. A second small group was still active in the vicinity of Gungu. By 1968, Mulele and his wife, Leonie Abo, were living alone in a forest camp from which they maintained infrequent contacts with local villagers and a handful of insurgents. In March and June 1968, government forces again caught up with Mulele and forced him to relocate his camp. In the previous three years of the insurrection, Kwilu Province had been devastated as a consequence of the ANC's pursuit of Mulele. An estimated 60 000–100 000 people had died as a result of the hostilities and related famine. The affected districts had had a total population of about 500 000 when the rebellion began. The ANC's initial counterinsurgency strategy had been predicated on a scorched-earth policy which included the burning of villages and crops of suspected Mulele supporters. As in the case of the Malgache rebellion, many of the displaced civilians fled into the forests. Mulele's forces failed to establish farms and grow crops to feed these refugees, however, and they eventually rallied to the government.[53]

With the loss of his military commanders and the evaporation of his civilian support throughout most of Kwilu Province, Mulele grudgingly abandoned the armed struggle. In early September 1968 he travelled to Brazzaville, capital of the neighboring Congo Republic. After several meetings with government emissaries from Leopoldville (by then renamed Kinshasa), Mulele returned on 29 September 1968 believing that he would be eligible for an amnesty decreed by President Mobutu. At a reception held in his honor by the Commander in Chief of the ANC, Mulele reportedly said he was convinced that President Mobutu was carrying out the policy of the late Patrice Lumumba. Mulele asserted that he himself had not fought for power but for an ideology. As this ideology had now been upheld, Mulele conceded there was no point in further struggle. Nevertheless, on 2 October Mobutu announced that Mulele would be tried as a 'war criminal' and pointed out that the amnesty applied to 'political prisoners' not 'war criminals'. Mulele was brought before a military tribunal on 7 October 1968 and executed by a firing squad of unidentified Army personnel the following day.[54]

MARXIST, 'MAGICAL' OR *MATÉRIEL* FAILURE?

As in the case of the Malgache and Kenyan insurgencies, the defeat of the Kwilu rebellion has been attributed to flaws in Mulele's leadership and the guerrillas' excessive reliance on traditional religious views. Mulele was faulted because he did not effectively pass on his Maoist/Marxist teachings to his followers. As one critic observed, the 'pronouncements of the forest camps were not put into practice in the brief period the rebels controlled parts of Kwilu.'[55] In essence, Mulele never really established a 'revolutionary' political organization charged with educating peasants and coordinating their actions. A related evaluation suggests that Mulele applied Maoist principles in an inappropriate context.[56] This perspective emphasizes his failure to appreciate the strength of traditional animistic religious sentiments. An alternative view of Mulele's behavior indicates that rather than underestimating traditional theology, Mulele actively chose to exploit and manipulate it. In so doing, he must have known that he was compromising the Maoist/Marxist principles he initially brought to Kwilu Province in 1963.

While personal and political factors undeniably contributed to the character and course of the rebellion, the guerrillas' lack of outside support was critical in accounting for their eventual failure. Because Mulele emphasized self-sufficiency, his forces made no concerted effort to acquire external support. Only a few of Mulele's colleagues made half-hearted attempts to contact insurgent groups active in Congo's eastern districts. Mulele's unwillingness to pursue actively the creation of an alliance or 'broad front' with guerrilla movements in the east stunted his forces' political and military growth and further limited their prospects. A coalition of guerrilla forces might have enabled Mulele's insurgents to obtain additional recruits as well as supplies and civilian support outside the boundaries of Kwilu Province. In 1966, Mulele finally made a feeble effort to propose the establishment of a coalition of Congolese dissidents. By this time, however, guerrilla forces in the east were already seriously weakened by their own internal splits and had little or nothing to offer Mulele's increasingly harried insurgents.

Mulele's opposition to obtaining outside aid, particularly in the early years of the insurgency, stemmed from a belief that such support would force him to accommodate external patrons who eventually would dominate or dictate policy to him and his commanders. His fear of a 'neo-colonial' conclusion to a successful rebellion led Mulele to avoid promising his followers any great riches after their victory. Instead, he told the insurgents they were fighting for a future in which they would have the possibility to make – by themselves – those things which the masses truly needed.[57]

This approach to the conduct of the insurgency severely limited the firepower Mulele's forces could bring to bear against the ANC. The government's military capability steadily proved more effective than the initial surge of unarmed enthusiasts who rallied to the Kwilu rebellion. Insurgents whose armory generally consisted of spears, bows and arrows and homemade rifles gradually proved to be insufficiently armed, even against a poorly led and trained government force. Moreover, the ANC quickly acquired an adequate supply of trucks and weapons to equip a conventional light infantry force capable of sustaining a dogged pursuit of Mulele. The ANC, whose troops originally were drawn from provincially based units (excluding those in the secessionist provinces of Katanga and Kasai), had grown from a force of 23 000 at independence to over 37 000 by 1962. By 1964, there were over 200 Belgian officers and about 100 American advisors assisting the ANC. The US and Belgium had delivered over $7 million worth of equipment to Congolese security forces.[58]

While Mulele's reasons for isolating his insurgency may have seemed politically sound, they ultimately proved disastrous militarily. In some respects, the constraints imposed on the insurgents by Mulele's isolationist impulse were compounded by contemporary geopolitical factors. Kwilu Province insurgents had no adjacent international boundaries across which they could have found safe havens. Their southern flank was on the border of the Portuguese colony of Angola. The right-wing Salazar regime in Lisbon, already confronted by two Angolan insurgent movements in 1963, was clearly incompatible with Mulele's Marxist/Maoist ideological preferences.

The Congo River and the ANC's control over territory on its southern bank likewise discouraged but did not necessarily prevent Mulele's forces from considering Congo-Brazzaville as a conduit for supplies or an area in which to establish rear bases. A logistic line running through Congo-Brazzaville, however, probably would not have been too difficult to establish. On the other hand, vast distances, and the existence of potentially hostile insurgent forces in eastern Congo, made Tanzanian, Ugandan, or Sudanese conduits seem less desirable though not implausible. In the late 1960s the insurgent Popular Movement for the Liberation of Angola (MPLA) established supply lines leading from Dar es Salaam, Tanzania, across Zambia into eastern Angola. The absence of external support and inadequate firepower notwithstanding, Mulele and his Kwilu insurgents have since passed into history as still another example of unsuccessful insurrections which failed because they were commanded by inept rural leaders or guided by parochial views.

The fact that they were unable to topple a weak independent African government, in addition to their poor performance against heavily armed colonial forces, underscored what have come to be viewed as inescapable personal and intellectual limitations in any insurgency which emphasizes traditional religious values and customs. For the remainder of the 1960s and early 1970s, the prevailing view in the analysis of guerrilla warfare held that only insurgents whose leaders espoused 'progressive'/modern world views could hope to wage a successful war. The success of such movements, however, presumably still depended on assured sources of outside support from sympathetic states such as U.S.S.R., China, and the former Soviet bloc governments of eastern Europe. This view became axiomatic for many observers who also assumed that no external power, even one motivated solely by self-interest, would support a revivalist/reactionary peasant movement because its prospects for success were considered minimal. Any investment in such a movement ultimately would be wasted and potentially even counterproductive in that it might undermine relations with the colonial or local government which eventually prevailed over its insurgent opponents. Subsequent events in recent African history suggest that this perspective was based on questionable assumptions about the adaptive and resilient quality of revivalist movements, particularly if they acquire external support.

6 Mozambique: From the NRM to Renamo, 1977–92

Nationalist movements in Mozambique originally bore the trappings of contemporary political parties and modern ideologies. When Portugal refused to accommodate the 'wind of change' sweeping colonial Africa in the early 1960s, the advocates of Mozambican independence launched a guerrilla war inspired by the teachings and success of Mao, Ho Chi Minh, and the Algerian insurgents of the previous decade. When Mozambique finally achieved its independence in 1975 the prospect of a revivalist guerrilla challenge to one of Southern Africa's most widely acclaimed 'progressive' political parties was unimaginable. A reconsideration of recent Mozambican history, however, reveals that the seeds of an opposition movement emphasizing traditional religious beliefs and social institutions had been planted long before independence.

A FRAGILE UNITY OF PURPOSE

One of the principal roots of contemporary Mozambican politics can be traced to the National Democratic Union of Mozambique (Udenamo) founded in 1958, and led by Adelino Gwambe and Uria T. Simango. On 25 June 1962, Udenamo merged with the Mozambique African National Union (Manu) and the National Union for Mozambican Independence (Unami) to form the Front for the Liberation of Mozambique (Frelimo). This merger reflected a realization that the three small proto-nationalist movements represented only a narrow segment of the Mozambican population whose growing urge for independence could be better represented by a broad, nationwide, coalition. Udenamo members Fanuel Mahluza, David Mabunda, and Paulo Gumane assumed prominent positions in Frelimo. Mabunda was appointed Secretary General, Gumane became Deputy Secretary General, and Mahluza was the Front's representative in Cairo. Less than a year later, personal and political disputes as well as debates concerning the movement's military strategy against Portuguese colonial rule undermined Frelimo. Gwambe, Mabunda, and Gumane left Frelimo and sought to reconstitute Udenamo.[1]

On 24 September 1964, Frelimo launched a guerrilla war to gain Mozambique's independence from Portugal. Although they did not form their own military wings, Udenamo, Manu, and other minor Mozambican movements continued to compete with Frelimo for power and influence in the leadership ranks of the anti-colonial struggle. In 1965, Zambian President Kenneth Kaunda invited Frelimo and several other Mozambican nationalist splinter movements to a meeting in Lusaka to promote a merger of Mozambican nationalists. Frelimo representatives walked out after the other movements refused to merge under Frelimo's leadership. Its military commanders continued the guerrilla struggle Frelimo had initiated in 1964.

Shortly thereafter, Frelimo experienced additional internal dissension which revealed regional and tribal fissures in the movement. Makonde tribe members from the north complained that they were being used as 'cannon fodder' in a war led by insurgent commanders drawn primarily from Shangaan tribe members in the south. Claims of racism and elitism emphasizing the educational qualifications of the movement's leadership exacerbated these divisions.[2] The tensions between various factions became particularly pronounced after the 3 February 1969 parcel bomb assassination of Frelimo's founder and first President, Eduardo Mondlane. Uncorroborated reports indicated that the presumed Portuguese assassination plot had been facilitated by disgruntled Frelimo members.

The uneasy triumvirate of Samora Machel, Marcelino dos Santos, and Uria Simango created a Presidential Council which briefly led the movement until May 1970 when Machel was appointed Frelimo's sole leader. The party was once again undermined by some of the same regional, racial, and tribal issues which had divided the anti-colonial movement in the first half of the 1960s. These debates soon came to a head, and in May 1970 Simango was expelled from the Presidential Council. Prior to his expulsion, Simango had publicized the debates which were dividing Frelimo. Among the most serious disputes Simango revealed, his appeal that 'the question of scientific socialism and capitalism in Mozambique should not be allowed to divide us' eventually proved to be one of the most crucial issues at the heart of the struggle for independence and the formation of a new Mozambican state.[3]

While Frelimo struggled on to resolve ideological and leadership disputes, the four movements which remained after the collapse of the 1965 Lusaka talks had merged and established the Revolutionary Committee of Mozambique (Coremo). Adelino Gwambe, former Udenamo leader, became Coremo's first President. Gwambe was expelled from Coremo in 1966, however, accused of being a Portuguese agent. He was succeeded by Paulo Gumane, Udenamo's former Deputy Secretary General. Coremo's Defense Minister was Fanuel Mahluza, who had once been

Udenamo's Vice President, underscoring the continuous influence of Udenamo adherents in the ranks of Mozambican nationalists alienated by Frelimo.[4] Coremo established its headquarters in Lusaka. Throughout the late 1960s and early 1970s, it waged a low-level guerrilla campaign, operating primarily in northwestern Mozambique. By the early 1970s, Coremo claimed to have 5000 members. This almost certainly was an exaggerated figure for a force that likely had no more than 1000–1500 insurgents. The movement, however, never articulated a coherent ideological platform although it voiced 'anti-imperialist' sentiments. Consequently, it was described, at times, as a pro-Chinese organization and on other occasions, a pro-Western movement.[5] Coremo also suffered from factionalism and, in 1968, Amos Sumane, the movement's Deputy President, broke away. Sumane formed the short-lived Rumbezi African National Union (UNAR) and, in 1974, the Revolutionary Party of Mozambique (PRM).

In the transition period between the April 1974 Portuguese revolution and Mozambican independence in June 1975 Frelimo emerged as the new nation's only effective political and military force. Coremo and several other newly formed political parties briefly coalesced in 1974 to form the National Coalition Party (PCN). The PCN called for a referendum to determine the composition of an independent Mozambican government. Former Frelimo Vice President Uria Simango was among the more prominent nationalist spokesmen who lent his voice to the new coalition. In September 1974, shortly after the new military government in Lisbon agreed to turn over power to Frelimo without an election, the PCN was implicated in disorganized and ultimately abortive coup-plotting. Simango and other PCN leaders were arrested and sent to 'reeducation' camps in northern Mozambique.

INDEPENDENCE, EXILE AND INSURGENCY

Fearing Frelimo reprisals, white and black Mozambicans who had co-operated with or served in the Portuguese colonial administration and those who owed their allegiance to several small nationalist movements fled to neighboring countries such as South Africa, Rhodesia, and Malawi, or to Portugal. By late 1976, white-ruled Rhodesia had assembled and armed a number of these exiles. This cadre was encouraged to assume the leadership of what soon became known as the National Resistance of Mozambique (NRM).[6] Reports of large-scale support from Salisbury initially convinced many observers that the NRM was little more than a large mercenary force fighting at the behest of Rhodesia's beleaguered white regime.

In its early years, the NRM or the Mozambican National Resistance Movement (MNRM) was widely viewed as an organization whose leaders' political aims were, at best, ambiguous. From 1977 to 1980, the NRM's ideological inclinations were frequently portrayed as nothing more than blind obedience to the orders of Rhodesia's Central Intelligence Organization (CIO). The NRM was regarded as a fifth-column force primarily used for counterinsurgency operations inside Mozambique against the guerrilla bases of the Zimbabwean African National Union (Zanu). In the aftermath of Mozambican independence, the Frelimo government had permitted Zanu insurgents to operate from bases in central Mozambique. Moreover, aid for Zanu which originated in eastern Europe or China transited the Mozambican port of Beira, thereby assuring the insurgents a more rapid delivery of outside support which had previously been transshipped from Dar es Salaam, Tanzania. This aid enabled Zanu to wage an increasingly effective guerrilla campaign. The white Rhodesian regime jumped at the chance to manipulate exiled Mozambican dissidents in a counterinsurgency campaign against Zanu's rear bases with little regard for the internal Mozambican consequences.

In the late 1970s NRM personnel often infiltrated central Mozambique to acquire information on the location and strength of Zanu insurgent camps. The results of these reconnaissance missions were passed on to Rhodesian security forces which used the information to plan cross border raids on Zanu bases. NRM attacks on Mozambican government outposts and economic facilities were a secondary mission which the white regime in Salisbury rationalized as retaliation for Mozambique's participation in the international trade and arms embargo against Rhodesia. Documents captured in later years revealed that NRM military commanders found this relationship with Rhodesia to be one which compromised their tactical initiative as well as their political integrity.

A British-mediated resolution of the Rhodesian war in 1979 was expected to sound the NRM's death knell. The end of white rule and the election of a Zanu-dominated government led by Robert Mugabe presumably would leave the NRM without external aid and the loss of rear bases. With the transition in April 1980 from Rhodesia to independent Zimbabwe, South Africa emerged as the NRM's new patron. Pretoria also saw the movement as a useful means to destabilize the Mozambican government. Frelimo supported the insurgent African National Congress (ANC) and Mozambique's ports and rail lines offered landlocked Zimbabwe and Zambia an alternative to dependence on South African facilities for the movement of their imports and exports. Supporting the NRM offered South Africa's military planners the opportunity to weaken several of its most hostile neighbors.

South Africa's increasingly aggressive politico-military intervention throughout Southern Africa distracted many observers from significant internal Mozambican trends in the late 1970s. In the first few years of Mozambican independence, it was clear that the NRM and its external patrons were not the only threat to Maputo. Dissatisfaction with Frelimo's rule spawned several small dissident movements, many of whose members later provided support and recruits for the evolving NRM. In late 1975, violent incidents in northern Mozambique were attributed to a Frente de Cabo Delgado (FCD), a Makonde group loyal to the imprisoned former Frelimo official Lazaro Kavandame. By the late 1970s, press reports also hinted that members of a 'Rumbezia separatist' movement, presumably the moribund UNAR, and residual elements of the PRM had evidently merged to form a group calling itself Africa Livre. This movement conducted low-level guerrilla operations in western Zambezia Province until 1982, when it reportedly merged with the NRM.[7] None of these dissident movements, which cumulatively revealed a current of discontent that reached from the central to the far northern provinces, had more than a few hundred armed members. Most of their supporters appeared to be motivated by ethnic or regional interests and many evidently opposed Frelimo's unilateral imposition of Marxist-Leninist inspired social and economic policies after 1977.

Still another manifestation of dissatisfaction with the Maputo government was a shadowy movement known as 'Magaia' which took its name from Frelimo's first military commander, Felipe Magaia, who died in 1966. Some Frelimo dissidents claimed Magaia was murdered by fellow insurgents while others insist he was assassinated by Portuguese agents. In 1976, publications bearing the title *Voice of Magaia* appeared in Maputo. These tracts recalled some of the intra-Frelimo disputes of the mid-1960s. 'Magaia' sympathizers apparently figured prominently in a December 1975 mutiny by several hundred troops in the newly created Mozambican Armed Forces (FAM) at the Machava barracks in Maputo. Suspected 'Magaia' members were said to have been purged from the ranks of the military in subsequent months. These former soldiers joined the ranks of thousands of other veterans who had fought for the Portuguese colonial army and were demobilized en masse in 1975. Collectively, this disgruntled force found little economic opportunity in post-colonial Mozambique and many of them undoubtedly formed a sizeable pool of recruits for the NRM.[8]

A RISING TIDE OF REBELLION

As insurgent activity spread in the central Mozambican countryside, additional voices from the pre-independence era joined the chorus of dissent increasingly dominated by the NRM. Some of the individuals who initially held key leadership positions in the early years of the NRM's existence confirmed that at least a portion of the movement's political roots, in fact, pre-dated Mozambique's 1975 independence. Veterans of the anti-colonial struggle included Fanuel Mahluza and Artur Vilankulu, both of whom had played prominent roles with Coremo. Mahluza became the NRM's Foreign Secretary and Vilankulu served as a principal overseas spokesman in the early 1980s. Further gestures of support from other elements of the Mozambican political spectrum demonstrated that the NRM had come to represent nationalists whose vision had been suppressed by Frelimo's Marxist wing. Eventually the United Democratic Front of Mozambique (Fumo) also announced its support for Renamo, the acronym adopted by NRM leaders in 1983.[9] Fumo originally had been comprised of disgruntled Frelimo members who left the party in the early 1970s due to disagreements over leadership and ideological issues. Fumo briefly worked from an office staffed by Mozambican exiles in Nairobi before relocating to Lisbon.[10]

Renamo rarely claimed to be the political heirs of Coremo, Fumo or any of the other smaller factions of the pre-independence era. Virtually all of the nationalists who opposed Frelimo were tarnished by varying degrees of collaboration or association with Portuguese colonialists. The latter had made repeated efforts to manipulate Frelimo's opponents in order to compromise the independence movement in the vain hope that they could preserve their colonial-era power and privilege. This may account for occasional NRM claims of allegiance to the legacy of Eduardo Mondlane and their commitment to a 'second struggle for independence'. These bore a striking resemblance to the earlier Kwilu insurgents' quest for a 'second independence' and Mulele's avowed loyalty to Lumumba's ideals. In any event, the ideological and leadership splits of the 1960s and early 1970s which had plagued the anti-colonial movement seemed to be coming back to haunt Frelimo.[11] While the urban, intellectual, pro-Soviet, Marxist element eventually dominated the latter years of the anti-colonial struggle, it evidently had not completely persuaded or suppressed a more moderate, rurally based, leadership faction. The emergence of these obscure and excluded forces slowly began to shape the NRM's military identity and contribute to its evolution as a nationalist movement.

The depth of anti-Frelimo sentiments in rural Mozambique had surprised even the NRM's white Rhodesian patrons. The late Ken Flower, chief of Rhodesia's Central Intelligence Organization (CIO) and 'godfather' of the NRM, indicated that he and his colleagues were surprised at the large number of rural Mozambicans who were willing to take up arms against the Frelimo government. While Rhodesia may have armed and trained many of the movement's early members it did not, in the most fundamental sense, create the NRM. The rebellious sentiment which motivated many of the early NRM guerrillas was based on a rejection of ideological preferences dictated by certain elements within Frelimo before and shortly after independence. As Flower had pointed out, 'The undoubted success of the movement [i.e. the NRM] also signified that Frelimo in Mozambique (as between the MPLA and Unita in Angola) lacked that essential measure of support that they needed from the population: or the Portuguese had acted too hastily in transferring power to a liberation movement which could not establish popular support through elections.'[12]

AN AMBIGUOUS POLITICAL-MILITARY IDENTITY

The early prominence of figures such as the NRM's Secretary General, Orlando Christina, a white Portuguese with previous ties to the former Portuguese colonial administration and the Portuguese secret police, clouded the issue of who the guerrillas' true leaders were and to whom their allegiance was owed. This remained a problem for the NRM even after Christina was murdered in South Africa in 1983, possibly as the result of an intra-NRM power struggle. Evo Fernandes, a Mozambican of Goan descent who had also had ties to the former colonial government, replaced Christina. Several other early NRM spokesmen, such as Paulo Oliveira, who claimed to represent the movement in Lisbon and elsewhere in Europe, had similar backgrounds.

Over time, it became increasingly clear that the organization's ineffective external wing, dominated by former members of the colonial administration or a moderately educated elite associated with some of the small independence movements of the 1960s, was not representative of the NRM's military wing. At best, Christina, Fernandes, and others served as opportunistic middlemen for Portuguese citizens who formerly resided in Mozambique. These former colonialists saw the NRM as a movement which might eventually moderate Frelimo's Marxist policies and enable them to reclaim the properties and other assets lost during the transition to

Mozambican independence. NRM ties to this community, like its relationship with Rhodesia and South Africa, were mixed blessings and further distracted overseas attention from the goals sought by the insurgents.[13] As the insurgency grew in size, its combatants and rural supporters became much more influential in determining the NRM's ideology as well as its military strategy and tactics.

It is the NRM's military commanders whose personal and political backgrounds link the insurgency to its Malgache, Kenyan, and Congolese predecessors. André Matsangaisse, the insurgents' first military leader, had joined Frelimo during the war for independence. He deserted the fledgling Mozambican Armed Forces (FAM) after independence, accused by the government of embezzling funds. Matsangaisse maintained that he had been alienated by the government's establishment of a Marxist-oriented regime and its social and economic policies. After Matsangaisse's death, during a skirmish with government forces in 1979, Afonso Dhlakama became the NRM's commander-in-chief. Dhlakama, the son of an Ndau chief, also had deserted the FAM and had opposed the new government's ideological leanings. The insurgents' second commander came from a rural background with limited education and little experience with the formal workings of modern political parties or nationalist movements. In a 1983 interview, alluding to his political views, the 32-year-old Dhlakama said 'I need a crash course in almost everything except fighting. My forces will win the war and guarantee peace, but we'll let the intellectuals and civilians govern.'[14]

Like their first two military commanders, many of the NRM's original members were deserters from the Mozambican army. Political prisoners from 'reeducation' camps established by Frelimo for Mozambicans associated with the colonial administration or some of the small dissident movements which emerged after 1975 also proved to be an occasional source of recruits. One of the NRM's first major attacks, in May 1977, was on such a camp in central Mozambique. The guerrillas freed several hundred inmates, many of whom subsequently joined the NRM. In some of their subsequent press statements, the insurgents designated this attack as the 'official' beginning of the struggle to oust the Frelimo government.[15]

THE EVOLUTION OF AN IDEOLOGY

Whereas the political background of the movement's external wing had obfuscated the motivation of many of the insurgents' internal leaders and early supporters, the NRM's belated publication of a formal policy statement also raised doubts about their political or ideological aspirations. Initially, some NRM spokesmen rationalized their failure to articulate an elaborate political program because, they claimed, the insurgents were pursuing a strategy which emphasized military over political concerns. As late as 1984, Evo Fernandes, Renamo's Secretary General, described the organization as a 'popular mass movement' whose military arm was Renamo. Although Fernandes explicitly stated that the movement was not a political party, he also described the organization's aims as 'democratic, fundamentalist and nationalist'.[16] The earliest sign of an insurgent political agenda was the promulgation, in 1979, of a document entitled simply *Statutes*. These pronouncements may have been an edited version of the Udenamo manifesto originally prepared by Fanuel Mahluza in the early 1960s. On 17 August 1981 the twelve members of the insurgent's National Council, including external representatives and military commanders, agreed on a program which addressed issues of politics, economics, justice, constitutional affairs, health and education, public works, and foreign policy.[17]

In a leaflet found in Maputo in the mid-1980s, Renamo described itself as an organization fighting for the creation of a multiparty democracy, a free market economy based on private property, a government of laws with respect for the individual, civil rights, and equality under the law. The insurgents also declared their commitment to the rights of all citizens to health care and to a public or private education, a state with a secure economic infrastructure, the subordination of military power to political authority, and the immediate dismantlement of the forces that repress civil rights. Renamo furthermore avowed respect for international organizations, friendly and cooperative relations with all people, non-interference in other countries, and a freely elected assembly that would approve a new constitution based on principles of democratic politics and economics.[18] The infrequent appearance of such leaflets in Maputo or elsewhere in Mozambique also raised doubts about whether the guerrillas' commitment to this program was sincere. Skeptics continued to suggest that such formulations were designed to further distract potential sympathizers from the NRM's South African connections.

Renamo statements of principle may have gained the support of some former Frelimo dissidents in exile. However, Renamo's grass-roots support was based on an appeal to the revival of traditional religious, social, and political practices which Frelimo had denounced as reactionary or counter-revolutionary. The reluctance of sympathetic traditional tribal chiefs in northern Mozambique to fully surrender their authority to more radical Frelimo members had been a source of friction in the early years of the anti-colonial insurgency.[19] Similarly, in the name of 'scientific socialism', the Frelimo government later denounced the beliefs and practices of *feitiçeiros* (spirit-mediums) and *curandeiros* (traditional healers). These individuals were considered the embodiment of a perspective which perpetuated a colonial-era mentality that thwarted the eventual social and intellectual 'liberation' of the masses.

By the early 1980s, it was clear that deposed and disenfranchised tribal and religious leaders, as well as their local supporters, had become a significant source of Renamo sympathizers and recruits. Moreover, as the movement became more widespread and began to consolidate its position in various areas of the countryside, Renamo's commanders used the traditional tribal system of governance to administer the local civilian population. Gradually, the insurgents established an infrastructure whereby guidance was passed from Renamo's leadership to various civilian liaison officers attached to guerrilla units. These cadres subsequently served as the primary link to the reconstituted traditional tribal chiefs and passed Renamo directives to them, or in some cases, to the *regulos* (Portuguese-appointed chiefs) as they were called in the colonial era.[20]

Buttressing their appeals to traditional values and leadership, Renamo blamed the devastating drought of the early 1980s on Frelimo's alienation of the 'ancestors'.[21] In the late 1980s, Renamo insurgents claimed that 'our struggle is of the spirit', or that 'our struggle is for the ancestors'.[22] A similar commitment had been evoked by the movement's Secretary General, Evo Fernandes, when he defined his characterization of Renamo as 'fundamentalist' as an implied respect for 'the national traditions of a society which speaks several languages and professes several faiths.'[23]

GROWTH AND CONSOLIDATION OF THE INSURGENT FORCE

Like their Malgache, Kenyan, and Congolese counterparts, Renamo's principles and practice of military organization also reflected a synthesis of traditional and modern precepts. The latter influence was readily apparent in the command and control network the insurgents developed to accommodate their rapid growth and an expanding area of operations. In the late 1970s, the movement's armed strength was estimated to number between 700 and 1000 with an operational area limited to central Mozambique. By 1981, there were thought to be 6000–7000 guerrillas active over an increasingly larger expanse of the countryside. In 1984, the insurgent force had grown to some 10 000–12 000 and was operating, with varying degrees of intensity, in all ten Mozambican provinces. Two years later, Afonso Dhlakama claimed the movement had more than 20 000 armed members and another 4500 unarmed trainees, a figure which remained constant throughout the latter years of the war.[24] Renamo appeared to be one of Africa's, if not the world's, fastest growing insurgencies in the mid-1980s. Its growth contrasted sharply with that of Frelimo's anti-colonial struggle from 1964 to 1974, which never exceeded 10 000–11 000 armed members and had conducted extensive operations in only five provinces by the time the war for independence ended.[25]

As the insurgent force grew larger, its organizational structure became more complex. In addition to Dhlakama serving as the movement's 'commander in chief', Renamo forces divided the country into three commands, each led by a 'general'. The general staffs associated with the northern, central, and southern commands were further subdivided into 'regional', 'sector', and 'zone' commands.[26] In the mid-1980s, Renamo commanders placed some 2000 men into conventional battalion-sized formations. Four battalions were active by 1986 and deployed for large-scale attacks on towns and government garrisons. By early 1990, Renamo already had trained and deployed 13 semi-conventional battalions. The guerrillas also had established a 200 man 'special force' commando unit which was trained to operate in three-man teams throughout the Mozambican countryside.[27]

What had begun as a lightly armed force also acquired a much more diverse and potent combination of armaments, including 60 mm and 80 mm mortars, 82 mm B-10 recoilless rifles, 122 mm Grad P (B-11) rockets, and rocket-propelled grenade launchers (RPG-7). This increase in firepower stemmed from large South African deliveries in the early 1980s and a growing arsenal of weapons captured in attacks against FAM and militia units. By the mid-1980s, the guerrillas had captured a limited number of 12.7 mm and 14.5 mm guns as well as a few SA-7 surface-to-air missile launchers, which provided them with a modest anti-aircraft capability. Renamo forces also had seized a handful of 120 mm M-1943 mortars and 76 mm field guns in attacks on government positions. An elaborate network of high-frequency radios facilitated communications from Dhlakama's mobile headquarters in central Mozambique. The guerrillas also relied on couriers, travelling on foot or by motorcycle, to relay messages.[28]

Although Renamo spokesmen continued to insist, throughout most of the 1980s, that the movement was not a conventional political party, the insurgents nevertheless developed an embryonic administrative infrastructure in areas they controlled or dominated. This hierarchical system gradually became as elaborate as its military network and later served as the foundation for the transition from a guerrilla movement to a post-war political organization. Civilian officials in the movement were appointed as heads of 'Departments' of Ideology, Education and Culture, Agriculture, Health and Internal Administration. Each department was organized at provincial, regional, district, and zonal levels. At the district level and below, Renamo created a parallel, traditionally based, structure which included a paramount chief assisted by local chiefs, subchiefs, and headmen of zones. The latter official supervised four or five families.[29]

Renamo also established a Youth League and a Women's League. In addition to the latter, the guerrillas also had established, in the early years of their insurgency, a 'Feminine Detachment'. Various journalists who visited Renamo camps reported seeing armed female guerrillas active in a variety of leadership roles. According to one account, women members served as instructors in numerous subjects, while another reporter claimed the female members also went into combat.[30] The role of women in the Renamo insurgency provides an interesting note of continuity in the history of modern guerrilla warfare in Mozambique. During its anti-colonial struggle, Frelimo also relied on female members who had joined the movement in the early years of the war. In 1967, militant females pressured the organization to create a female detachment and, in general, to give women a greater voice in the decision-making processes of the movement. Women nevertheless encountered continuing opposition from among male members of the movement.[31] Whether Renamo's armed female members achieved any greater degree of power and liberation from traditionally inferior roles is unclear from the sketchy accounts of a handful of journalists. Renamo's insistence on the restoration of polygamy and the bride-price, which Frelimo had outlawed as feudal and sexist practices, suggested a lingering ambiguity in the status of female insurgents.

In late 1989, a Renamo representative provided some statistics pertaining to the guerrillas' 'state within a state'. Allegedly, the insurgents had established 3000 hospitals at regional, provincial, district, local, and zonal levels. What were probably no more than rudimentary clinics or dispensaries purportedly employed some 8000 civilian and military nurses. Renamo's education department was said to be administering 45 'secondary' schools with classes up to the sixth grade as well as 9373 primary schools. The Agriculture Department deployed agrarian technicians, trained by Renamo, to assist peasant farmers. Each family in Renamo-dominated areas cultivated a six hectare plot of grains and produced an average of 2.5 tons per hectare. While these statistics could not be verified, and most were no doubt greatly exaggerated, they supported frequent, albeit impressionistic, observations by journalists and other visitors that civilians in Renamo areas had far better food supplies than many of their compatriots in government-controlled areas of rural Mozambique.[32]

FLECHAS AND FEITIÇEIROS

Renamo's military and administrative structures reflect at least three and probably four modern organizational influences. During the latter years of its efforts to stem the anti-colonial tide, Lisbon had recruited large numbers of black Mozambicans into the ranks of its colonial army. Many of these troops were trained as commando forces known as *flechas* (arrows); some were deployed in airborne units as paratroopers. At the end of the anti-colonial war, Lisbon had recruited some 10 000–20 000 Mozambicans to buttress its metropolitan army. This force included an estimated 4000-man elite airborne brigade.[33]

The counterinsurgency skills these soldiers acquired were easily converted to guerrilla warfare by those who later decided to oppose Frelimo. Mozambicans who fled to Rhodesia and received military training were likewise exposed to a contemporary military doctrine which reflected British influence from an earlier colonial era. By the late 1970s, Rhodesian instructors, many of whom had studied the British campaign in Kenya against Mau Mau, already had developed a thorough doctrine of guerrilla and counterinsurgency warfare. These contacts influenced the organization, strategy, and tactics of the NRM's early commanders. Additional influences, as well as skills in the operation of Soviet bloc weapons systems, were no doubt brought into the insurgents' ranks by those Frelimo soldiers who had deserted the FAM in the first few years after independence. Finally, the training and doctrine passed on by South African instructors and advisors in the early 1980s also played a significant role in shaping Renamo's infrastructure and its operational style.[34]

Nevertheless, beneath all these modern, conventional, influences which molded the insurgency into a force comparable to most contemporary guerrilla organizations, there remained a stubborn adherence to a magico-religious world view. The persistence of this widely held view clearly places Renamo into the more narrowly defined tradition of guerrilla warfare as it was practiced in Madagascar, Kenya, and Congo. Comparable manifestations of a traditional religious influence on Renamo's rank and file members appear throughout the fifteen-year war.

Like other leaders of earlier rural rebellions, Renamo's first military commander, André Matsangaisse, was surrounded by an aura of supernatural power. Matsangaisse reportedly had acquired supernatural powers from a local *feiticeiro* (spirit-medium) which protected him and his men from bullets. One legend asserts Matsangaisse was hit by a machine gun burst at point-blank range without suffering any wounds. Instead, some of his followers maintain he was killed by a bazooka round or a rocket-propelled grenade and that the gunner who killed him immediately went insane. Alternative accounts, reminiscent of UPC leader Ruben Um Nyobe's demise, suggest that Matsangaisse died because his bulletproof powers had been negated shortly before the attack in which he was killed.[35] Like the 'Mulelists' of the Kwilu rebellion, local press reports continued to refer to the guerrillas as *matsangas* (supporters of Matsangaisse) long after the first commander's death. Seven years after Matsangaisse's death, unsubstantiated rumors of an occasional insurgent attack led by his wife, seeking to avenge his death, still surfaced in central Mozambique. Moreover, she was thought to be 'invulnerable to anything'.[36]

Afonso Dhlakama did not acquire a reputation comparable to Matsangaisse's. In 1986, a captured Renamo member claimed that Afonso Dhlakama paid visits to a Malawian 'witch doctor', but the purpose of these consultations is unknown. Several Renamo commanders, however, reputedly had a variety of magical powers. At least three senior insurgent commanders in Zambezia Province reportedly claimed the ability to forecast the future, the power to 'disappear and reappear at will or fly, and the ability to turn bullets into water.'[37]

While the average Renamo combatant usually was not thought to have received the full range of powers attributed to some of their commanders, they did participate in religious rites which were expected to provide at least a modicum of similar benefits. In the early 1980s, a former Renamo member described a guerrilla camp at which a so-called *cupwacha* ceremony was performed, presumably for the propitiation of local ancestral spirits. This occasion included the ritual spreading of tobacco, cornmeal, and *cabanga* (local drink) on the ground, accompanied by clapping and singing. At the same camp, 'witch doctors' and 'priests' performed tasks such as the forecasting of events during combat or logistic operations.[38] Several years later, a civilian who had been a prisoner at a Renamo camp in northern Mozambique reported that 'before each battle, they [the guerrillas] would kneel around a special clearing surrounded by flowers and clap their hands three times. Then a *curandeiro* (traditional healer) would wave a goat tail dipped in magic liquid at each one as they marched off. Some believe the liquid stops bullets.'[39]

Renamo's reliance on spirit mediums initially seemed to be limited to members of the Ndau tribe in central Mozambique. The insurgents' obsessive efforts to assure that they removed their dead and wounded members from the battlefield was not only meant to keep them from being captured and interrogated by government forces. This practice, which observers had noticed in the earliest years of the war, was also intended to convince their opponents that a long-standing local belief in the supernatural powers of Ndau warriors was still valid. In addition to their reputation for an ability to make themselves bulletproof, the Ndau reportedly also relied on a medication which enabled them to be resurrected as spirits with the ability to retaliate against those who had killed them. Nearly all of Renamo's Ndau troops purportedly had taken this medication.[40]

Within less than a decade after they expanded from their Ndau-dominated core areas in central Mozambique the insurgents had recruited from among an ethnically diverse peasantry whose local or regional religious beliefs contained common themes regarding supernatural powers. This process readily enhanced a nationwide campaign. Renamo commanders allegedly based virtually all major decisions, particularly those concerning military matters, on previous consultation with ancestral spirits. The guerrillas' pantheon included the spirits of Frelimo founder Eduardo Mondlane and André Matsangaisse as well as the ancestral spirits of both men. Renamo also successfully assimilated a preexisting synthesis of Ndau spirits from central Mozambique and Zulu-speaking spirits from the south. The insurgents evidently made similar efforts to merge Shona spirit-mediums with religious traditions and influences prevalent in the northern provinces of Tete and Zambezia. These attributes of the insurgency prompted one skeptical observer to define them as Renamo's formulation of a 'neo-traditionalist culture of insurgency', or alternatively, a 'traditionalist and ethnically structured vision of Mozambican political realities'.[41]

MOBILITY IN GORONGOSA, DEMORALIZATION IN MAPUTO

Over the course of the fifteen-year war, Renamo's blending of traditional religious belief and practice with the strategy and tactics of modern guerrilla warfare proved to be a devastating and ultimately unstoppable military challenge to Maputo. Mobility was a key factor in accounting for Renamo's effectiveness. Large government offensives forced the guerrillas to abandon their principal military headquarters in the Gorongosa Mountains of central Mozambique on at least four or five occasions in the 1980s. After leading their pursuers on an exhausting and eventually futile chase across the countryside, the insurgents regrouped not far from their original location. Despite the disruption of logistics and communications that these tactical setbacks caused, the insurgents continued to acquire new recruits, thereby expanding the territorial scope of the war and intensifying the level of hostilities.

By the end of the 1980s, Renamo's guerrillas had disrupted or stopped traffic on virtually every major road network and rail line in the country. By sabotaging hundreds of pylons, Renamo shut off the flow of electricity to South Africa from the Cabora Bassa Dam on the Zambezi River. The guerrillas attacked power lines supplying Maputo and several provincial capitals, as well as striking large agricultural projects, collective village farms, light industrial facilities, and other economic installations. As the insurgent force grew in size and deployed its semi-regular battalions, they assaulted larger district capitals and army garrisons.[42] In the mid and late 1980s, Renamo occasionally launched simultaneous protracted offensives in several provinces, suggesting a fairly sophisticated level of command and control of their forces.

Nevertheless, it would be misleading to suggest that Renamo's effectiveness was solely the result of more competent leaders or more capable fighters. The insurgents' impact was significantly magnified by several serious flaws and shortcomings in the FAM. In the years immediately after independence, Maputo had far greater reason to fear a conventional external military threat from its white Rhodesian and South African neighbors. Consequently Soviet, East European, and Cuban advisors who trained the first generation of FAM officers concentrated on conventional military operations. They prepared the FAM to defend against an aggressor equipped with aircraft, tanks, armored vehicles, and mechanized infantry units. Within a few years it was obvious that a military establishment equipped with World War II and Korean War vintage tanks, surface-to-air missiles, and the attendant strategy and tactics provided to such a force was largely useless against Renamo.

Simple quantitative considerations also began to weigh against the FAM. Ever since the British experience in countering the Malay insurgency in the 1950s it has become a truism of counterinsurgency warfare doctrine that a successful counterinsurgent force must outnumber its opponent by a ten-to-one ratio.[43] In the war's early years, the government's 35 000-man army and 30 000-man border guard and militia force may have approached this theoretical requirement. However, as Renamo grew in size and approached a figure of 20 000 insurgents, the numerical advantage which Maputo once enjoyed could not be sustained despite occasional efforts at creating additional local militia forces to defend isolated villages.

Qualitative shortcomings often compounded Maputo's quantitative problems. FAM troops usually suffered from a lack of education, low morale, and, as the war dragged on, diminishing loyalty. The vast majority of the FAM was a conscript force, many of whom were unwilling to join and indeed were probably impressed into service. Not surprisingly, this often resulted in an undisciplined and poorly led force, particularly after long periods without pay and adequate rations. Consequently, there were frequent reports of FAM troops stealing food and other goods from civilians. Government troops on occasion also beat and killed peasants suspected of being Renamo sympathizers. In an increasingly desperate effort to 'drain the water' in which the Renamo 'fish' swam, rural civilians were sometimes forced to leave their ancestral homes for 'protected villages' not unlike the *aldeamentos* (strategic hamlets) favored by the Portuguese during their counterinsurgency campaign against Frelimo in the 1960s and 1970s.[44]

Frelimo acknowledged these and other shortcomings at various stages of the war. In the early 1980s, the government began to promote a new generation of officers trained in contemporary techniques of counterinsurgency warfare. These freshly trained officers were expected to be more innovative and daring than their colleagues whose primary military experience had been acquired as guerrillas in the anti-colonial struggle. President Machel also launched an ambitious campaign to establish village militia units throughout the countryside. The training offered these units was inadequate, however, and many of the weapons provided to militia members may quickly have made their way into Renamo's hands. In 1987, Maputo attempted a further reorganization of the armed forces in an effort to purge the army of a sizeable cadre of corrupt and inefficient officers.[45]

The government was much more reluctant to acknowledge the large-scale desertion of FAM conscripts throughout most of the war. Many FAM deserters likely made their way to Renamo camps, often providing valuable intelligence as well as experience in the use of weapons and military operations. Renamo's critics insisted, and interviews with former insurgents were usually cited to support them, that most of the insurgents were also an unwillingly conscripted force.[46] While many may indeed have been threatened with execution if they deserted, the insurgents' performance in combat frequently was better than their government opponents. If death threats kept large numbers of Renamo from deserting, they did not account for the insurgents' repeated willingness to engage in combat for more than a decade, and their generally superior performance under fire.

As Maputo and many other African government military forces have learned to their dismay, press-ganged and intimidated troops assigned to rural areas far from home may not desert in large numbers but they are notoriously poor fighters. Renamo cadres on the other hand, whether motivated by traditional religious precepts or old political allegiances, demonstrated a commitment to their cause which seemed more profound than that inspired by Maputo's commitment to Marxism-Leninism or a belated pursuit of 'democratic centralism'.

That the morale of the insurgent force seemed higher than that of the FAM was an observation borne out not only by reporters who visited Renamo camps but also by expatriates occasionally captured by the guerrillas and forced to travel with them before their release in a neighboring country. Even more telling was the apparent difference in the extent to which Renamo suffered from desertion compared to that experienced by FAM. Ultimately, far fewer guerrillas deserted than did government forces and, despite two clemency offers and one protracted amnesty offer, Maputo never enticed a significant number of insurgents to lay down their weapons.

By late 1988, only some 3000 purported 'bandits' had accepted the government's amnesty offer. The fact that many of those who surrendered failed to turn in weapons suggests that they may have been civilian sympathizers or supporters rather than combatants. This factor considerably reduced the significance of a figure that ostensibly represented as much as 15 percent of the Renamo force.[47] Moreover, evidence that Renamo continued to grow in size during most of the years in which the amnesty was available indicates that those insurgents who availed themselves of Maputo's offer were readily replaced by conscripts, volunteers, or FAM deserters.

POWERFUL PATRONS

What sets Renamo apart from its Malgache, Kenyan, and Congolese predecessors, however, is the role of outside support in accounting for the movement's survival in the early years of the war. From 1976 until 1980, Rhodesian military personnel trained, supplied, and armed the movement. Salisbury also provided a site from which the Voz da Africa Livre (Voice of Free Africa) radio station transmitted propaganda broadcasts into Mozambique. During the first few years of the war, when the insurgents numbered under 1000, they probably relied far more on Rhodesian support than on captured supplies to meet their operational needs.

By various Renamo accounts, this relationship proved to be a mixed blessing for the insurgents. According to a captured document found in

1981, Afonso Dhlakama claimed, 'We were oppressed by the Rhodesians and the leaders of our movement were not allowed to make any of the decisions.... We worked for the English, neither I nor the deceased André could plan any military operations. It was the English who determined the areas to attack and where to recruit.'[48] Many of Renamo's harshest critics cite the latter sentence in this document as proof that the organization was nothing more than a mercenary force created, directed, and solely subservient to its Rhodesian patrons. Dhlakama's use of the word 'oppressed', however, suggests that the insurgents were already developing a military and political agenda of their own which they were increasingly eager to pursue.

After April 1980, when Rhodesia became Zimbabwe, Renamo found a patron willing to support their expansion well beyond the confines of central Mozambique and, probably unwittingly, initiated a process whereby the insurgent military commanders evolved from reluctant puppets to increasingly independent partners. South African military personnel already had made contact with NRM leaders in Rhodesia by 1979, and Pretoria was well prepared to compensate for the loss of the insurgents' Rhodesian support. One week before Zimbabwean independence, a South African aircraft flew Dhlakama and other commanders to South Africa.

At bases near the Mozambican–South African border, the insurgents reestablished a site for their Voz da Africa Livre radio station. South African Defence Force (SADF) personnel acted as advisors and trainers for Renamo commanders and a core group of 250–300 members who were transferred from Rhodesia. Prospective guerrillas were recruited from among migrant Mozambican laborers who worked in South African mines as well as other Mozambican immigrants in South Africa. Pretoria also helped establish a radio network to facilitate insurgent communications between base camps in Mozambique as well as contact with facilities in South Africa. South African advisors and medical personnel were also flown into Renamo camps in Mozambique.[49]

In the early 1980s, South African support for Renamo was substantial and included large quantities of rifles, mortars, ammunition, and a host of other kinds of equipment. Transport aircraft or ships reportedly made deliveries to insurgent base camps every few days. This effort not only supported Renamo's growth from a 1000 to a 10 000 man force between 1980 and 1984, but also replaced weapons and *matériel* lost when government offensives forced the insurgents to abandon their main base camps in central Mozambique. Like their Rhodesian predecessors, SADF officers used their support for Renamo as a screen for clandestine operations inside

Mozambique. SADF commando raids damaged rail and harbor facilities, thereby forcing Mozambique's neighbors to continue relying on South African trains and harbors for many of their exports and imports. SADF personnel also launched several attacks on suspected African National Congress (ANC) facilities in Maputo. These raids were usually rationalized by Pretoria as preemptive counterinsurgency operations and SADF spokesmen made no effort to attribute these attacks to Renamo.[50]

However, South Africa's largesse also carried a price which Renamo's commanders found onerous. SADF advisors occasionally also insisted that the guerrillas target rail lines from Mozambique to Zimbabwe and Malawi, thereby contributing to Pretoria's notorious policy of destabilization throughout Southern Africa. Renamo commanders allegedly were reluctant to do so because they thought the risk of large personnel losses was too great and that such operations would primarily benefit South Africa and not the insurgents.[51] Whatever initial disagreements there may have been between Renamo and their SADF advisors, these disputes probably were much less burdensome than the 'oppressive' experience they had had with their white Rhodesian patrons.

In addition to acting as a conduit for financial support provided by former Portuguese colonists who had fled from Mozambique to South Africa after 1975, Pretoria also helped introduce Renamo to potential supporters outside Southern Africa. In November 1980, Afonso Dhlakama made a trip to Portugal, West Germany, and France.[52] Whether Dhlakama succeeded in garnering any significant degree of financial support from private or government sources in Western Europe is uncertain. Throughout the 1980s, occasional reports linked politically conservative private citizens in Portugal and elsewhere in Western Europe to Renamo.[53] Details of the kinds or volume of support Renamo obtained through such channels are not available, but they generally were assumed to be much more limited than that provided by South Africa.

Despite what appeared to be a durable commitment to Renamo, by late 1983 South Africa offered to terminate its assistance to Renamo in exchange for an end to Maputo's support for the African National Congress (ANC). Pretoria was enticed by the prospect of acquiring a degree of regional and international legitimacy, and on 16 March 1984 South Africa and Mozambique signed the N'komati Accord. Under the terms of the accord, Pretoria pledged to cease all forms of aid and assistance to Renamo in exchange for a similar commitment by the Maputo government which expelled all ANC members from Mozambique except for a small political office. Shortly before the signing of the accord,

Pretoria provided Renamo with a supply of ammunition and *matériel* estimated to be sufficient for at least six months of military operations. Moreover, Renamo members remaining in South African base camps were infiltrated back into Mozambique.[54] Even though South Africa promptly shut down the insurgent's *Voz da Africa Livre* radio transmitter and participated in the operation of a bilateral Joint Security Commission to monitor the accord, there were violations within weeks after it was signed.

Pretoria frequently asserted that while the accord had bound the South African government, it could not account for the activities of all private citizens, particularly the expatriate Portuguese community, and other elements of the white community sympathetic to Renamo. The latter may even have included a rogue element of the SADF which decided to circumvent state policy and continue providing assistance to the insurgents. In 1985, an offensive against Renamo's headquarters resulted in the capture of documents revealing the continuation of South African government aid to the insurgents. Pretoria acknowledged its role in delivering what it claimed were only medical supplies. Government spokesmen asserted that all other South African support was limited to maintaining the insurgents' radio station. South African officials also acknowledged arranging numerous visits by SADF officers to Renamo bases as well as bringing Renamo officers into and out of Mozambique. The latter function presumably was intended to facilitate insurgent representatives' onward travel to other parts of Africa and the West in search of additional outside support. South Africa regarded these as 'technical' violations of the accord.[55]

Aside from several eyewitness accounts of aircraft landings or seaborne deliveries, and a handful of documents, there is a paucity of evidence from which to deduce an accurate set of figures for the tonnage of supplies or an inventory of the number and types of weapons which South Africa provided to Renamo. An estimate of the proportion of Renamo's supplies which were externally provided and the related figure for *matériel* captured from government forces is equally difficult to calculate. Mozambican aircraft and air defense forces never intercepted or shot down a single South African aircraft delivering supplies to Renamo. Nor could Maputo claim that it lacked the ability to carry out such operations. In 1982 an air defense battery shot down a South African remotely piloted reconnaissance aircraft over Maputo. Between 1980 and 1988, however, FAM air defense units only managed to accidentally shoot down a French chartered aircraft performing survey work over southern Mozambique. In 1988, they mistakenly downed a Malawian transport near the

Mozambican–Malawian border. This consistently inept, but lethal, performance casts doubt on many of the numerous sightings of 'suspect' aircraft overflying Mozambique reported by government troops and civilians. In any event, by the mid-1980s South African aid reportedly had diminished, whether from private citizens or renegade SADF elements. Nonetheless these reports proved to be as impressionistic and sketchy as those prior to the signing of the N'komati Accord. Evidence that Renamo's armed forces had grown from some 10 000 in early 1984 to over 20 000 in the next four years was much more alarming to Maputo than any residual ties to South Africa. The surge in the number of Renamo's armed members suggested that outside aid from South Africa and other sources may have become proportionately smaller and militarily less significant than it had been in the early 1980s.

MORE SUPPORT, LESS SUCCESS

While Renamo appeared to be growing less dependent on outside aid and more able to capture what it needed from government forces, Maputo became more dependent on its allies. After an ineffective performance by 1000 Zimbabwean troops committed to augment FAM defenses in 1982, Harare increased its force in Mozambique from 2500 to some 12 000 in 1985. The Zimbabwean National Army (ZNA) contingent launched major offensives against large Renamo base camps in central Mozambique. ZNA troops also became increasingly responsible for the security of vital roads and rail lines as well as the oil pipeline across central Mozambique, collectively referred to as the 'Beira Corridor'.

In early 1987, Tanzania sent more than 2000 Tanzania Peoples' Defense Force (TPDF) troops to north-central Mozambique to defend the port of Quelimane as well as nearby roads and a small rail line.[56] This deployment was a response to a large-scale Renamo offensive in the central Zambezi River valley which threatened to cut northern Mozambique off from the southern provinces. Neighboring Malawi also committed an estimated 500 troops to assist in the defense of Mozambique's northernmost rail line which served as Lilongwe's link to the port of Nacala. Earlier Renamo attacks had crippled the rail line and forced Lilongwe to resort to longer and more costly trade routes through Zimbabwe and Zambia.

Supplementing these efforts, in 1986, Britain started to train several hundred FAM officers per year. Mozambican officer candidates were sent to Zimbabwe where they were instructed by members of the British

Military Advisory and Training Team. London reportedly also gave Malawi more than $1 million to purchase non-lethal supplies in support of the Malawian troop contingent guarding the Nacala rail line.[57] Finally, in a gesture that seemed even more startling to some observers than the signing of the N'komati Accord, South Africa began to provide aid to the FAM. On 28 November 1988, the South African Navy supply ship *Drakensberg* delivered 139 tons of non-lethal aid to the port of Beira. Pretoria's assistance included 30 trucks, four communications vehicles, radios, boots, clothing, tents, blankets and a variety of other *matériel* intended for Mozambican troops. An additional delivery was scheduled for March 1989. Pretoria did not follow up on these initiatives, however, and South Africa's military assistance to Maputo never assumed as significant a role as Frelimo's traditional allies.[58]

During the years of Mozambique's growing dependence on its African neighbors, Maputo continued to receive a steady supply of Soviet and Eastern European arms, ammunition, and logistic support for all branches of the Mozambican armed forces. Between 1978 and 1982, Moscow had provided an estimated $175 million in economic assistance to Maputo. In the mid-1980s, Moscow rescheduled Mozambique's external debt and provided greater quantities of oil on favorable economic terms. By 1986, Moscow had supplied an estimated $1 billion in military hardware to Mozambique. Deliveries in 1985 alone included Mi-24 Hind helicopters, PT-76 amphibious tanks, BTR-60 armored personnel carriers, artillery pieces, and BM-24 multiple rocket launchers. An estimated 850 Soviet advisors were involved in planning and supporting Maputo's campaigns against Renamo as well as training FAM troops in the use of a variety of weapons.[59]

A comparison of the trends in outside support to the combatants in the Mozambican war clearly favored Maputo. Renamo allegedly continued to receive aid from renegade elements within South African military intelligence and elements of the Portuguese community in South Africa throughout the 1980s. Members of the Malawian security establishment, particularly the police, were also thought to be supportive of the insurgents and facilitated the flow of outside aid to Renamo.[60] Moreover, the insurgents had also managed to elicit modest amounts of assistance from private American citizens who belonged to a variety of religious denominations or whose business and political affiliations made them sympathetic to Renamo's cause.[61] Renamo's advocacy of religious freedom for all denominations in Mozambique, including a sizeable Muslim community in the far north, also may have prompted Saudi Arabia and Oman to provide the guerrillas some financial support.[62]

Despite their cultivation of an internationally more diverse support network than the insurgents had in the early years of the war, the total amount of assistance supplied to Renamo on an annual basis seemed to have levelled off by the late 1980s, and may even have begun to decline from the peak reached in the first half of the decade. This was partially reflected in the fact that Renamo ceased enlarging the number of its armed members. From 1986 to 1990, Afonso Dhlakama and other spokesmen repeatedly asserted that the movement had some 20 000–22 000 armed members. The number of unarmed 'recruits' undergoing training likewise stayed within a 4000–7000 range. This most likely stemmed from the fact that the insurgents failed to acquire or capture a sufficient number of weapons and supplies to arm additional guerrillas. At best, Renamo continued to replace deserters and casualties suffered as a result of hostilities which were taking a mounting toll on the population of Mozambique and its neighbors.

A LONG AND DEVASTATING TRANSITION FROM WAR TO PEACE

Throughout the last few years of the war, Maputo and its allies made several attempts to capture key Renamo base camps and sought to engage large concentrations of insurgents. The guerrillas likewise continued to demonstrate an ability to mass sizeable forces and attack towns and garrisons throughout Mozambique. In 1986, Afonso Dhlakama also declared war on Zimbabwe in reaction to Harare's earlier deployment of an additional 10 000 ZNA troops. Renamo guerrillas began to conduct raids across the Mozambique–Zimbabwe border in early 1987. For the next three years, the insurgents inflicted hundreds of casualties on Zimbabwean civilians, police, and military personnel in eastern Zimbabwe.

While Maputo and its allies repeatedly sought to prove that Renamo could not win an outright military victory, the insurgents finally demonstrated that they could not be defeated on the battlefield. The cost of proving these points was measured not only in the devastation of the Mozambican economy but also in the number of casualties suffered by the civilian population. In late 1986, a Mozambican government official estimated that over 100 000 had died as a result of the war.[63] By 1989, the casualty figures were variously reported as 600 000 and 900 000. These totals probably included fatalities due to combat as well as disease and famine. As the war drew to a close, casualties were widely assumed to have exceeded one million. The precision of these figures was frequently challenged.[64] As in the case of the 1947 Malgache rebellion, exact figures probably will never be determined.

Similar controversies are likely to rage for years regarding the number of unarmed Mozambican civilians intentionally killed by both combatants during the course of a war in which neither side had a monopoly on virtue. According to a survey, conducted in 1987, of Mozambican refugees from various regions of the country, Renamo had murdered possibly as many as 100 000 civilians in the previous twelve months. These executions were largely directed at Frelimo party members and their families as well as other civilians perceived by the guerrillas as being active government collaborators.[65] In 1986, it was alleged that more than 75 000 Mozambicans had died in government prison camps established after independence.[66] By 1989, approximately one million Mozambicans had fled the country to refugee camps in South Africa, Swaziland, Zimbabwe, Malawi, and Tanzania. An additional one million citizens abandoned their home districts and resettled in other parts of the country to escape the hostilities. This dislocation and the attendant destruction of the economy, estimated to be more than $7 billion, threatened some 6 million Mozambicans, nearly half the population, with severe food shortages if not starvation.[67]

More than a decade after it began, the nature of the war had evolved from a strictly military to a political-military struggle. This evolution was implicitly acknowledged in the changing behavior of Maputo's allies and neighbors. By the end of the 1980s Zimbabwe's military presence had been reduced to nearly half the size of the force deployed in 1985, leaving only about 5000–6000 ZNA troops to concentrate primarily on the defense of road and rail lines vital to the Zimbabwean economy. Harare had recognized that the war was militarily unwinnable and chose to limit its involvement to the protection of economic facilities important for its own national interests. Similarly, faced with an increasingly costly commitment to a protracted conflict, Tanzania had pulled out its entire 2000-man force. Rather than acknowledge that budgetary constraints made it impossible to continue, Dar es Salaam rationalized its withdrawal by emphasizing the fact that its troops had saved some of Mozambique's larger northern towns from falling into Renamo's hands, thereby forestalling an even greater military crisis for Maputo.

The Zimbabwean reduction and the Tanzanian pullout forced FAM units to assume the duties their allies had performed. This requirement stretched an already overextended FAM even further at a time when Renamo still showed no sign of reducing the nationwide military pressure it had put on Maputo since 1986. Compounding the problems generated by a diminishing allied African effort, the Soviet Union too seemed to be unwilling or unable to deliver military supplies and other assistance at levels recorded a few years earlier. By 1989, it became increasingly clear that a negotiated settlement rather than a decisive military victory was the only way to end 13 years of war.

Grudgingly but gradually, Frelimo acknowledged Renamo's assertion that its leadership and support represented a genuine Mozambican nationalist sentiment, notwithstanding all the doubts raised by earlier links to the Rhodesian Central Intelligence Organization and the South African military establishment. Between 1989 and 1990, public pronouncements by President Chissano and other officials changed the lexicon of Mozambican politics by referring first to 'armed bandits', then to 'so-called Renamo', and finally to Renamo. More importantly, as a result of a major reform endorsed at Frelimo's fifth Party Congress in July 1989, the government subsequently abandoned Marxism-Leninism, and agreed to a redrafted constitution which called for multiparty elections and a host of other changes which coincided with nearly all the positions for which Renamo claimed it had fought. The new constitution was approved in early November 1990. While Portuguese would still be the nation's official language, the newly defined state was committed to the survival and cultivation of other national languages. The government was also required to tolerate and respect the country's numerous religious denominations. Maputo, however, never described these reforms as an accommodation of the insurgents' demands but rather a revision or modification of what some Frelimo adherents still seemed to believe was a continued commitment to democratic socialism.

Renamo and Frelimo representatives subsequently agreed, at a December 1990 meeting held in Rome, to a limited ceasefire contingent on the confinement of Zimbabwean National Army troops to the Beira and Limpopo road and rail 'corridors'. Renamo also ceased its cross-border attacks into eastern Zimbabwe and at subsequent negotiating sessions in Rome, various Western mediators encouraged both parties to broaden this agreement to a nationwide ceasefire. Despite the generally favorable trends of the next two years, there remained lingering doubts about Renamo's ability to be as effective politically as it was militarily.

THE STRUGGLE CONTINUES, VICTORY IS UNCERTAIN

The insurgents may have won the war, only to lose the peace. As the 1994 elections approached, Renamo had not conclusively demonstrated that it would necessarily avoid the same fate as that of the Malgache, Kenyan, or

Kwilu insurgents. Although Renamo's 15-year campaign demonstrated that a guerrilla war waged for 'traditional' or 'revivalist' aims can be militarily successful, if given significant external support, it remains to be seen whether this success can be carried over into a peacetime political arena. Key events in Renamo's political history reveal the persistence of what may be irreparable fissures. It was not until July 1989 that Renamo held its 'first Party Congress' at a base in central Mozambique. At this assembly the organization, for the first time, explicitly described itself as a political party as well as an armed nationalist movement.[68] Like its Malgache, Kenyan, and Congolese forerunners, however, Renamo did not emerge from its protracted struggle as a politico-military monolith. There had been evidence of tension within the ranks of the movement's leadership in its earliest years. Afonso Dhlakama succeeded André Matsangaisse after a bitter internal struggle. The succession may have included a shootout with at least one other contender for the position of chief military commander of the guerrilla force.[69]

Chronic leadership struggles between members of the movement's external wing were compounded by splits within the guerrillas' military ranks. In late 1987 a Renamo commander, Gimo Phiri, led a breakaway force of several hundred insurgents which called itself the Mozambican National Union (Unamo). Phiri reportedly broke with Renamo over what he perceived to be an excessive number of officers from the Ndau tribe in the organizations' upper ranks. Unamo subsequently carried out limited operations and occasionally skirmished with Renamo along the southeastern Malawi border.[70] Unamo's willingness to ally itself with government forces raised doubts about the solidity of Renamo's pan-Mozambican ethnic coalition.

The emergence of 'Naprama' posed equally serious questions concerning the extent to which Renamo had alienated members whose principal aim was a revival of traditional religious beliefs and social institutions. In March 1990, a *curandeiro* named Manuel Antonio announced to his followers in north-central Mozambique that he had a divine mission to end the war in Mozambique.[71] Within several months, Antonio recruited a 400-man militia force known as 'Naprama', a Macua word which translated as 'irresistible force'.

Naprama members were vaccinated by Antonio, who used razor blades and the ashes of a 'secret plant', to make a 'magic potion' which was said to make his followers invisible and impervious to bullets if they also observed certain prohibitions. The potion reportedly would be rendered ineffective if those who had been vaccinated ate the meat of a certain type of deer, engaged in sexual intercourse, or killed another person, among a variety of other strictures. By the end of 1990, Naprama's machetes and spears had proven to be far more effective in attacks on Renamo bases in Zambezia Province than any operations carried out by local FAM garrisons.[72]

Until his death in a battle with Renamo forces in early December 1991, Manuel Antonio's Naprama represented a formidable challenge to Renamo's hold over large areas of the Mozambican countryside northeast of the Zambezi River. At the height of his influence, Antonio claimed that he had raised a 30 000-man force. This figure undoubtedly was exaggerated and it is likely that many of the several thousand combatants who did obey Antonio were part-time soldiers who tended their farms between battles. By early 1991, Naprama claimed to have resettled 100 000 peasants who previously had been under Renamo's authority or influence throughout much of Zambezia Province. Antonio's success gradually prompted the government to offer a modest degree of support and Naprama briefly appeared to be evolving into a paramilitary or auxiliary militia force.

The conflict between Naprama and Renamo, however, was not simply a conventional political and military contest. In early 1991, Renamo officials told a foreign correspondent that they had moved additional forces, sending possibly as many as 3000 troops, to the northeast to challenge Naprama and prove that the 'ancestors' who supported Renamo were more powerful than those who favored Manuel Antonio. Afonso Dhlakama is said to have personally taken charge of the counteroffensive against Naprama between August and September 1991. Renamo claimed to have devised an anti-Naprama vaccine for use in areas it recaptured from Naprama. This vaccine supposedly made Naprama members visible and deprived them of their bulletproof powers. By early 1992, Renamo had regained much of the ground it lost to Naprama in the previous two years.[73] In some respects the Renamo campaign against Naprama reflected an underlying tension between the insurgents' avowed commitment to multiparty democracy and a completely tolerant attitude towards all Mozambican religious traditions and authorities.[74]

Movements such as Unamo and Naprama represented cleavages in Mozambican society which threatened to undermine Renamo and frustrate Frelimo's efforts to reestablish a post-war national consensus. Moreover, the emergence of a variety of other small political parties from among exiled Mozambicans who formerly were Renamo representatives abroad, or disaffected Frelimo members, raised the possibility that Renamo might experience further fragmentation after a national election.[75] Tensions within Renamo promised to bear out a forecast made by the late Evo

Fernandes who boasted in 1984 that 'when we win the final victory, we plan to hold a congress out of which will come a party, or even two parties.'[76] At present, it is unclear whether this outcome will reflect the maturation or the further disintegration of the Mozambican body politic. The history of Angola, Chad, Sudan, and Uganda during the past three decades provide ample evidence for the assertion that the birth and development of a nation-state can sometimes require the resolution of more than one major civil war. It was certainly unrealistic to expect that violence, whether politically inspired or conducted for criminal purposes, would simply come to a halt in Mozambique upon the signing of a peace accord and a ceasefire. Personnel loosely affiliated with Renamo or elements of the FAM which have recently engaged in brigandage are likely to plague various areas of the countryside for some time to come, regardless of the composition of a post-war government. The extent to which this predictable law and order problem undermines a new government will not only be a reflection of the former combatants' control of their troops but the rate at which the country's ravaged economy recuperates. A fortunate combination of an effective military demobilization and a revived economy will reduce the likelihood of an inevitable law-and-order problem evolving into a serious security threat to Mozambique's newly elected government.

7 Conclusion

NOSTALGIC HEROES OR MISGUIDED VILLAINS?

The legacy of revivalist insurgencies in Africa, whether militarily success-ful or not, is frequently subject to revision. The Malgaches have been reluctant to recall or fully assess the 1947 rebellion. Those who died in the uprising were not officially recognized as 'martyrs' or 'heroes' of the nationalist cause until several years after independence in 1960. Independent Kenya's attitude to the Mau Mau uprising seems subject to the fluctuating political fortunes and power balances within and among its various tribes.[1] Pierre Mulele's memory appears to have survived with a greater, if somewhat vague and romanticized, aura of respectability than that of his supporters. Zaire's President Mobutu demonstrated a striking ability to coopt leaders and supporters from a variety of insurgent move-ments throughout the two decades following the tumultuous events of the early 1960s, including those who had fought in Kwilu Province. Dissidents who chose to collaborate with Mobutu managed to rationalize their decision. Like Mulele, many insisted that what had been historically correct acts of resistance to the state were no longer relevant or appropri-ate options, due to changing national and international circumstances.

The aftermath of Mozambique's first multiparty elections, held in late October 1994, will be instrumental in determining whether future accounts reassess the multitude of myths and misperceptions which surrounded Renamo and Frelimo. Renamo's post-war political shortcomings will likely confirm the view that 'where the peasantry has successfully rebelled against the established order – under its own banner and with its own leaders – it was sometimes able to reshape the social structure of the coun-tryside closer to its heart's desires; but it did not lay hold of the state, of the cities which house the centers of control, of the strategic nonagricul-tural resources of the society.'[2] Alternatively, if Renamo succeeds as a political organization, its role in Mozambican history may put it in the more ambiguous ranks of those uprisings which one author described as 'forward – as well as backward – looking rebellions [which] at times con-stitute last gasps of an old order, at other times first breaths of a new.'[3]

Still another perspective on a successful Renamo political-military cam-paign might be one which views it as the harbinger of a new, post-Cold

War, Third World trend characterized by the triumph of 'movements of rage'. These have been described as 'revolutionary movements with ... an ethos akin to the thought of Franz Fanon. Their motivating spirit is nihilistic rage against the legacy of Western colonialism.'[4] This conclusion, however, may overstate the significance of the Cold War's demise and its impact on warfare in the Third World. Insurgencies which might have been described as 'movements of rage' appeared long before the Cold War ended and could often be reactionary or revivalist rather than revolutionary in their aims. Furthermore, associating Franz Fanon's thought with 'nihilistic rage' may be akin to mistaking the means for the ends of violent struggle. Fanon himself was acutely aware of this distinction and pointed out that 'radicalism, hatred, and resentment cannot sustain a war of liberation ... Intense emotion of the first few hours will fall to pieces if it is left to feed on itself ... Even very large-scale peasant uprisings need to be controlled and directed into certain channels ...'[5]

The implications of Fanon's insights were not lost on subsequent generations of guerrilla leaders even if historians and politicians occasionally overlooked or underemphasized them. There are several instances of successful insurgent movements in modern Africa whose effectiveness was, in part, due to a creative synthesis of traditional theology and modern techniques of political and military organization. The earliest example of such a campaign is the war fought by the partisans of the Partido Africano da Independência da Guiné e Cabo Verde (PAIGC) from 1963 to 1974. Founded by Amilcar Cabral in late 1956, the PAIGC launched what proved to be one of the most successful anti-colonial guerrilla struggles in all of sub-Saharan Africa during the next two decades. Motivated by socialist principles and the vocabulary of 'liberation' movements, the PAIGC appeared to be one of Africa's most functional 'vanguard' parties. The PAIGC's ideological orientation also encouraged Moscow and some of its Eastern European allies to provide the insurgents with military support.

Cabral's struggle was not without its problems, however, not the least of which was arriving at a successful accommodation of magico-religious beliefs and practices. Although the PAIGC's leaders attempted to come to grips with the problem at an early party congress in 1964, the synthesis of traditional and modern views was one which continually had to be addressed for the remainder of the decade. Ultimately, the PAIGC appears to have arrived at a successful combination based on tolerance and expediency. This was done at the risk of compromising the party's reputation for ideological purity and alienating external support.[6]

The history of the guerrilla campaigns waged by the Zimbabwean African National Union (Zanu) against the Ian Smith regime in Rhodesia as well as the pre-and post-independence struggle of the National Union for the Total Independence of Angola (Unita) are also characterized by the formulation of a pragmatic *modus vivendi* between magico-religious and modern secular perspectives.[7] This synthesis does not insure a politically and militarily successful insurgency of its survival in the transition to post-war politics. Nor does an eclectic approach to ideology provide any guarantee that such a movement's place in its nation's history will be free of controversy.

Insurgent movements which advocate an ecumenical approach to the religious views of actual or potential supporters run the risk of being characterized as opportunistic, manipulative, and amoral. An approach which seemed politically and even militarily sensible in the context of a nationalist guerrilla war may ultimately be untenable in post-war civil society. The problems and the risks inherent in the transition from a predominantly military movement to a political party often are more pronounced for 'reactionary' or 'revivalist' movements than for those describing themselves as 'revolutionary' or 'progressive'.

As in the case of their Congolese, Kenyan, and Malgache predecessors, a political failure by Renamo likely will be viewed by skeptics as further evidence that the movement was simply the reflection of dysfunctional social behavior, exacerbated by Mozambique's catastrophic drought and resultant famine in the early 1980s, and manipulated by outside powers with ulterior motives. Despite indications the Mozambican government had discarded such explanations by 1989, recent assessments continue to suggest that Renamo should be seen as a manifestation of psychopathological behavior by an essentially criminal element of Mozambican society. Three months before Renamo representatives signed peace accords in Rome in October 1992, the movement was still being characterized as one which '... had more to gain through fighting and pillage than it could gain politically through negotiations or elections.'[8] The characterization of violence perpetrated by Renamo as a reflection of depravity represents an ironic contrast to the view fervently espoused by Frelimo in its anti-colonial struggle. In the 1970s Frelimo celebrated the 'liberating and transforming' effects experienced by long-suffering peasants who finally resorted to armed force against their colonial oppressors.[9] After nearly thirty years of warfare in Mozambique, none of the combatants alluded to the therapeutic value of violence, regardless of the perpetrators' ideological motivations.

In its late stages, however, the Renamo insurgency frequently was characterized as an organic dysfunction in the Mozambican body politic. The insurgency was described as a cancerous growth which gradually invaded the healthy political and economic 'cells' that had been created by Frelimo. Related interpretations hinted at the possibility that Renamo was a vehicle for the expression of a cult of 'black magic' or that its members had become 'locked into a negative culture of evil'.[10] Modern African insurgencies emphasizing traditional religious themes often have elicited such extreme interpretations. Unfortunately, these analyses frequently betray a status quo bias on the part of those who propose them. Authors who supported the French presence in Madagascar denigrated the 1947 rebellion by calling it a 'sorcerers' revolt'.[11] Similarly, conservative white British settlers and many British military officers regarded the Mau Mau insurgency as evidence of '... the latent terror-laden primitivism in all Africans, the Kikuyu especially.'[12] The Kwilu and Renamo insurgencies' reactionary or revivalist features made them equally as susceptible to similar criticism from African officials as their predecessors had been to the detraction of European colonial governments. The military defeat of these insurgencies generally has delayed a balanced historical assessment of the extent to which such rebellions represented a genuine national, or at least regional, political impulse or whether they were primarily a psychological-sociological 'illness' in the otherwise healthy body of a nation-state.

In some respects, these views found a paternalistic echo in the explanations frequently offered by white settler regimes in Rhodesia and South Africa to explain indigenous rebellions. White settlers often claimed that 'their natives' would not have been so politically aroused if they had not been influenced by 'outside agitators' who were generally branded as generic 'Communists'.[13] The demonology of insurgency is equally as prone to finding 'foreign devils' or domestic 'sorcerers'. In the case of the Renamo insurgency, those who sympathized with the government could readily find evidence of both evils.

Underlying all these highly emotive assessments is the fundamental issue of legitimacy. With the exception of the UPC, none of the insurgencies discussed in this study received official foreign acclaim or recognition as belligerents in a civil war or war of independence. Even in the context of their own country, the political acumen of those who joined movements such as Jina, Panama, Mau Mau, Savoir Vivre or Mpeve was frequently in doubt. Legitimacy, like sovereignty, often reflects an acknowledgement of political and military success based on the effective use of bullets rather than ballots. Debates over the 'legitimacy' of Renamo or any other insurgent movement all too often impede an objective assessment of what such an organization represents in the context of a particular nation's history and culture.

Similar legalistic distinctions emerge in discussions of 'social bandits' as opposed to 'bandits'. This line of analysis also conjures up the issue of internal legitimacy. Those who employ the term 'social bandit' suggest that when an armed dissident force shares its plunder with some of the most impoverished and oppressed members of society, it acquires the status of a legitimate political movement. However, armed forces often described as 'social bandits' rarely assault military garrisons. So-called 'social bandits' seldom, if ever, propose political reforms of the oppressive regime whose economic facilities, tax collectors, and other unarmed institutions or representatives they are willing to attack. While their short-lived careers may economically enrich their members and temporarily relieve the suffering of those to whom they distribute their spoils, 'social bandits' rarely stand for, or bring about, fundamental or lasting change. The appearance and spread of 'social banditry' is, to some extent, a measure of the incumbent governments' internal loss of legitimacy and can potentially begin to erode its sovereignty.

Unfortunately such terminology also may lend itself too easily to partisan assessments which overstate the legitimacy of an incumbent regime or underestimate the legitimacy of its armed opponents. Thus a serious security threat to a particular government in the throes of a civil war is dismissed by its supporters as nothing more than a matter of reestablishing law and order. For those who seek to delegitimize a regime's opponents, the term 'predatory bandits' is an appropriate alternative to 'social bandits'. When dissidents appear to enjoy a degree of local or regional support and the central government has lost most or all of its ability to govern a remote district, the terminology may shift from 'bandits' to 'warlords'. These are not simply abstract theoretical distinctions.[14] They often form the basis of decisions by neighboring or more distant governments to support one side or the other in such conflicts.[15]

ON THE NECESSITY OF EXTERNAL SUPPORT

From a strictly military standpoint it may be more useful, though not necessarily less controversial, to attempt an assessment of the role played by external actors, particularly those who chose to supply the insurgents. Without Rhodesian and South African assistance, Renamo commanders might have found it much more difficult, if not impossible, to move beyond the confines of central Mozambique. Indeed, they might ultimately have shared the fate of their Malgache, Kenyan, and Congolese predecessors. Moreover, with no cross-border rear base to retreat to, unaided Mozambican guerrillas might not have been nearly so able to fend off government forces eventually augmented by thousands of troops from neighboring Malawi, Tanzania, and Zimbabwe. Nevertheless, it is inaccurate to assume that Renamo's military effectiveness was solely a function of outside support. At least two other insurgencies in recent Southern African history demonstrate the limitations which external patrons face when attempting to foment a rebellion. In the 1960s and 1970s, Lesotho's Chief Leabua Jonathon pursued an opportunistic foreign policy which oscillated between subservience to Pretoria and later appeals for support from the Soviet Union, Cuba, China, and North Korea. The cumulative impact of an erratic foreign policy and controversial domestic policies made Jonathon unpopular with Basotho citizens across a fairly broad political spectrum. Only a very small number of those who were dissatisfied with Jonathon, however, chose to rally to the Lesotho Liberation Army (LLA). The LLA was recruited, armed, trained, and based in neighboring South Africa from 1979 until the mid-1980s. By 1986, following a limited number of raids and sabotage operations, it had finally ceased to operate as an insurgent movement when Pretoria resumed closer ties with the military junta which ousted Jonathon.

While Pretoria might have been pleased if the LLA had evolved into a genuine insurgent organization, the SADF was satisfied to have it serve as a coercive tool and potential bargaining chip in its relations with the Jonathon government. South African military planners could also use the LLA as a screen for attacks against African National Congress (ANC) targets in Lesotho. The LLA never posed a credible military threat to the Maseru government and did not seriously attempt to mobilize a significant element of the population. Unlike Renamo, the LLA was truly a 'creation' of South Africa and did not represent a potent political force inside Lesotho. Outside support was not sufficient to create or sustain a genuine armed Lesotho opposition movement.[16]

A South African backed dissident force in post-independence Zimbabwe suffered a similar fate. In the early 1980s, Pretoria sought to exploit long-standing disputes between Ndebele tribe members loyal to the Zimbabwean African People's Union (ZAPU) and the ruling Zanu, dominated by the Shona tribe. Dissatisfied with the outcome of the 1980 elections which had resulted in a Zanu-dominated government, demobilized ZAPU guerrillas fled to refugee camps in Botswana where they were contacted by South African military personnel who offered them weapons, training, communications gear, and other support. Pretoria armed and supplied possibly several hundred former ZAPU guerrillas. Between 1981 and 1984, South Africa made several arms deliveries to a movement known as 'Super-ZAPU'. This force never developed into a cohesive military organization, much less a political movement. The vast majority of its attacks on civilian targets can best be described as acts of banditry or the conduct of personal vendettas in Ndebele areas of southern Zimbabwe. Like the LLA, the demise of Super-ZAPU demonstrated that external support, while it may be necessary, is not sufficient to create a genuine insurgent movement out of a disparate group of self-styled 'social bandits' or loosely organized dissidents.[17]

In any event, it is clear that external support, as Pierre Mulele so adamantly pointed out, is always a mixed blessing for any guerrilla force. For Frelimo and other Southern African insurgent movements which received Soviet or Chinese aid in the 1960s, the price of such support included being labelled 'Communist puppets', 'stooges', and surrogates. For Renamo, and similarly for Unita in Angola, taking South African assistance also carried the cost of being described as 'lackeys of apartheid', 'mercenaries', and 'surrogates' for Pretoria's policy of regional destabilization. In effect, the involvement of external powers in Southern African insurgencies frequently distorted what were essentially nationalist struggles by portraying them as principally racial or ideological conflicts.

External involvement may also have a comparable affect in determining whether the insurgents or their supporters are responsible for setting ultimate goals. Outside aid can also be instrumental in the cessation or prolongation of hostilities. South African military officials were quite often thought to have no desire to see Renamo win its war against Maputo. Pretoria's interest in the insurgents was presumably limited to perpetuating Mozambique's economic dependence on South Africa and denying the ANC a safe haven.[18] By the early 1990s, however, many observers could not even be sure that Renamo's own commanders, much less some outside agent, could exercise effective control over all the combatants in the Mozambican countryside. Ultimately, the 'South African puppet' perspective was no less presumptuous than a comparable claim, often made in the late 1970s and early 1980s, that Moscow's support for Southern African insurgents was intended to produce a region full of governments willing to withhold strategic minerals such as cobalt, chromium, manganese, and platinum from the West. Clearly, external support for insurgents engaged in a nationalist struggle is neither a guarantee of military success nor a reliable patron–client relationship.

DOES 'TRADITION' HAVE A FUTURE?

Neither the earlier failure of insurgencies emphasizing traditional goals elsewhere in sub-Saharan Africa nor the apparent modifications to the character of the Renamo insurgency provide any definitive answers for those who question the capability or viability of guerrilla movements guided by a magico-religious worldview. The Ugandan Holy Spirit Movement (HSM), now referred to as the Lord's Resistance Army, and the National Patriotic Front of Liberia (NPFL) insurgencies both show signs of an enduring blend of traditional spiritual perspectives and modern guerrilla warfare. The persistence of such perspectives in various African states in the early 1990s suggests that this approach to the world in general, and to warfare in particular, have not yet been discredited. Moreover, the appeal of this worldview may not be limited to the more remote rural areas of Africa. In early 1991, South African members of the ANC living in Soweto reportedly were being anointed with *muti*, a potion expected to protect them against bullets, spears, and knives.[19] Rather than viewing this as the appearance of additional 'movements of rage' in a post-Cold War African context, it may be more pertinent to consider the politico-military ramifications of such developments rather than their psychological significance.

It seems likely that a magico-religious worldview will continue to influence many combatants in Africa who would use modern weapons and contemporary techniques of warfare, possibly even into the next century. Indeed, one might ask whether the chiliastic myth of Marxism, with its deterministic view of history and an anticipated transformation of human nature, was even more counterproductive for recent African insurgents and less likely to survive than the traditionally rooted beliefs and values of African religion. Committed Marxists claim that the changes sweeping Russia and Eastern Europe do not represent the failure of Communism but a failure to properly implement Marx's teachings. This disclaimer sounds very much like those made by African spirit-mediums who told insurgents that their failure to become bulletproof was due to their lack of faith and not the failure of their rituals and amulets. The repeated and widespread manifestation of a belief in spirit-mediums and religious rites which can provide combatants with an unconventional advantage over their enemies bears witness to the fact that the worldview from which they evolved has much deeper and stronger roots than those planted by the African disciples of Marx and Lenin.

The outcome of the war in Mozambique suggests that neither incumbent governments nor politico-military analysts can afford to dismiss the phenomenon of religiously inspired insurgents or consign it to the category of esoteric chapters in military history texts. As a Mozambican minister acknowledged to a visiting journalist in 1988, 'We didn't realize how influential the traditional authorities were, even without formal power. We are obviously going to have to harmonize traditional beliefs with our political project. Otherwise we are going against things that the vast majority of our people believe – we will be like foreigners in our own country. I think we are gathering the courage to say so aloud. We will have to restore some of the traditional structures that at the beginning of our independence we simply smashed, thinking that we were doing a good and important thing.' The minister went on to point out that 'Traditional beliefs are a point of reference for all those people caught in the middle of the road between Westernization and African society. In a state of flux like a war, the beliefs become even stronger. This war of ours has certainly underlined the shortcomings of our choice to ignore those beliefs.'[20]

The persistent applicability of traditional African religious belief to modern warfare suggests that the impact of secular Western culture on traditional African beliefs has been overstated. Many analysts seem to have assumed that the imposition of Western institutions would lead to an inevitable erosion of all pre-colonial cultural, political, and religious principles and their replacement by secular, scientific, and rational-legal values. Recent literature suggests that previous explanations of Africa's response to the Western concept of the nation-state need to be revised and modified as thoroughly as the analyses of the manner in which imported ideologies of communism and socialism were expected to shape Africa's future.[21]

The ambivalent assessments of the insurgencies in Madagascar, Kenya, Congo, and Mozambique often are derived from an unspoken assumption that these revolts were fundamentally 'anti-modern' and therefore 'anti-nationalist'. Secular nationalists could acknowledge or accept that the traditional religious or social values which inspired Jina or Mau Mau insurgents may have contributed to campaigns against colonial powers. However, insurgents who called for the restoration of the *fokonolona* or the empowerment of *feiticeiros* ultimately were considered irrelevant to the long-term struggle because they failed to provide a comprehensive replacement for the institution of the nation-state whose governments they opposed. Those who dismiss traditional religion's relevance to contemporary politics and warfare further marginalize the theological or spiritual realm because they assume that individuals only reactivate their faith at times of economic or social stress. As one anthropologist said of Mau Mau, theirs was a 'magic of despair'.[22] The possibility that traditional African religious beliefs could form a constant and desirable point of reference in anyone's life is only implicitly dismissed, presumably because it is considered insulting to repeat Marx's tired characterization of religion as a popular opiate. Alternatively, one can argue that students of modern African politics often are excessively restrained in addressing the persistence of traditional African religious belief and ritual. These subjects are thus left to historians and anthropologists to study. Contemporary analyses of political and military matters often avoid confronting these factors, perhaps in part out of a fear of offending African leaders who consider themselves a secular elite destined to lead their fellow citizens into a bureaucratic national future free of 'superstition' and other 'irrational practices'.

The perspective offered here does not support a forecast of endless revivalist insurgencies in Africa. A dynamic mixture of Islam, Christianity, and animist religious perspectives in sub-Saharan Africa seems likely to result in the appearance of additional syncretic theologies. Whether the impact of these evolving worldviews will eventually intensify or lessen the potentially volatile debate between the secular and the sacred is uncertain. The debate is unlikely to end altogether in the near term. Those who seek a better understanding of the values which inspire the current generation of African soldiers as well as statesmen must continue to look to their traditional sources. The already extensive body of sociological studies of the roots of contemporary insurgencies might benefit from the addition of an equally close scrutiny of the relationship between traditional African religion and warfare.

An early assessment of the 1947 Malgache rebellion suggested that the insurgency rapidly assumed the character of a *'lute sacrée'* (holy war).[23] The concept of a 'Holy War' or Jihad, as it is understood in the modern Middle East for example, frequently is used to describe the campaigns of religiously inspired fanatics. At the very least, this usage suggests the participation of combatants whose morale is high and whose commitment to combat is perhaps more profound than that experienced by soldiers serving a secular state and ideology. Such a limited definition of 'holy wars' probably would understate the impact of African religion on many of the combatants who fought in Madagascar, Kenya, Congo, and Mozambique. The participants in these wars often seem to have drawn political and philosophic, as well as tactical military, inspirations from their pre-colonial traditions.

Further study may reveal that religious traditions in sub-Saharan Africa are the well-spring out of which a 'military mythology' and a 'military ethic' have flowed. Studies of religion and mythology which support the idea of Oriental and Occidental military myths and a related military ethos possibly could be extended to past as well as recent wars in sub-Saharan Africa. This perspective might yield a more objective analysis of combat in Africa which reveals unique attitudes towards war, the manner in which warfare is to be conducted, and the balance between religious and secular motives of its participants.[24] Modern African military history demonstrates that a substantial body of African religion and mythology has survived the impact of Western political institutions, ideology, and military technology. While bullets may never be turned into water, oppressive alien ideas and their corrupting influence on indigenous tradition continue to be diluted by those who retain their faith in ancestral spirits and institutions.

Notes

1 INTRODUCTION

1. Kenneth W. Grundy, *Guerrilla Struggle in Africa*. New York: Grossman Publishers, 1971. See pp. 57 and 59, for a relatively optimistic outlook on the prospects for guerrilla war in Africa. With the passage of time, a more pessimistic view began to prevail. For a fairly typical expression of the latter, more pessimistic, view, see Robert Buijtenhuis, *Essays on Mau Mau, Contributions to Mau Mau Historiography*, Leiden: African Studies Centre, Research Report No. 17, 1982. According to Buijtenhuijs, 'It is extremely difficult, under the conditions prevailing in Africa south of the Sahara to launch a successful peasants revolt. This was already so during the colonial era when the situation was relatively clear, because it was easy to identify the common enemy. The failure of the Mau Mau revolt in Kenya, of the 1947 Madagascar war and the UPC insurrections in Cameroun strongly remind us of this difficulty. As far as one can judge, conditions are even less favorable in post colonial Africa.' This quote appears in Terence O. Ranger, *Peasant Consciousness and Guerrilla War in Zimbabwe*. London: James Currey, 1985, p. 138. For an early assessment of the greater likelihood of coups in Africa, see Ruth First, *Power in Africa; Political Power in Africa and the Coup d'Etat*. Harmondsworth, Middlesex: Penguin Books, 1972. pp. 20–23. Ruth First discussed the 'contagion of the coup' in Africa and concluded 'the continent wide cycle is far from complete.'

2. Claude E. Welch Jr, 'Obstacles to Peasant Warfare in Africa', *African Studies Review*, Vol. 20, no. 3, December 1977, pp. 121–130.

3. Thomas Hodgkin, *Nationalism in Colonial Africa*. London: Muller, 1956. p. 114.

4. Gerard Chaliand, *Armed Struggle in Africa: With the Guerrillas in 'Portuguese Guinea'*. New York: Monthly Review Press, 1969, p. 116. Indeed, Che Guevara's own brief encounter with the ethnic and magico-religious dimensions of insurgency in the Congo between 1964 and 1965 purportedly convinced him that these factors more than thwarted the conduct of effective insurgency; they made guerrilla warfare in Africa impossible. See Thomas H. Henriksen, *Revolution and Counterrevolution; Mozambique's War of Independence, 1964–1974*. Westport, Connecticut: Greenwood Press, 1983. p. 4.

5. Basil Davidson, *Africa in Modern History*. London: Allen Lane, 1978, p. 350.

2 MADAGASCAR: THE 1947–48 REBELLION

1. Nigel Heseltine, *Madagascar*, Praeger, New York, 1971, pp. 174. The MDRM's immediate forerunner originally appeared in 1945 under the name

of the Party of the Restoration of Malgache Independence (PRIM). PRIM very quickly established local branches throughout the island. See Henri Grimal, *Decolonization.* Boulder, Colorado: Westview Press, 1978, pp. 354–355.

2.   Maureen Covell, *Madagascar: Politics, Economics and Society.* London: Frances Pinter, 1987, p. 25, and Mervyn Brown, *Madagascar Rediscovered.* Hamden, Conn.: Archon Books, 1979, p. 267.

3.   Jacques Tronchon, *L'insurrection malgache de 1947.* Paris: Editions-Diffusion Karthala, 1986, p. 92.

4.   Heseltine, op. cit., p. 176.

5.   Tronchon, op. cit., p. 29.

6.   Ibid. pp. 147–148.

7.   Ibid. pp. 211–216. Raseta and Ravoahangy's affiliation with an early Malgache nationalist movement gave them considerable stature in the eyes of many of their colleagues who sought an early end to French colonialism. In 1912, a small group of students founded the Vy Vato Sakelika (Iron and Stone), known as the VVS. This movement operated as a clandestine organization of several hundred students subdivided into small groups in Tananarive and elsewhere in the central highlands. In 1915 French authorities claimed to have uncovered a VVS plot to poison all Europeans on the island. Several dozen members were arrested. Prosecutors never revealed evidence of weapons caches or poison but more than thirty VVS members were nonetheless sentenced to long periods of hard labor. Among those later released as part of a general amnesty in 1921 were two medical students, Joseph Raseta and Joseph Ravoahangy. For additional details on the early stages of modern Malgache nationalism, see Virginia Thompson and Richard Adloff, *The Malagasy Republic.* California: Stanford University Press, 1965, pp. 21–24.

8.   Heseltine, op. cit., pp. 179–182, and Tronchon, op. cit., pp. 31. For a discussion of anti-MDRM provocations by settlers and colonial officials, as well as the creation of the PADESM, see Pierre Boiteau, *Contribution à l'Histoire de la Nation Malgache.* Paris: Editions Sociales, 1958, pp. 358–362, 366–367.

9.   Tronchon, op. cit., pp. 162–163. For a further discussion and details on splits within the MDRM and the debate over tactics, see Raymond K. Kent, *From Madagascar to the Malagasy Republic.* New York: Frederick A. Praeger, 1962, pp. 108–112. At their 1948 trial, French officials accused the three Malgache parliamentarians of fomenting the rebellion. Their last minute telegram was portrayed as a 'secret signal' to begin the uprising, not an attempt to thwart it. See Hubert Deschamps, *Histoire de Madagascar.* Paris: Editions Berger-Levrault, 1961, p. 271.

10.   Tronchon, op. cit., pp. 315–317 and Heseltine, op. cit., p. 179. Insurgent forces assaulted numerous small towns and economic targets in the opening phase of the rebellion. The town of Ambila was burned, Vatomandry, Manakara, and Farafangana were attacked, and colonial settlers living in the Mananjary, Faraony, and Matitana area were murdered. Sahasinaka, Vohipeno, Fort Carnot, and Ifanadiana were seized. At Vohilava, near Mananjary, the local Merina governor and all his administrators were massacred. See Deschamps, op. cit., p. 269. For a French settler's account of

insurgent attacks on his estate during the first days of the insurgency, see Henry Casseville, *L'île ensanglantée (Madagascar 1946–1947)*. Paris: Fasquelle Editeurs, 1948, pp. 140–148.

11. Tronchon, op., cit., p. 45
12. Ibid. p. 75.
13. Ibid. pp. 207–210 for additional biographical data on all three insurgent commanders. See also Brown, op. cit., pp. 268–269. Brown says most of the insurgents' military leaders were Jina members.
14. Tronchon, op. cit., pp. 47–48. Malgache civilians employed in the colonial postal and communications systems may also have served as the nucleus of a communications network which facilitated the transmission of messages between insurgent members throughout northern and central Madagascar. For this line of speculation, see John T. Gordge, 'The Outlook in Madagascar', *African Affairs*, Vol. 48, no.191 (1949), pp. 133–141
15. Arthur Stratton, *The Great Red Island*. New York: Charles Scribner's Sons, 1964, pp. 248, 255.
16. National Archives, Washington, DC. Despatch no. 351, American Consulate, Tananarive, Madagascar, 30 April 1947. Record Group 59. General Records of the Department of State, 851 W.00/4-3047. Initial counterinsurgency sweep operations a few hundred miles south of Moromanga netted several combatants who proved to be former members of the French Resistance. See also Despatch no. 332, American Consulate, Tananarive, Madagascar, 31 March 1947, RG 59, 851 W.00/3-3147. For the text of the insurgent communiqué, see Despatch no. 401, American Consulate, Tananarive, Madagascar, 5 July 1947, enclosure no. 1, RG 59, 851 W.00/7-547.
17. Tronchon, op. cit., pp. 158–159.
18. Heseltine, op. cit., p.180, and Brown, op. cit., p. 267. Stephen Ellis, *The Rising of the Red Shawls; A Revolt in Madagascar 1895–1899*. Cambridge: Cambridge University Press, 1985, pp. 66–73 provides an extensive discussion of the religious restoration movement behind the 1895 rebellion.
19. Tronchon, op. cit., pp. 169–170. While the appearance of the *fokonolona* coincides with the early years of the Merina monarchy, it may not have spread far beyond the island's central plateau.
20. Ibid. p. 171–173. Tronchon notes that this tradition already had been compromised by the last two Merina monarchs and their associated nobility.
21. Ibid. pp. 247. See also pp. 350–352 for examples of some of the oaths used.
22. Stratton, op. cit., pp. 245–246 and Tronchon, op. cit., pp. 358–359, 368. See also Despatch no. 349, American Consulate, Tananarive, Madagascar, 22 April 1947, RG 59, 851 W.00/4-2247.
23. Heseltine, op. cit., p. 180 and Tronchon, op. cit., p. 59.
24. Stratton, op. cit., p. 245. For a discussion of the mutinous Malgache conscripts, see Despatch no. 83, American Consulate, Tananarive, Madagascar, 20 April 1948, RG 59, 851 W.00/4-2048. The only loyal battalion, which later participated in counterinsurgency operations, was comprised of troops from the southwest, an area of the island ultimately untouched by the uprising.
25. Tronchon, op. cit., pp. 260, 262. According to Boiteau, op. cit., French settlers were increasingly concerned by the prospects of an armed uprising by early

1947. Months before the rebellion began, many were said to be arming them-selves and some had turned their homes into veritable 'blockhouses'. See p. 371. For additional details on the augmentation of colonial forces, see Despatch no. 425, American Consulate, Tananarive, Madagascar, 1 August 1947, RG 59, 851 W.00/8-147 and Despatch no. 439, American Consulate, Tananarive, Madagascar, 16 August 1947, RG 59, 851 W.00/8-1647

26.   Information on French counterinsurgency operations is available in Despatch no. 414, American Consulate, Tananarive, Madagascar, 18 July 1947, RG 59, 851 W.00/7-1847, Despatch no. 434, American Consulate, Tananarive, Madagascar, 9 August 1947, RG 59, 851 W.00/8-947, Despatch no. 495, American Consulate Tananarive, Madagascar, 15 November, 1947, RG 59, 851 W.00/11-1547, and Despatch no. 12, American Consulate, Tananarive, Madagascar, 17 January 1948, RG 59, 851 W.00/1-1748.

27.   French military operations in 1948 are described in Despatch no. 74, American Consulate, Tananarive, Madagascar 8 April 1948, RG 59, 851 W.00/4-848, Despatch no. 164, American Consulate, Tananarive, Madagascar, 7 September 1948, RG 59, 851 W.009-748 and Despatch no. 221, American Consulate, Tananarive, Madagascar, December 8 1948, RG 59, 851 W.00/12-848.

28.   Heseltine, op. cit., p. 180.

29.   Tronchon, op. cit., pp. 53, 63. This included a region estimated to have been 800 kilometers long and, on average, 180 kilometers wide. Brown, op. cit., p. 268, estimates the area to have been roughly one-third of the island.

30.   Covell, op. cit., pp. 26–27.

31.   Tronchon, op. cit., pp. 70–71.

32.   Stratton, op. cit., p. 246.

33.   Covell, op. cit., pp. 27–28. Notwithstanding the rebellions' nationalist character, rare incidents of tribal antagonism were recorded. The insurgency veiled at least one instance in which members of the Zafisoro tribe attacked Farafangana, a town inhabited by the Antefasi, their traditional enemies. At least one tribal group, the Antesaka, remained completely loyal to the French, reflecting a collaborative relationship with the colonial power dating from the nineteenth century. See Deschamps, op. cit., p. 269.

34.   Tronchon, op. cit., p. 173.

35.   Ibid. p. 175. For an appreciation of 'Malagasey Nationalism' by a contem-porary observer of the rebellion, see J. T. Hardeyman, *Madagascar on the Move*. London: Livingstone Press, 1950, pp. 99–102. Hardeyman observed that 'there is an almost mystical regard for the *Tanindrazana*, that is, the land of the ancestors or fatherland. The years have broadened the former parochialism of this idea, and more and more (though the process is by no means complete) the "land of the ancestors" is coming to refer not simply to the family tomb and the village lands, but to Madagascar as a whole.' See p. 99.

36.   Tronchon, op. cit., pp. 163–164.

37.   Ibid. p. 111. Tronchon notes that a small number of colonialists did supply clandestine support to the insurgents, in the form of either guns, spears, or money. This assistance came mainly from those settlers whose economic assets, whether mines, plantations, rice paddies, or other ventures, were located in active insurgent zones.

38. Thompson and Adloff, op. cit., p. 59.
39. Ibid. pp. 47–48.
40. Ali A. Mazrui and Michael Tidy, *Nationalism and New States in Africa*. London: Heinemann Educational Books, 1984, pp. 118.

3 KENYA – THE MAU-MAU INSURGENCY (1952–60)

1. Donald J. Barnett and Karari Njama, *Mau Mau From Within*. New York: Monthly Review Press, 1966, pp. 38–42.
2. Ibid., pp. 41. For a description of the KAU's modest reform program in the late 1940s, see Frank Furedi, *The Mau Mau War in Perspective*. London: James Currey, 1989, pp. 133–135.
3. Ibid. For a more detailed discussion of the KCA's role in the years immediately prior to the start of the insurgency, see Furedi, op. cit., pp. 78–80, 105. Furedi describes the KCA's metamorphosis into a rurally based mass movement in the late 1940s as well as the generational split between moderate elders and radical youth which finally changed the KCA from a vanguard/elitist organization into a mass movement.
4. Carl G. Rosberg, Jr. and John Nottingham, *The Myth of Mau Mau: Nationalism in Kenya*. New York: Frederick A. Praeger, 1966. See pp. 331–332. See also Barnett and Njama, op. cit., pp. 51–55.
5. Barnett and Njama, op. cit., pp. 54. Wunyabari O. Maloba, *Mau Mau and Kenya; An Analysis of a Peasants Revolt*. Bloomington: Indiana University Press, 1993, pp. 128–129. By 1953 at least a few insurgents evidently were occasionally using the term 'Mau Mau' to describe themselves and their colleagues. However, this seems to have been an acknowledgement of the fact that white settlers and the outside world had come to know the movement by this name rather than an official acceptance of the term by the insurgents themselves. Of the five insurgencies discussed in this study the Mau Mau uprising has generated the most extensive academic literature covering a broad spectrum of factors accounting for the rebellion and assessing its outcome. For an appreciation of the ever expanding number of studies produced in the first two decades after the insurgency ended, see Marshall S. Clough and Kennell A. Jackson, Jr., *A Bibliography on Mau Mau*. California: Stanford University, 1975. See Thomas pp. Ofcansky, 'The Mau Mau Revolt in Kenya, 1952–1960: A Preliminary Bibliography', *Africana Journal*, Vol. 15 (1990), 97–126, for a more recent bibliographic essay on Mau Mau which highlights a wealth of additional journalistic sources.
6. Barnett and Njama, op. cit., p. 5.
7. Ibid. pp. 55–56. The authors note that oath taking also played a traditional role as a form of social sanction in Kikuyu society.
8. Claude Welch, Jr., *Anatomy of Rebellion*, Albany: State University Press of New York, 1980, p. 261.
9. John Lonsdale, 'Mau Maus of the Mind: Making Mau Mau and Remaking Kenya', *Journal of African History*, Vol. 31 (1990), 393–421. See p. 416.
10. Barnett and Njama, op. cit., p. 199.

11.   Rosberg and Nottingham, op. cit., p. 261.
12.   Welch, op. cit., pp. 258–259.
13.   Barnett and Njama, op. cit., p. 202.
14.   Ibid. p. 70.
15.   Rosberg and Nottingham, op. cit., pp. 282. The authors assert that, in many respects, the remaining leadership did manage to fill this void, eventually espousing many of the same goals and ideals as the educated elite that had been detained. See pp. 300. For a description of the movement's embryonic 'military wing' see Furedi, op. cit., p.111. Furedi notes that the nationalists had established a paramilitary element known as *Kiama Kia Bara* (the fighting group) in late 1951. Some of the men in its ranks had previous military experience with British forces in World War II.
16.   Lonsdale, op. cit., p. 418.
17.   Robert B. Edgerton, *Mau Mau: An African Crucible*, New York: The Free Press, 1989. See pp. 62–63. The ambivalence, if not the irony, of Kenyatta's denunciations of Mau Mau would not have been lost on those who had read his celebrated book, *Facing Mount Kenya*, first published in 1938. Kenyatta had dedicated it 'To Moigoi and Wamboi and all the dispossessed youth of Africa: for perpetuation of communion with ancestral spirits through the fight for African Freedom, and in the firm faith that the dead, the living, and the unborn will unite to rebuild the destroyed shrines.' See Jomo Kenyatta, *Facing Mount Kenya*, London: Martin Secker & Warburg, 1953.
18.   Rosberg and Nottingham, op. cit., p. 275. Kenyatta was considered more of a liability than a political asset by a few of his colleagues, however, and in 1952, some militant Kenyan nationalists considered assassinating him. Bruce J. Berman, 'Nationalism, Ethnicity and Modernity: The Paradox of Mau Mau', *Canadian Journal of Modern African Studies*, Vol. 25, no. 2 (1991),181–206. See p. 201. Maloba, op. cit., pp. 98–100 provides an informative discussion of Kenyatta's trial.
19.   Barnett and Njari, op. cit., p. 152.
20.   Ibid. p. 151. The oathing rituals also proved to be a counter-productive measure as a means of mobilizing potential supporters in some instances. See Rosberg and Nottingham, op. cit., p. 261. The oathing rituals evidently alienated Kikuyus who were leaders of various mission churches or members of Christian revival groups. Moreover, the modification of traditional Kikuyu oaths also angered Kikuyu traditionalists who did not condone the presence or participation of women and children in the rituals.
21.   Barnett and Njari, op. cit., p. 66. See Edgerton, op. cit., pp. 63–64 and David Throup, *Economic and Social Origins of Mau Mau, 1945–1953.* London: James Currey, 1988, p. 224, for a listing of incidents attributed to Mau Mau prior to September 1952. See also p. 248 of Throup's study which concurs with Furedi, op. cit., p. 105 in dating the start of the revolt from 1947 when Mau Mau members began conducting widespread oathing ceremonies. Throup provides an extensive discussion of the mounting economic pressures on Kikuyu squatters in the late 1940s. Maloba, op. cit., p. 62 notes that local authorities had some difficulty distinguishing between criminal and political activity in accounting for rural and urban violence between 1950 and 1952.

22. Edgerton, op. cit., p. 70. Maloba, op. cit., pp. 64–65. Militant Kikuyus also relied on criminal networks in Nairobi to buy or steal weapons prior to 1952.
23. Rosberg and Nottingham, op. cit., p. 274.
24. Edgerton, op. cit., p. 77.
25. Welch, op. cit., pp. 298–299. Welch notes that Mau Mau's gunsmiths proved to be quite prolific. By 1958, British forces had captured some 3000 homemade weapons. Maloba, op. cit., p.121. During the insurgency, Mau Mau also managed to buy a modest number of weapons from African troops and members of the Home Guard.
26. Barnett and Njari, op. cit., pp. 157 and 172. See also Edgerton, op. cit., p. 73.
27. Edgerton, op. cit., p. 81. See also Julian Paget, *Counterinsurgency Operations: Techniques of Guerrilla Warfare*. New York: Walker, 1967, pp. 90–91. Paget concurs with the 12 000–15 000 estimate for guerrilla strength and suggests there may have been a cadre of 30 000 additional members which comprised a 'passive wing' of supporters living in the Kikuyu Reserves.
28. See Barnett and Njari, op. cit., pp. 66 and 360. The insurgents had planned but ultimately were unable to mobilize members of the Turkana, Suk, and Kalenjin tribes.
29. Edgerton, op. cit., pp. 78–79.
30. Rosberg and Nottingham, op. cit., pp. 290–292. The authors suggest the attacking force may have numbered as many as 3000. Edgerton, op. cit., cites an estimate of 1000–3000.
31. Edgerton, op. cit., pp. 87, 93–94.
32. Ibid. pp. 112–113. The insurgents' largest camp in the Aberdare Mountains may, at times, have held as many as 5000 members.
33. Ibid. pp. 82. See also Barnett and Njari, op. cit., pp. 245 and 329. The Kenya Defense Council was superseded by a 'Kenya Parliament' in February 1954. The latter was envisioned as an alternative African government and represented an effort to separate political and military functions.
34. Edgerton, op. cit., see p. 113.
35. Ibid. pp. 21. See also Throup, op. cit., p.151 for evidence that demobilized veterans were also active in the early stages of non-violent protest against colonial policy concerning agriculture and land holding which adversely affected Kikuyu peasant farmers.
36. See Oginga Odinga, *Not Yet Uhuru*, New York: Hill & Wang, 1967, p. 110. For additional details on Kimathi's brief, and less than distinguished, military career, see Edgerton, op. cit., pp. 112.
37. Edgerton, op. cit., pp. 120 and 140.
38. Ibid. p.121.
39. Maloba, op. cit., p.125. Barnett and Njari. op. cit., p.137.
40. Barnett and Njari, op. cit., p. 205.
41. Ibid. p. 216.
42. Ibid. p. 136. Maloba, op. cit., pp. 138–150 provides an extensive discussion of the 'rehabilitation' program for Mau Mau prisoners.

43.   Ibid. pp. 211–212. See also Edgerton, op. cit., pp. 67, 87. For a discussion of the reorganization of the British colonial force command structure subsequent to this influx of troops, see Paget, op. cit., pp. 95–96. The arrival of British units did not signal an immediate improvement of the security situation. Some of the first troops deployed to Kenya were not properly trained or equipped for counterinsurgency operations in the local terrain. See Anthony Clayton, *Counter-Insurgency in Kenya 1952-1960.* Nairobi: Transafrica Publishers, 1976, p.16. These shortcomings were compounded by a serious lack of intelligence which required a major reform and reorganization of police and military units responsible for gathering information on the insurgency. Randall W. Heather, 'Intelligence and Counter-Insurgency in Kenya, 1952–1956', *Intelligence and National Security,* Vol. 5, no. 3 (1990), pp. 57–83. See pp. 58, 65, 69.

44.   Edgerton, op. cit., p. 91. Rosberg and Nottingham, op. cit., p. 303 give a figure of   27 000. Maloba, op. cit., pp. 81–83 discusses British tactics and operations under General Hind in early 1953.

45.   Edgerton, op. cit., pp. 92–93. and Barnett and Njari, op. cit., p. 332. The tactical initiative very quickly shifted from Mau Mau to British forces. Heather, op. cit., p. 76 notes that 'During 1953 Mau Mau held a 2:1 advantage in the number of incidents initiated against the Security Forces (including Home Guard), while in 1954 the advantage shifted to the Security Forces by a 2.8:1 margin.'

46.   Edgerton, op. cit., pp. 98–99 and Maloba, op. cit., pp. 88, 94–95. 'Operation Dante' is described in John Newsinger,' A counter-insurgency tale: Kitson in Kenya', *Race and Class,* Vol. 31, no. 4 (1990), 61–72. See p. 67. For a discussion of 'pseudo-gangs' and related efforts to induce large-scale Mau Mau surrenders, see Paget, op. cit., pp. 102–103, 105–106 and Newsinger, op. cit., pp. 64–65. Clayton, op. cit., pp. 33–34 discusses the conversion techniques used in recruiting 'pseudo-gang' members. Heather, op. cit., p. 75 notes that 'counter-gangs' had been used during previous British campaigns in Palestine and Malaya.

47.   Maloba, op. cit., pp. 132–133 and Barnett and Njari, op. cit., pp. 455–456. The latter also noted that divisions in the movement coincided with evidence of what loosely may be called schisms in the traditional religious beliefs and practices of some of the insurgents. Some members chose not to observe certain traditional taboos concerning foods or other ritual requirements. At one camp, the *mundo mugo* had appointed an eleven year old boy as a general, and changed traditional prayer rituals. Members of the camp refused to eat or live with a person who had not been cleansed by their own religious authorities. See pp. 316, 382.

48.   Lonsdale, op. cit., pp. 418–419.

49.   Edgerton, op. cit., pp. 99–102.

50.   Welch, op. cit., pp. 106, 343. Barnett and Njari, op. cit., p. 440, claim a much greater number already had died by early 1955. They cite a figure of 22 000 killed as of early 1955.

51.   Edgerton, op. cit., p. 86. The effectiveness of air power is a chronically contentious issue in the conduct of counterinsurgency operations and the

Mau Mau rebellion was no exception. See Paget, op. cit., pp. 95–96. The crash of four Harvard bombers, caught in mountain valley down drafts, raised further doubts in the minds of some critics as well as boosting insurgent morale. See Clayton, op. cit., p. 24.

52. Barnett and Njari, op. cit., p. 67. These and other shortcomings are frequently overlooked by a small group of analysts who insist that Mau Mau should be seen as one of the most successful and influential instances of a nationalist movement in post World-War II Africa. See John Walton, *Reluctant Rebels; Comparative Studies of Revolution and Underdevelopment*, New York: Columbia University Press, 1984, p.130 for a relatively recent example of this perspective.

53. Edgerton, op. cit., pp. 82–83. Analysts have listed a variety of political, economic, and theological factors as decisive in accounting for Mau Mau's failure to sabotage rail and power lines. For a more elaborate discussion of this point, particularly with respect to the vulnerability of the Kenyan railroad, see Clayton, op. cit., pp. 31–33. The insurgents may, however, have considered a functional rail line of greater tactical value. See Guy Campbell, *The Charging Buffalo; A History of the Kenya Regiment, 1937–1963*. London: Leo Cooper in association with Secker & Warburg, 1986, p. 49. Campbell claims 'It was known that throughout the Emergency the Mau Mau used the railway like commuters. No stops or searches were ever made as far as I know, although the trains passed through several battalion areas and police posts.' See also Maloba, op. cit., pp. 122–123, and 127. Maloba rejects the arguments of captured Mau Mau commanders who asserted that they refrained from sabotage of the Kenyan economic infrastructure because they did not want to inflict further hardships on fellow Kenyans living in towns and cities. Instead, Maloba claims that 'There is, therefore, good reason to argue that the absence of any substantial sabotage is attributable to Mau Mau's reliance on seers, prophets and witch doctors for strategic calculation and planning. These seers failed to realize the military significance of electricity, railways and roads and since the guerrillas relied on the seers for guidance they could not embark on unsanctioned exploits. Lack of sabotage must be seen in retrospect as one of the most costly prices the revolt paid for relying on witch doctors.' Maloba's argument may be reasonable but it appears to be uncorroborated by other accounts of the insurgency's strategy and tactics. The colonial forces' rapid seizure of the tactical initiative, their superior firepower, command control and mobility, combined with Campbell's observations and Mau Mau commanders' political assessments provide a compelling list of factors which would readily account for Mau Mau's failure or unwillingness to attack economic targets.

54. Barnett and Njari, op. cit., p. 359. Maloba, op. cit., p.112, cites former Colonial Secretary Oliver Lyttelton's unsubstantiated claims, published in 1963, that Mau Mau had received assistance and money from the Soviet embassy in Addis Ababa.

55. Edgerton, op. cit., p. 216.

56. Ibid. pp. 218, 222–223.

4   CAMEROON: THE UPC INSURRECTION (1956–70)

1.   Basil Davidson. *Africa in Modern History*, London: Allen Lane, 1978, p. 258.
2.   David E. Gardinier, *Cameroon – United Nations Challenge to French Policy*. London: Oxford University Press, 1963, p. 69.
3.   Victor T. LeVine, *The Cameroons: From Mandate to Independence*. Los Angeles: University of California Press, 1964, pp. 147–148.
4.   Ibid. pp. 149–150.
5.   Ibid. pp. 152–155.
6.   Ibid. p. 156. See also Neville N. Rubin, *Cameroon: An African Federation*. New York: Praeger, 1971, p. 68. See also Richard A. Joseph, 'Ruben Um Nyobe and the "Kamerun" Rebellion', *African Affairs*, Vol. 73, no. 293 (1974), pp. 428–448, especially pp. 437–438.
7.   Rubin, op. cit., p. 68. See also Willard R. Johnson, *The Cameroon Federation: Political Integration in a Fragmentary Society*, Princeton, NJ: Princeton University Press, 1970, pp. 360. Moumie's statement about Um Nyobe appears in Willard Johnson, 'The Union des Population du Cameroun in Rebellion: The Integrative Backlash of Insurgency', in *Protest and Power in Black Africa*, edited by Robert I. Rotberg and Ali A. Mazrui. New York: Oxford University Press, 1970, pp. 671–692. See p. 673. A thorough discussion and analysis of the events of May, 1955 appears in Richard A. Joseph, *Radical Nationalism in Cameroun*. Oxford: Clarendon Press, 1977. See pp. 269–288, 316.
8.   Smith Hempstone, *Africa – Angry Young Giant*. New York: Frederick A. Praeger, 1961, pp. 202–203. Although the early stages of the UPC insurgency are sometimes characterized as a Bassa revolt, this description is not precise. Initial UPC insurgent activity is thought to have been conducted under the command of Abel Kingue, a Bamileke, working with Bassa related groups in the Sanaga Maritime Région. See Rubin, op. cit., p. 69. Rubin notes that no official estimate of casualties for the 1955–1956 phase of the insurgency was ever provided. For additional detail, see also Johnson, op. cit., p. 350.
9.   Rubin, op. cit., p. 95 and Johnson, op. cit., p. 350.
10.   Hempstone, op. cit., p. 204.
11.   LeVine, op. cit., p. 270. See also Special Operations Research Office, *Casebook on Insurgency and Revolutionary Warfare*. Washington, DC: The American University, 1962, pp. 289–290, and Joseph, op. cit., p. 346.
12.   Gardinier, op. cit., p. 210.
13.   LeVine, op. cit., p. 170 and Johnson, op. cit., pp. 351–352.
14.   Johnson, op. cit. See p. 244 for the UPC's 1959 statements and p. 195 for its post-independence aims and grievances.
15.   Gardinier, op. cit., p. 94.
16.   Rubin, op. cit., p. 98 and Johnson, op. cit., p. 356. Moumie's poisoning was widely attributed to right-wing French nationalists who either had acted independently or at the behest of the French Secret Service. For a recent account which implicates French officials in Moumie's assassination, see Roger Faligot and Pascal Krop, translated by W .D. Halls, *La Piscine; The*

French Secret Service since 1944. New York: Basil Blackwell, 1989, pp. 186–190.

17. LeVine, op. cit., p. 292. For a discussion of the political parties and various positions they espoused concerning independence, secession, or unification for the British Cameroons during the course of the insurgency, see Bongfen Chem-Langhee and Martin Z. Njeuma, 'The Pan Kamerun Movement, 1949–1961', in Ndiva Kofele-Kale, *An African Experiment in Nation Building: The Bilingual Cameroon Republic Since Reunification.* Boulder, Colorado: Westview Press, 1980, pp. 25–64.

18. Johnson, op. cit., pp. 251–252.

19. Special Operations Research Office, op. cit., pp. 290 and 295. See also Johnson, op. cit., pp. 357–358.

20. Rubin, op. cit., p. 155.

21. Johnson, op. cit., p. 355.

22. Zbigniew Brzezinski (ed.), *Africa and the Communist World*, California: Stanford University Press, 1963 – see pp. 38, 192. The total number of weapons and supplies provided to the UPC is uncertain.

23. LeVine, op. cit., pp. 149–150.

24. Johnson, op. cit., p. 61.

25. Special Operations Research Office, op. cit., pp. 291–292, and 296. See also LeVine, op. cit., p. 171.

26. Hempstone, op. cit., p. 211.

27. Johnson, op. cit., pp. 156, 359.

5   CONGO/ZAIRE: THE KWILU REBELLION (1963–68)

1.   Herbert F. Weiss, *Political Protest in the Congo: The Parti Solidaire Africain during the Independence Struggle.* Princeton: Princeton University Press, 1967. See pp. 79, 82.

2.   Ibid. p.185.

3.   Ibid. p.193.

4.   Ibid. p. 291.

5.   Ibid. pp. 118–120, 126–127.

6.   Ibid. pp. 152–153. Weiss also points out that the PSA created a 'paramilitary organization' used to protect party delegations in late 1959. However, the PSA never approved the creation of a militia and its own paramilitary force never became as large as the militia units established by some other parties. See pp. 228, 254.

7.   Ibid. p. 266.

8.   Renee C. Fox, Willy de Craemer and Jean Marie Ribeaucourt, 'The "Second Independence": A Case Study of the Kwilu Rebellion in the Congo', *Comparative Studies in Society and History*, Vol. 8, no. 1 (1965), 78–109. See p. 87.

9.   Ibid. pp. 80, 91.

10. Ibid. p. 97.

11. Ibid.

12.   Ibid. pp. 85–86. See also Thomas Turner, 'Congo-Kinshasa', in Victor A. Olorunsola (ed.), *The Politics of Cultural Sub-Nationalism*. Garden City, NY: Doubleday, 1972, pp. 195–283. Turner states that Mpeve was the off-shoot of a secret society known as Lupambula, which first appeared in 1947. See p. 246. Numerous authors also refer to the influence of the Bapende Revolt of 1931–1932. This rebellion lasted for several months and stemmed from a workers' protest against harsh working conditions and the exploita-tion of laborers on local palm-oil plantations. This uprising reportedly was still recalled by Kwilu Province residents in the early 1960s and some observers see this as evidence of a 'tradition of revolt' which was an import-ant factor in explaining Bapende support for Mulele. See Centre de Recherche et d'Information Socio-Politique (CRISP), *Congo, 1964; Political Documents of a Developing Nation*. Princeton, NJ: Princeton University Press, 1966, pp. 7–8.

13.   Benoit Verhaegen, *Rébellions au Congo*, Brussels: CRISP, 1965, pp. 48–49.

14.   Fox et al., op. cit., pp. 90–91.

15.   Crawford Young, *Politics in the Congo*, Princeton, NJ: Princeton University Press, 1965, p. 435.

16.   Ibid. See also Fox et al., op. cit., p. 90.

17.   Benoit Verhaegen, 'La rébellion muleliste au Kwilu: chronologie des événe-ments et essai d'interpretation (janvier 1962–juillet 1964)', in Catherine Coquery-Vidrovitch and Alain Forest, *Rébellion-Révolution au Zaire, 1963–1965, Tome 1*. Paris: Harmattan Editions, 1987, pp. 120–167. See pp. 122–123.

18.   Ibid. p. 125.

19.   Ibid. p. 127.

20.   Ibid. p. 142.

21.   Verhaegen, *Rébellions au Congo*, op. cit., p. 59.

22.   Ibid. pp. 72, 83. These individuals may, of course, have been trying to save themselves from arrest. Similar concerns probably also motivated Gizenga who chose not to rally to Mulele after then President Tshombe released the former from prison in July 1964.

23.   M. Crawford Young, 'Rebellion and the Congo', in Robert I. Rotberg and Ali A. Mazrui (eds), *Protest and Power in Black Africa*. New York: Oxford University Press, 1970, pp. 968–1011. See pp. 971, 991–992. See also Ludo Martens, *Pierre Mulele, ou la seconde vie de Patrice Lumumba*. Berchem, Belgium: Editions EPO, 1985, pp. 97, 132. According to Martens, Felix Mukulubundu, who later became one of Mulele's key commanders, attended classes in guerrilla warfare in March 1961 while serving as the 'military attaché' to China for the Stanleyville-based Gizengist government. Mulele began his course of instruction in April 1962.

24.   Young, op. cit., p. 992

25.   Fox et al., op. cit., p. 96.

26.   Ibid.

27.   Verhaegen, 'La rébellion muleliste au Kwilu', op. cit., p. 128 and Verhaegen, *Rébellions au Congo*, op. cit., pp. 107. Mulele called together local Bambunda chiefs and persuaded them to provide him with a select group of young men from each village who would then be sent to Mulele's camps. Mulele promised to provide training which would help them con-

tribute to the prosperity of their village. He also seemed to imply that he could mint currency and would pass this knowledge on to his trainees and eventually to all their relatives. For the approximate location of Mulele's camps in the Gungu–Idiofa–Kikwit triangle, see CRISP op. cit., p. 11.

28. Verhaegen, 'La rébellion muleliste au Kwilu', op. cit., p. 130 and Verhaegen, *Rébellions au Congo*, op. cit., p. 70.
29. Claude E. Welch, Jr., *Anatomy of Rebellion*. Albany: State University Press of New York, 1980, p. 304 and Young, op. cit., p. 971. For a chronology which includes the location and details of the first four weeks of guerrilla attacks in 1964, see op. cit., pp. 13–16.
30. Claude E. Welch, Jr., 'Ideological Foundations of Revolution in Kwilu', *African Studies Review,* Vol. 18, no. 2 (1975), 116–128. See pp. 122–123. For additional details on the insurgent's political and military structure, see CRISP, *Congo, 1965; Political Documents of a Developing Nation.* Princeton, New Jersey: Princeton University Press, 1967, pp. 91–93 and Martens, op. cit., pp. 208–222.
31. Fox et al., op. cit., p. 104.
32. Ibid. pp. 104–105.
33. Verhaegen, *Rébellions au Congo*, op. cit., pp. 79–80. See also Herbert Weiss and Adrienne Fulco,'Les partisans au Kwilu: analyse des origines sociales des membres et cadres des équipes de base', in *Rebellions-Révolution au Zaire*, op. cit., pp. 168–181. See pp. 169–170. The authors estimated the average size of an 'équipe' at approximately 50. They ranged in strength from 9–160 insurgents. Each 'équipe' had a 'political commissar' appointed by Mulele as well as a military leader selected by the équipe's own men. For additional information on équipes and the strength figures in other units, see CRISP *Congo, 1965*, op. cit., pp. 93–94.
34. Thomas Kanza, *The Rise and Fall of Patrice Lumumba.* London: Rex Collings, 1978, pp. 110–111. Kanza claims that Mulele briefly served in the same battalion with Joseph Mobutu in 1951–1952. See also Martens, op. cit., pp. 42–52 for a biographic sketch of Mulele's early life, including his service in the colonial Force Publique and his subsequent encounter, in the late 1950s, with the works of Mao and Lenin. Theotime Ntsolo, a former ANC member, trained an 'elite battalion' of troops for Mulele, and ANC deserters, Pierre Ngwensungu and Eugene Mumvudi were insurgent zone commanders. See Martens, op. cit., pp. 210, 253.
35. Verhaegen, *Rébellions au Congo*, op. cit., pp. 126–127, Young, op. cit., p. 989 and Fox et al., op. cit., p. 98. For a critique of this widely held view, see Martens, op. cit., pp. 230–232. Martens claims that only some of the movement's early members believed in 'magic' and fetishes. Martens asserts that Mulele himself did not advocate a traditional religious world-view and told his followers as much. According to Martens, the story of Mulele shooting himself with blanks was propagated by ANC officers to convince credulous troops that Mulele was not invulnerable. Moreover, the battle cry 'Mai' was simply intended as a signal to the enemy that the insurgents did not fear their bullets. Martens' sources for this interpretation are undocumented interviews with unidentified insurgents. His effort to minimize the role of an animistic religious perspective seems to reflect Marten's personal preference for the Maoist and Leninist influences which he perceives as the principle ideological components of the rebellion.

36. Fox et al. op. cit., p. 85. The legacy of the 'talking snake' cult was not pervasive in Kwilu Province, however. Furthermore, some residents who still believed in it did not necessarily support Mulele's revolt. See Verhaegen, *Rébellions au Congo*, op. cit., p. 30 where it is noted that at least one tribe which ascribed to the cult also opposed Mulele.

37. Welch, 'Ideological Foundations of Revolution in Kwilu', op. cit., pp. 120–121 and Fox et al., op. cit., p. 100.

38. Verhaegen, *Rébellions au Congo*, op. cit., pp. 124–126.

39. Fox et al. op. cit., pp. 98–99, 105.

40. Verhaegen, *Rébellions au Congo*, op. cit., pp. 124–126.

41. Young, op. cit., pp. 1001. According to the testimony of a Kwilu insurgent captured in 1966, Mulele opposed the rebellion in the east and especially the local insurgents' August 1964 occupation of Stanleyville. Mulele evidently considered this a strategically inappropriate move for an insurgency which had just begun to mobilize popular support. See CRISP, *Congo, 1965*, op. cit., p.107.

42. See Fox et al., op. cit., p. 101 for a discussion of their reasons for siding with Mulele.

43. See Weiss and Fulco, op. cit., pp. 169–170 for evidence supporting a range of 90 000 or more partisans. For Mobutu's assessment, see Verhaegen, *Rébellions au Congo*, op. cit., p. 114. For an early 1964 estimate that Mulele had enlisted 9000–10 000 youths ranging in age from 15 to 20, see CRISP *Congo, 1964*, op. cit., p. 29. Martens, op. cit., p. 154 states that Mulele had already recruited 5000 supporters by December 1963.

44. Welch, *Anatomy of Rebellion*, op. cit., p. 344. For details of the attack on Kimpata Eku, see Martens, op. cit., pp. 192–193.

45. Young, op. cit., p. 971. See also CRISP, *Congo, 1964*, op. cit., pp. 18–19, 24.

46. Welch, *Anatomy of Rebellion*, op. cit., pp. 268, Verhaegen, *Rébellions au Congo*, op. cit., p. 119 and Martens, op. cit., pp. 255, 282, 291–293.

47. CRISP *Congo, 1965*, op. cit., pp. 89, 91, 120, 128–130. See also Welch, *Anatomy of Rebellion*, op. cit., pp. 305–306 and Martens, op. cit., pp. 206, 276, 282.

48. Welch, *Anatomy of Rebellion*, op. cit., p. 305 and CRISP *Congo, 1965*, op. cit., p. 119. Some female Kwilu insurgents claimed, under interrogation, to have seduced ANC soldiers and stolen their weapons and ammunition while the troops slept. Welch also reports that unspent cartridges were carefully retrieved after every engagement.

49. Weiss, op. cit., p. 299 and Verhaegen, *Rébellions au Congo*, op. cit., pp. 115, 171. Kandaka later accused Mulele, among other things, of giving more weapons to Bambunda members, led by Louis Kafungu, than to Bapende insurgents. Kafungu was one of Mulele's chief commanders and was also responsible for the movement's personnel and administrative affairs. See CRISP, *Congo, 1965*, op. cit., pp. 91–95. Martens, op. cit., pp. 202–207 describes the origins of Kandaka's disaffection in the last months of 1964. Kandaka's subsequent effort at reconciliation failed. Martens asserts that Kandaka was executed by insurgents loyal to Kafungu who acted on their own initiative and not under Mulele's orders. Mulele was said to be ready to reconcile with Kandaka in early 1965.

50. Young, op. cit., p. 1002.

51. Fox, et al., op. cit., p. 107.

52. Benoir Verhaegen, 'Le rôle de l'ethnie et de l'individu dans la rébellion du Kwilu et dans son echec', in *Rébellion-Révolution au Zaire*, op. cit., p. 155.

53. Ibid. pp. 164–165. See Weiss and Fulco, op. cit., for the total population figure of the Kwilu districts affected by the rebellion. For the details of the ANC's pursuit of Mulele, see Martens, op. cit., pp. 294–298, 300, 304. The status of the Kwilu rebellion in late 1967 is also briefly described in M. Crawford Young, 'Congo-Kinshasa Situation Report', *Africa Report*, Vol. 12, no. 7 (1967),12–18. See p. 17.

54. Colin Legum and John Drysdale, *Africa Contemporary Record; Annual Survey and Documents, 1968–1969*. Africa Research Limited: London, 1970. pp. 441–445. See also *Keesing's Contemporary Archive*, Vol. 16, 1967–1968. London: Keesing's, 1968, p. 22958. Martens, op. cit., pp. 331–333 offers a very different account of Mulele's death including graphic details of torture and dismemberment.

55. Welch, 'Ideological Foundations of Revolution in Kwilu', in *Anatomy of Rebellion*, op. cit., p. 123. Martens, op. cit., pp. 255–259, 264–268 provides an extensive critique of Mulele's political and administrative failures. In Martens' view, Mulele did not sufficiently appreciate the need for a 'vanguard' political wing to lead the insurgency along the lines advocated by Lenin in his theoretical tracts. The leaders of the Kwilu rebellion also failed to understand the proper relationship between political and military struggles and did not prepare the 'masses' for a long war.

56. Verhaegen, 'Le rôle de l'ethnie et de individu dans la rébellion du Kwilu et dans son echec', op. cit., pp. 165–166. The 'intellectuals' who answered Mulele's May 1964 call to join his movement and supplement the ranks of his illiterate section leaders were mainly school teachers and high school students. These intellectuals later became some of the first members to abandon the movement as well as having been part of the last to join it. As the rebellion began to collapse, in late 1965 and early 1966, it was the students and teachers who were among the first to rally to the government, leaving their rural compatriots to continue the struggle. This further suggests that the core membership of the rebellion had come from the ranks of those who had previously been inspired by Mpeve and Savoir Vivre. See CRISP, *Congo, 1965*, op. cit., pp. 107–108, 120.

57. Ibid. p.162. Mulele may not have felt this way in the early weeks of the insurgency. Immediately after he decided to launch the rebellion, in August 1963, one of the movement's founding members, Leonard Mituditi, went abroad on what proved to be an unsuccessful mission to acquire aid. In the early months of the rebellion, uncorroborated reports alluded to *matériel* and modern weapons deliveries to Mulele's forces via Brazzaville. See Verhaegen, *Rébellions au Congo*, op. cit., pp. 69 and 119. Martens, op. cit., pp. 305, 318 reports that Mituditi and Thomas Mukwidi made two, evidently unsuccessful, trips in early 1964 to China, Algeria, Guinea, and other unidentified 'progressive' countries in search of support. Whether Mulele authorized these ventures is uncertain. For an account of various Mulelist representatives' efforts to establish contacts with insurgents in eastern

Congo between late 1963 and 1965, see Martens, op. cit., pp. 156–157, 308, 318–324. For a brief moment, at a conference held in Cairo in April 1965, Congolese dissidents from the east and Kwilu nearly succeeded in establishing a 'Supreme Council of the Revolution' which designated Mulele as a ranking officer. Factionalism within the ranks of the eastern Congolese dissidents subverted these efforts. In the mid-1960s the previously 'revolutionary center' of Brazzaville became little more than a useful meeting place rather than a source of supplies for a variety of insurgents from Congo-Kinshasa and other African countries. Congolese insurgents briefly met and exchanged information with members of the Popular Movement for the Liberation of Angola (MPLA) and the Cameroonian UPC in early 1964. Efforts by Mukwidi and other Mulelist representatives to rejoin their colleagues in Kwilu Province by infiltrating from Brazzaville were thwarted in 1965 and 1967. The guerrillas had failed to mobilize local civilian support in advance of their efforts to move through territory separating Brazzaville and Kwilu.

58.   Jean Claude Willame, 'Congo-Kinshasa: General Mobutu and Two Political Generations', in Claude E. Welch, Jr. (ed.) *Soldier and State in Africa.* Evanston, Illinois: Northwestern University Press, 1970, pp. 124–151. See p. 139.

6   MOZAMBIQUE: FROM THE NRM TO RENAMO (1977–92)

1.   Allen Isaacman and Barbara Isaacman, *Mozambique: From Colonialism to Revolution, 1900–1982.* Westview Press: Boulder, Colorado, 1983. See pp. 82–83. For additional details on the membership and leaders of Udenamo, Manu and Unami, see Barry Munslow, *Mozambique: The Revolution and Its Origins.* New York: Longman, 1983, pp. 79–80, 83–84. Munslow points out that the decision to unify the three movements and form Frelimo reflected a growing sentiment that the smaller parties were wasting their time, in exile, writing petitions to the United Nations asking that pressure be applied to Lisbon to grant Mozambique its independence. A younger generation of Mozambican nationalists was convinced that only more militant solutions would end colonial rule.

2.   Joseph Hanlon, *Mozambique: The Revolution Under Fire.* London: Zed Books, 1984, p. 33. For a more extensive discussion of the various issues which undermined the coalition which Frelimo claimed to represent, see Hanlon's account on pp. 28–33.

3.   Notwithstanding a frequent claim that they comprised a more cohesive group than their Angolan counterparts, Mozambican nationalists and their foreign supporters eventually had to acknowledge that 'Despite the united front Frelimo presented to the world, it was really two entities throughout much of this early phase ... . The first, rooted in a narrow nationalist tradition, sought merely to capture the colonial state. The second increasingly saw the struggle as an opportunity to transform basic social and economic as well as political relations.' See Isaacman and Isaacman, op. cit., p. 86. For details on the controversy over elitism, see Munslow, op. cit., pp. 97–99.

4. Richard Gibson, *African Liberation Movements: Contemporary Struggles Against White Minority Rule,* New York and London: Oxford University Press, 1972, pp. 287–288.
5. Ibid. pp. 288–289.
6. Colin Legum, 'The MNR', *CSIS Africa Notes,* No. 16, 15 July 1984, p. 2. See also Hanlon, op. cit., p. 220.
7. Alex Vines, *Renamo: Terrorism in Mozambique,* Centre for Southern African Studies, University of York, 1991. See p. 54.
8. Ibid. pp. 14–15. For the name of Magaia's alleged assailant, see Africa Watch, *Conspicuous Destruction; War Famine and the Reform Process in Mozambique.* New York: Human Rights Watch, 1992, p. 16. See also Munslow, op. cit., p. 103. For details on the political and economic tensions between Frelimo and the newly created Mozambican Armed Forces which led to the 1975 mutiny, see Annette Seegers, 'From Liberation to Modernization: Transforming Revolutionary Paramilitary Forces into Standing Professional Armies', in Bruce E. Arlinghaus and Pauline Baker (eds), *African Armies: Evolution and Capabilities.* Boulder, Colorado: Westview Press, 1986. pp. 52–83. See pp. 65–66.
9. Fumo spokesmen issued a communiqué in Lisbon in 1986. See 'Fumo declares support for Renamo; U.S. Policy Criticized', *O Diabo* (Lisbon), December 30, 1986, p. 17.
10. This information is available in a Fumo document, a copy of which Professor John Marcum, University of California, Santa Cruz, kindly made available to the author. The organization's officials enumerated Fumo's complaints against Frelimo and sent them to the Organization of African Unity in a letter dated 21 June 1971.
11. Paul Fauvet, 'Roots of Counter-revolution: The Mozambique National Resistance', *Review of African Political Economy,* no. 29 (1984), 108–121. See p. 119. In 1982, NRM insurgents captured six Bulgarian cooperants during an attack in northern Mozambique. NRM representatives claimed they would release their captives in exchange for 28 political prisoners including Uria Simango, Mateus Gwenjere, Joana Simiao, and others previously associated with Coremo and other small splinter movements discredited by Frelimo during the anti-colonial struggle. Maputo refused the offer and the Bulgarians were later released. In December 1987 a Renamo Newsletter, *Bulletin 14,* published in January 1988 in Washington, DC, by the Renamo Department of Information called for the release of Simango, Gwenjere, and Simiao in exchange for a British journalist, Nicholas de la Casa, who had been captured by the insurgents and accused of spying in mid-1987. The journalist was eventually released without an exchange for Simango or others held in Mozambican jails. See also Africa Watch, op. cit., pp. 19 and 158. In April 1992 the government acknowledged that Simango, Simiao, Gwenjere, and other prominent dissidents had been executed. Africa Watch surmises they were executed in May 1983, possibly because the Mozambican government feared that South African special forces might have staged a prison raid to free them and turn them over to Renamo in order to bolster the insurgent's claim to legitimacy as a nationalist movement.
12. Ken Flower, *Serving Secretly: An Intelligence Chief on Record: Rhodesia into Zimbabwe, 1964–1981.* London: John Murray, 1987. See

p. 302. Flower's text is taken from a document dated April 1974, more than two years before the NRM was established. However, the language in the cited paragraph suggests that it may have been written several years after the original document was prepared. Alternatively, the document may have been backdated or mistakenly dated when it was prepared for publication. See Africa Watch, op. cit., p. 18. In an April 1987 interview, Flower stated that '... we in turn [developed] this movement, which we ourselves generated, it is true, but to a certain extent was self generating ...' For further evidence that Mozambican government officials were well aware of the fact that NRM recruits represented the continuation of unresolved intra-Frelimo disputes from the earliest days of the independence struggle, see Colin Darch, 'Are there Warlords in Mozambique? Questions of the Social Base of MNR Banditry', *Review of African Political Economy*, no. 45/46 (1989). 34–49. See p. 41. Darch cites a Mozambican journalist who claims that 'Samora Machel dated the roots of Renamo back to the foundation of Frelimo in 1962, arguing that "there are problems which Frelimo dragged along with it right up to the day it won, and were taken on board by the ultra-racists who used to be around here".' Africa Watch, op. cit., p. 55 cites a Renamo commander's 1991 account of the origins of the insurgency which also traces its origins back to the independence struggle.

13. Paul Fauvet, op. cit., See pp. 109–110 for biographic information on Christina and Fernandes.

14. Interview with Afonso Dhlakama, *International Herald Tribune*, 14 September 1983. Fauvet, op. cit., p. 114 provides biographic sketches of Matsangaisse and Dhlakama. Renamo spokesmen have disputed allegations that both insurgent commanders left Frelimo while under investigation for criminal or politically suspect behavior.

15. *Africa Confidential* (London), No. 15, 21 June 1982, pp. 1–5.

16. Paradela de Abreu, interview with Evo Fernandes, in Lisbon, undated, reported in *O Dia* 24, 27 December 1984, pp. 2, 13–14. Christian Geffray, *La cause des armes au Mozambique; Anthropologie d'une guerre civile*. Paris: Edition Karthala, 1990, pp. 24 and 203. Geffray provides a detailed examination of the political and social tensions which fostered Renamo's growth in the northern Mozambican province of Nampula and turned it into what he characterizes as a 'popular military movement'.

17. Piet Gouws, 'Renamo's Long Path of Struggle, Strife and More Success', *Beeld* (Johannesburg), 6, 8 November 1984, pp. 13 and 19.

18. This program was also spelled out in greater detail in news bulletins released in the US and Western European capitals by Renamo's Department of Information. For a complete transcription, see also 'Manifeste et programme de la Résistance nationale mozambican', *Politique Africaine*, no. 3, June 1988, pp. 106–112.

19. Isaacman and Isaacman, op. cit., pp. 89–91.

20. Evidence of Renamo's embryonic administrative system was recorded by several journalists. See Sharon Behn, 'The Unknown Side', *Africa Events*, May 1987, pp. 24–26, and an article by Richardo de Melo in *The Star* (Johannesburg), 27 May 1986, p. 18. See also Geffray, op. cit., pp. 54–55, 80–88, 120 and 154–160. Geffray notes that in Nampula Province quite a few former *regulos* remained loyal to Frelimo. Geffray also

refers to Renamo's use of *capeceiros* – former colonial era police/militia members – as intermediaries between the guerrillas and local chiefs. According to Geffray, the insurgents more often used the term *mambo* than *regulo* to designate sympathetic local leaders. Anders Nilsson, 'From Pseudo-Terrorists to Pseudo-Guerrillas: the MNR in Mozambique (Part II)', *Review of African Political Economy*, no. 58 (1993), 34–42. In Inhambane Province, according to Nilsson, it was the former *cabos de terra*, the subordinates of the former *regulos*, who may have been more readily recruited by Renamo. See pp. 38–39.

21. Isaacman and Isaacman, op. cit., p. 178.
22. Karl Maier, 'The Battle for Zambezia', *Africa Report*, March–April, 1989, pp. 13–16. See p. 14.
23. Paradela de Abreu interview with Evo Fernandes, op. cit..
24. Holger Jensen, 'Resistance chief plans "diplomatic offensive"', *The Washington Times*, 17 December 1986, pp. 1A and 6A. See Vines, op. cit., p. 19, for the 1981 strength figure.
25. Isaacman and Isaacman, op. cit., pp. 105–106. Michel Cahen, *Mozambique La Révolution Implosée*. Paris: Editions L'Harmattan, 1987, p. 71. Cahen cites a figure of 8000 Frelimo guerrillas at the end of the war of independence in 1974.
26. 'Interview with Secretary General Evo Fernandes', *Journal of Defense and Diplomacy*, Vol. 3, no. 9 (1985), 45–49. See p. 49 for additional information on the duties of the various commands.
27. For further details of the insurgents' evolving organizational structure see, Almerigo Grilz, 'Rebels of Mozambique', *Jane's Defence Weekly*, 12 July 1986, pp. 20–22, and Sibyl Cline, 'Forgotten Freedom Fighters', *Soldier of Fortune*, January 1990, pp. 30–39, 88. See pp. 31–32.
28. See Grilz, op. cit., p. 22, Cline, op. cit., p. 32, and Jensen, op. cit., p. 6A.
29. See Cline, op. cit., p. 35.
30. See the article by Paul Moorcraft in *The Sunday Times* (Johannesburg), 30 November 1986, pp. 23, 25. Cline, op. cit., p. 32 also refers to female instructors. For one of the earliest references to a 'Feminine Detachment' see the Renamo journal, *A Luta Continua*, no. 3, June 1982, p. 14. This journal was an occasional publication prepared by the Department of Information of the Mozambique National Resistance, published in Portugal. Geffray, op. cit., p. 252 refers to a company-sized Renamo unit led by a female commander.
31. Isaacman and Isaacman, op. cit., pp. 91–92. For additional examples of organizational strengths and weaknesses common to both Renamo and Frelimo during their guerrilla campaigns, see Annette Seegers,'Revolutionary Armies of Africa: Mozambique and Zimbabwe', in *Military Power and Politics in Black Africa*, edited by Simon Baynham. New York: St. Martins Press, 1986, pp. 129–165. See pp. 140–141. Renamo's brutal treatment of female civilians ultimately gave the movement a greater degree of notoriety than any of the accomplishments of its 'feminine detachments'. Geffray, op. cit., pp. 111, 114–115 notes numerous references to civilian women held as sexual slaves in Renamo camps. K. B. Wilson, 'Cults of Violence and Counter-Violence in Mozambique', *Journal of Southern African Studies*, Vol. 18, no. 3, 1992, pp. 527–582. See pp. 535–537 for an effort to infer the

'sexual politics' implicit in Renamo's tactics. An equally ambivalent role for women in the ranks of the Kwilu rebellion was also noted by several observers. Female participants reportedly received military training and participated in combat. They also served as political instructors. Shortly after the Kwilu rebellion began, marriage ceremonies were conducted in the guerrilla camps. These rites reportedly were performed according to traditional custom and included the offering of dowries as well as the tolerance of polygamy. See CRISP, *Congo, 1965; Political Documents of a Developing Nation.* Princeton, New Jersey: Princeton University Press, 1967, pp. 122–124 and Ludo Martens, *Pierre Mulele, ou la seconde vie de Patrice Lumumba.* Berchem, Belgium: Editions EPO, 1985, pp. 209–210. Similar experiences were reported in the Mau Mau insurgency. See Robert B. Edgerton, *Mau Mau: An Africa Crucible.* New York: The Free Press, 1989, p. 128 and Tabitha Kanogo, *Squatters and the Roots of Mau Mau, 1905–1963.* London: James Currey, 1987, pp. 143–149. For a comprehensive study of women's roles in the Kenyan war, see Cora Ann Presley, *Kikuyu Women, the Mau Mau Rebellion, and Social Change in Kenya.* Boulder, Colorado: Westview Press, 1992, especially pp. 123–173. Presley notes that their participation in the Mau Mau rebellion ultimately gained women greater access to political power, though not parity, in independent Kenya. See p. 172.

32.   M. Martins de Almeida, interview with Manuel Frank, Renamo representative in Western Europe, *Jornal de O Dia* (Lisbon), 15 July 1989, pp. 4–5. For similar statistics on Renamo activity in Zambezia Province, see Behn, op. cit., p. 26.

33.   Isaacman and Isaacman, op. cit., p. 102. For additional details on the *flechas* and their performance, see Thomas H. Henriksen, *Revolution and Counterrevolution; Mozambique's War of Independence, 1964–1974.* Westport, Connecticut: Greenwood Press, 1983, pp. 62, 107, 136. When the anti-colonial war abruptly ended in 1974, some sixty percent of the Portuguese forces in Mozambique were black troops. As many as 10 000–12 000 of these troops may have been trained as *flechas* or members of other elite, special force, units. See Ian F. W. Beckett, 'The Portuguese Army: the Campaign in Mozambique,1964–1974', in *Armed Forces and Modern Counter-insurgency*, edited by Ian F.W. Beckett and John Pimlott. New York: St. Martin's Press, 1985, pp. 136–162. See pp. 149, 157.

34.   Paul Moorcraft, 'The Savage, Silent Civil War', *Army,* April 1987, 42–52. See p. 48. For further evidence of the direct connection between British and Rhodesian counterinsurgency strategy and tactics, see Randall W. Heather, 'Intelligence and Counter-Insurgency in Kenya, 1952–1956', *Intelligence and National Security*, Vol. 5, no. 3 (1990), 57–83. See p. 77. Heather points out that Ian Henderson, the official who formed the 'pseudo-gang' which eventually captured Mau Mau commander Dedan Kimathi, was appointed as a special security advisor to Rhodesian Prime Minister Ian Smith in 1966. Portugal also experimented with its own version of 'pseudo-gangs' by drawing from among some 2000 Frelimo members who deserted in the late 1960s. See Fauvet, op. cit., p. 114.

35.   Roger Job, 'Mozambique: The War Without a Name', *Le Soir* (Brussels), 30–31 January, 1 February 1990. See page 2 of the 31 January article. See

also Vines, op. cit., p. 74. For an account of Matsangaisse's death which alleges that the insurgent leader was betrayed by a disgruntled spirit-medium who terminated his bulletproof powers, see Hanlon, op. cit., pp. 221, 229.

36. J. M. C., 'Renamo Discredited in the West' in *Expresso* (International), 8 November 1986, pp. VII. Renamo supporters reportedly also commemorated the anniversary of Matsangaisse's death with 'traditional' religious ceremonies and feasts. See Africa Watch, op. cit., pp. 21–22. Like their 'Mulelist' predecessors who refused to speak French in their base camps, Renamo insisted on using Ndau as their principal language. Portuguese was forbidden in Renamo bases. All Renamo recruits and captives were required to learn Ndau. See Otto Roesch, 'Renamo and the Peasantry in Southern Mozambique: A View from Gaza Province', *Canadian Journal of African Studies*, Vol. 26, no. 3 (1992), 462–484. See p. 469.

37. Wilson, op. cit., p. 544. For the account of Dhlakama's consultation with a 'spirit-medium', see 'Captured MNR Bandit Describes Camp in Zomba, Malawi', *The Sunday Mail* (Harare), 21 December 1986, p. 2. The 'witch doctor' reportedly lived at the Malawian village of Migori-Phalombe.

38. *Diario de Mocambique*, (Beira), 27, 28, 29 December 1984, 3, 4, 5 January 1985. This is a series of six articles by Antonio Cesar which contains interviews with captured Renamo cadres. Geffray, op. cit., pp. 126–129 refers to reports that Renamo used magical powers which caused government troops to lose their way while conducting counterinsurgency operations. Some Frelimo administrators evidently shared the insurgents' belief in the use of such powers. Wilson, op. cit., pp. 548–551, chronicles Frelimo's own efforts to employ spirit-mediums during its counterinsurgency campaign against Renamo as well as evidence of occasional reliance on such powers during the anti-colonial struggle in the 1960s. These efforts generally were sporadic and incidental in nature reflecting a pragmatic rather than programmatic commitment to traditional religious beliefs and institutions.

39. Maier, 'The Battle for Zambezia', op. cit., p. 14.

40. Roesch, op. cit., pp. 476–477 discusses the Ndau's ability to return as a vengeful spirit known as a *fukwa*. W. Finnegan, 'A Reporter at Large', *New Yorker*, Part I, 22 May 1990, pp. 43–76; Part II, 29 May 1990, pp. 69–96. See p. 94. Corroborating reports of Renamo's support from non-Ndau spirit-mediums in southern Mozambique, Finnegan refers to a female *curandeiro* in Manhica, some 100 kilometers north of Maputo, who was said to give local Renamo members their 'power'. See also Gillian Gunn, 'The Chissano Era – Mozambique comes to Terms with itself', *Africa Insight*, Vol. 19, no.1 (1989), pp. 16–20. In late 1988, Gunn noted that 'observers say they see an increased evidence of witchcraft in MNR motivation and tactics.' See p. 20.

41. Roesch, op. cit., pp. 473 and 475. Wilson, op. cit., p. 541 discusses evidence of Renamo's effort to blend Ndau traditions with indigenous religious beliefs in northern Mozambique. Wilson notes that whereas Mondlane was called upon as the patron ancestor of Renamo's male troops, Josina Machel, the ex-wife of President Samora Machel, was invoked as the appropriate ancestor for the insurgents' 'feminine detachments'.

42. Grilz, op. cit., p. 20 and Cahen, op. cit., pp. 17–20, and 72. Cahen notes that the monthly rate of Renamo attacks, sabotage and other combat

operations had risen from less than 100 in 1983 to over 400 by July 1986. During the course of a September 1986 offensive in north-central Mozambique, Renamo combatants routed an entire FAM battalion, forcing troops to flee across the border into neighboring Malawi. This offensive also threatened to overrun government garrisons at numerous locations in the middle and lower Zambezi River valley, prompting officials in Maputo to claim Renamo sought to cut the country in half.

43.   What had long been a truism for many students of counterinsurgency warfare since World War II was decried as a misleading myth by one of the foremost experts in the field in the early 1960s. See Robert Thompson, *Defeating Communist Insurgency; Experiences from Malaya and Vietnam.* London: Chatto & Windus, 1966, pp. 48–49. Thompson observed that force ratios, which are usually fluid, are one of many vital indicators and trends in an insurgency rather than some predetermined prerequisite for a successful campaign.

44.   Joseph Hanlon, *Apartheid's Second Front: South Africa's War Against Its Neighbors.* New York, NY: Viking Penguin, 1986, p. 87. Geffray, op. cit., pp. 249–253 catalogs a sample of FAM atrocities and crimes against the civilian population.

45.   Glenda Morgan,'Violence in Mozambique: Towards an Understanding of Renamo', *Journal of Modern African Studies*, Vol. 28, no. 4 (1990), 603–619. See p. 617. See also Herbert Howe and Marina Ottaway, 'State Power Consolidation in Mozambique', in *Afro-Marxist Regimes: Ideology and Public Policy*, edited by Edmond J. Keller and Donald Rothchild. London: Lynne Rienner, 1987, pp. 43–65. See pp. 52–53. Hanlon, *Mozambique: The Revolution Under Fire,* op. cit., p. 232 also describes the Machel government's efforts to create a peasant militia. Frelimo may also have become increasingly concerned about the loyalty and commitment of key sectors of the officer corps as well as veterans of the independence struggle, some of whom evidently made tentative proposals for a negotiated settlement of the war with Renamo in late 1986. See M. Cahen, op. cit., p .72.

46.   William Minter, *The Mozambican National Resistance (Renamo) as described by ex-participants*, Washington, DC: Georgetown University, 1989. Minter interviewed approximately three dozen former Renamo combatants. Thousands of legal and illegal Mozambican migrant workers in South Africa, employed in mines and farms, became a ready pool of recruits or conscripts, many of whom reportedly were bribed or forced to join Renamo. See Paul Moorcraft, *African Nemesis; War and Revolution in Southern Africa (1945–2010).* London: Brassey's, 1990, p. 286. Determining the extent to which Renamo relied on voluntary or unwilling recruits has been a difficult issue for analysts since the earliest years of the war. For an example of evidence from both ends of the spectrum, see Hanlon, *Mozambique: The Revolution Under Fire,* op. cit., pp. 228–229. Roesch, op. cit., p. 470 stated that 'the vast majority of the non-Ndau people living on Renamo bases in Gaza Province, whether these be combatants or civilians, have been kidnapped by Renamo.'

47.   Maier, 'The Battle for Zambezia', op. cit., p. 16.

48.   Quoted in Isaacman and Isaacman, op. cit., p. 177. For additional details on the NRM's Rhodesian facilities, see Moorcraft, *African Nemesis*, op. cit., pp. 256–257.

49. Hanlon, *Apartheid's Second Front*, op. cit., p. 70. See also John Saul, 'Development and Counterdevelopment Strategies in Mozambique', in Keller and Rothchild, op. cit., pp. 109–153. See p. 130. The South African connection to the NRM in 1979–1980 is also discussed in Phyllis Johnson and David Martin (eds), *Frontline Southern Africa*, New York: Four Walls Eight Windows, 1988, pp. 9–12, and Moorcraft, *African Nemesis*, op. cit., pp. 261–262. South African Defense Force spotter planes allegedly also passed information on Mozambican Army troop movements to the NRM. See Hanlon, *Mozambique: The Revolution Under Fire*, op. cit., p. 224.

50. Hanlon, *Apartheid's Second Front*, op. cit., p. 71, and Moorcraft, *African Nemesis*, op. cit., pp. 265–266.

51. Saul, pp. 132–133. The obvious military value, to a guerrilla, of crippling a government's economic infrastructure and the relative ease of disrupting a largely undefended rail line suggests that the alleged differences of opinion may have been related to timing and location of the attacks.

52. *Africa Confidential* (London), 21 June 1982, pp. 1–5.

53. Ibid., 30 January 1985, pp. 4–7.

54. Saul, op. cit., p. 136. Many of the weapons transferred in Pretoria's pre-Nkomati Accord 'golden handshake' with Renamo were purportedly of Russian origin. These weapons allegedly had been captured by South African troops during raids against South West African People's Organization (Swapo) guerrilla camps in southern Angola. See Moorcraft, *African Nemesis*, op. cit., p. 272.

55. Saul, op. cit., p. 137.

56. William Claiborne, 'West Eyes Arms for Mozambique', *Washington Post*, 24 January 1988, p. A22. See also Lt. Gen. (Ret.) Emmanuel A. Erskine (Ghana), Brigadier (Ret.) B. L. Kapoor (India), and Lt. Col. Augustus Richard Norton (USA), *Peace Security and Humanitarian Relief in Northern Mozambique*. New York: International Peace Academy, 1987, pp. 15–16. The authors give a figure of 3000 Tanzanian troops and cite rumors that Tanzanian forces only deployed to rural areas in Zambezia and Niassa Provinces after elite Mozambican Army troops had cleared these zones of Renamo guerrillas. The International Peace Academy's observers also reported that the various foreign troops sent to Mozambique did not establish a joint command and that there appeared to be little joint coordination between the FAM and its allies.

57. 'War Aid For Mozambique: British Spit and Polish', *New York Times*, 18 May 1986, p. 18. British support for Malawi's troops in Mozambique is described in Moorcraft, *African Nemesis*, op. cit., p. 285.

58. Christopher S. Wren, 'Pretoria Aids Mozambique's Military', *New York Times*, 30 November 1988. See also Africa Watch, op. cit., p. 35.

59. Kurt Campbell, 'Southern Africa in Soviet Foreign Policy', *Adelphi Papers*, no. 227. London: International Institute for Strategic Studies, 1987/1988. See p. 19 for a discussion of Soviet aid to Mozambique. Moscow's aid generally was regarded as a paltry sum compared to the support offered to client governments in Angola and Ethiopia. For weapons deliveries to Mozambique in the mid-1980s, see *Soviet Military Power*, Washington, DC: Department of Defense, 1986, p. 132. Mozambique's annual military expenditures grew from an estimated $47 million in 1979 to $107 million in 1989. During this ten-year period, the nation's armed forces grew from

30 000 to approximately 65 000. Military expenditures rose from 27 percent to over 40 percent of central government expenditures. Similarly, annual arms imports grew from $120 million in 1979 to $400 million in 1983 and then gradually declined to an average of approximately $140 million between 1986 and 1989. See Arms Control and Disarmament Agency. *World Military Expenditures and Arms Transfers,1990.* Washington, DC: Government Printing Office, 1991, pp. 74, 116.

60. Mozambique: Time to talk', *Africa Confidential*, Vol. 30, no.13 (1989), 1–3. See p. 1. Moorcraft, *African Nemesis*, op. cit., p. 267 alludes to the Malawian connection to Renamo. Africa Watch, op. cit., p. 132 points out that Renamo was paid, presumably by Malawian and South African government officials, to refrain from attacking the Nacala rail line and the Cabora Bassa hydroelectric power lines.

61. Robert Pear with James Brooke, 'Rightists in U.S. Aid Mozambique Rebels', *New York Times*, May 22, 1988, pp. 1 and 14. Prexy Nesbitt, 'Terminators, Crusaders and Gladiators: Western (private & public) Support for Renamo and Unita', *Review of African Political Economy*, no. 43 (1988), 111–124. See pp. 118–124 for a list of known or suspected Renamo supporters and sympathizers.

62. Robert S. Jaster, 'The Security Outlook in Mozambique', *Survival*, Vol. XXVII, no. 6 (1985), 258–263. See p. 261.

63. Interview with Prime Minister Mario Machungo, in *Financial Mail* (Johannesburg), December 12, 1986, pp. 34–35. Diana Cammack, 'The "Human Face" of Destabilization: The War in Mozambique', *Review of African Political Economy,* no. 40 (1987), 65–75, also cites a figure of 'at least 100 000'. See p. 65 as well as p. 67 for figures on Mozambican refugees in neighboring countries.

64. Finnegan, 'A Reporter at Large', op. cit., p. 69 and Job, op. cit., 30 January 1990, p. 2. Finnegan's estimate of 600 000 covers the period 1981–1989. Considering the limited nature of the war between 1977 and 1980, it is highly unlikely that an additional 300 000 Mozambicans died during that time frame. The discrepancy between the figure cited in Finnegan's account and the 900 000 noted by Job must be due to differences in information available for the years from 1980–1989. Africa Watch, op. cit., pp. 103–113 provides a detailed summary of assessments of casualty figures by several humanitarian organizations.

65. Robert Gersony, *Summary of Mozambican Refugee Accounts of Principally Conflict-Related Experience in Mozambique*, Washington: Bureau for Refugee Programs, Department of State, 1988. At the time of its publication, the Gersony report probably engendered as much controversy as French accounts of the Malgache rebellion in the early 1950s. For a recent indication of the lingering debates surrounding the Gersony report, see Andrew Roberts, 'Mozambique Pique', in *The American Spectator*, Vol. 25, no. 3, (1992), 48–49. Of all the wars which have plagued Lusophone Africa, before and after independence, Mozambique evidently has the dubious distinction of having the greatest number of terrorist tactics committed against its civilian population. Between 1964 and early 1973, Frelimo guerrillas reportedly conducted at least 689 deliberate assassinations, in addition to

2000 woundings and 6500 abductions. The guerrillas were accused of murdering 55 local chiefs in Tete Province alone in 1971. By the time the war ended, the incidence of terrorist tactics was rising. See Beckett, op. cit., p. 159 For a further discussion of atrocities against civilians by both FAM and Renamo, see Africa Watch, op. cit., pp. 50–59.

66. Jack Wheeler, 'Renamo: Winning One in Africa', *Soldier of Fortune*, February 1986, pp. 64–69, 117–118. See p. 67. Wheeler claims 200 000–300 000 Mozambicans were held in prison camps in the mid-1980s. See also Alexander R. Alexiev, *Marxism and Resistance in the Third World*, Santa Monica, California: The Rand Corporation, April 1988, p. 22. Alexiev cites a press report asserting that 100 000 people were held in 'reeducation' camps by 1978. Africa Watch, op. cit., p. 142. In 1988, the government approved an amnesty law which reportedly freed many prisoners and reduced the number of 'security detainees' to 1400.

67. Finnegan, 'A Reporter at Large', op. cit., p. 69. and Africa Watch, op. cit., pp. 104.

68. See Martins de Almeida interview with Frank, op. cit., p. 5. Frank announced that the Congress had revised Renamo's program and statutes as well as changing the movement's flag and anthem.

69. *Africa Now* (London), no. 28 (1983), p. 25. Intra-Renamo disputes were also thought to have led to the murders of the movements' first two General Secretaries – Orlando Christina in South Africa in 1983 and Evo Fernandes in Portugal in 1988. *The Weekly Mail* (Johannesburg), 8–14 July 1988, pp. 10.

70. *Africa Confidential*, op. cit., Vol 30, no. 13, 23 June 1989, p. 1. According to this article, Unamo had contacted the Mozambican government's intelligence service to elicit support and cooperation in their struggle against Renamo.

71. Karl Maier, 'Healer in Mozambique Leads Attack on Rebels', *The Washington Post*, August 4, 1990, p. 19.

72. Karl Maier, 'A Traditional Revival', *Africa Report*, Vol. 36, no. 4 (1991), 64–67 for additional details on the social bases of Naprama. See also Vines, op. cit., pp. 117–118. Manuel Antonio's assertion that his powers were derived from Jesus Christ indicates a syncretic religious phenomenon that differs considerably from those associated with most of the *feiticeiros* and *curandeiros* who supported Renamo elsewhere in the Mozambican countryside. In several areas of rural Mozambique, *feiticeiros* had chosen to carve out small pockets of territory which Frelimo and Renamo agreed to respect as neutral zones exempt from combat. Roesch, op. cit., pp. 478–479 provides an account of how the 'spirit of Mungoi' managed to create a small demilitarized zone in Gaza Province. Wilson, op. cit., pp. 553–557 documents similar efforts elsewhere in the Mozambican countryside. Unlike Ruben Um Nyobe or Pierre Mulele, Dhlakama and Matsangaisse generally seem to have been more effective in mobilizing conservative peasants by adopting a sympathetic and tolerant attitude towards their religious beliefs rather than trying to cynically manipulate them or suppress them, at least in the early years of the war. For a dissenting view, however, see Hanlon, *Mozambique: The Revolution Under Fire*, op. cit., p. 229. Hanlon claims

that Dhlakama told recruits that the 'spirits' of the NRM would kill anyone who defected.

73.   Alex Vines, 'Diary', *Southern African Review of Books,* July–October 1991, pp. 31–32. For details on the size of Naprama's forces and their campaign claims, see William Finnegan, *A Complicated War: The Harrowing of Mozambique,* Los Angeles: University of California Press, 1992, p. 255. See also Wilson, op. cit., pp. 560–570 and 575–581.

74.   Wilson, op. cit., pp. 572–573 provides additional details on the disintegration of Naprama. See also pp. 558–560 for further evidence of the limits of Renamo's religious tolerance, particularly concerning their relations with Mozambican members of the Jehovah's Witnesses.

75.   Witney W. Schneidman, 'Conflict Resolution in Mozambique: A Status Report', *CSIS Africa Notes,* no. 121, February 28, 1991. See p. 8.

76.   Interview with Evo Fernandes, *O Dia,* December 1984, op. cit., p. 14.

7   CONCLUSION

1.   The myths surrounding rebellions such as Mau Mau are likely to be manipulated and distorted in a variety of ways. Some of these may contribute to nation-building processes while others can prove to be disruptive. Neither outcome is assured. For a thorough discussion of this phenomenon in Kenya, see Robert Buijtenhuijs, *Mau Mau Twenty Years After – The Myth and the Survivors,* The Hague, Netherlands: Mouton and Company, 1973, pp. 43–86. For more recent examinations, see E.S. Atieno-Odhiambo, 'The Production of History in Kenya: The Mau Mau Debate', *Canadian Journal of African Studies,* Vol. 25, no. 2, (1991), 300–307 and Wunyabari O. Maloba, *Mau Mau and Kenya; An Analysis of a Peasants Revolt.* Bloomington and Indianapolis: Indiana University Press, 1993, pp. 169–180.

2.   Eric R. Wolf, *Peasant Wars of the Twentieth Century,* New York: Harper & Row, 1969, p. 294.

3.   Claude E. Welch, Jr., *Anatomy of Rebellion,* Albany: State University Press of New York, 1980, p. 333.

4.   Ken Jowitt, 'The New World Disorder', *Journal of Democracy,* Vol. 2, no. 1 (1991) 11–20. See p. 19. Jowitt also points out that '... one cannot gauge the potential for future movements of rage by generalizing from their earlier failures.' See p. 19.

5.   B. Marie-Perinbam, 'Fanon and the Revolutionary Peasantry – the Algerian Case', *Journal of Modern African Studies,* Vol. 11, no. 3 (1973), 427–445. See p. 437. The quotes are taken from Fanon's *Wretched of the Earth.*

6.   Patrick Chabal, *Amilcar Cabral; Revolutionary leadership and people's war.* London: Cambridge University Press, 1983. See pp. 80–81. The difficult balancing act which an ecumenical approach entails is vividly portrayed in comments made by Cabral at various points in the war after the 1964 Congress. Thus, in 1969, Cabral stated that 'Our cultural resistance consists in the following: while we scrap colonial culture and the negative aspects of our own culture, whether in our character or our environment, we

have to create a new culture, also based in our own traditions but respecting
everything that the world today has conquered for the service of mankind.'
On another occasion, however, Cabral underscored the need to reject traditional practices which impeded the nationalist struggle and added the observation that 'The armed liberation struggle therefore implies a veritable
forced march along the road to cultural progress.' Both quotes appear in
Basil Davidson, *The People's Cause; A History of Guerrillas in Africa.*
Harlow, Essex: Longman, 1981. See pp. 160, 167–168. The coercion
implied in Cabral's choice of the term 'forced march' surfaced explicitly in
the late 1980s. The political heirs to the PAIGC, then the ruling party of an
independent Guinea-Bissau, forcefully closed the temples of the 'Yank
Yank' (shadow of God) cult which had emerged in the early 1980s. Cult
members were also beaten and jailed. Justifying this campaign, a government official told a journalist 'African culture is rich, vast and beautiful, but
there are times when you have to be implacable.' See James Brooke,
'Guinea Bissau Tries to Deprogram a Popular Cult', *New York Times*,
3 January 1988, p. 10.
7. David Lan, *Guns and Rain; Guerrillas and Spirit Mediums in Zimbabwe.*
London: James Currey, 1985, pp. 164–165. See also Fred Bridgeland, *Jonas
Savimbi; A Key to Africa.* New York: Paragon House, 1986, pp. 246–248.
In a 1984 interview, Savimbi told a reporter 'We should assimilate from
other cultures and other nations, but not be assimilated. We should conserve
our values, defend them at all times, but we should not be hostile to other
values. We have to ensure that the essence of our own traditions, customs
and languages remain intact.' See Fred Bridgeland, 'Savimbi's Respect for
Indigenous Customs "Secret of Success"', *Diamond Fields Advertiser*
(Kimberley, South Africa), 2 October 1984. p. A2.
8. *Conflict and Conflict Resolution in Mozambique* (Washington, DC: United
States Institute of Peace, April 1993), p. 28. Descriptions of Renamo's
organizational and ideological attributes continued to vary from one account
to another in the early 1990s. For a recent description which tended toward
one end of the spectrum and refers to the movement's emphasis on a 'kind
of primitive communalism' and a 'strict revolutionary discipline', see David
B. Ottaway, 'Mozambican Describes Detention by Rebels', *Washington
Post*, 25 May 1992, p. A21 For an example of how notions of criminality or
widespread psychopathology readily have been used to account for the
emergence of comparable movements, see Pierre Bettez Gravel, 'Of Bandits
and Pirates: An Essay on the Vicarious Insurgency of Peasants', *Journal of
Political and Military Sociology*, Vol. 13, (1985), 209–217. Gravel,
assessing an earlier European context, suggests that '... when peasants are
shamelessly exploited, as in seventeenth century Europe, the alternatives to
social banditry are: ... a kind of collective insanity, whereby masses of
people turn to preternatural solutions such as in revitalization movements .'
see p. 216.
9. Thomas H. Henriksen, *Revolution and Counterrevolution; Mozambique's
War of Independence, 1964–1974.* Westport, Connecticut: Greenwood Press,
1983, p. 216. See Davidson, op. cit., p. 80 for a similar view regarding the
'... vivid and acutely democratic process of fighting and supporting ...'
insurgencies whose members claimed to be waging a war of 'liberation'.

This view also seemed to have lost some of its persuasive power by the end of the 1980s.

10.   These interpretations, as well as several others, are discussed at length in Margaret Hall, 'The Mozambican National Resistance Movement (Renamo): A Study In The Destruction Of An African Country', *Africa,* Vol. 60, no. 1 (1990), 39–68. See pp. 59–61. C. Geffray, *La Cause des armes an Mozambique; Anthropologie d'une guerre civile.* Paris: Editions Karthala, 1990, p. 220 refers to the metastasis and pathology implied in the growing network of Renamo bases in rural Mozambique. Over the past four decades, the use of a medical metaphor to describe revivalist insurgencies also has had its appeal to prominent figures in the world of contemporary literature. For example, see Elspeth Huxley, 'The Cause and Cure of Mau Mau', *New Commonwealth,* Vol. 27, 18 January 1954, pp. 62–64. Huxley chose to describe Mau Mau as '… a symptom of a wasting disease of the spirit'. See p. 62. A brief visit to Mozambique evoked a similar reaction from Kurt Vonnegut 35 years later when he concluded that 'Renamo had become an incurable disease'. See Kurt Vonnegut, 'My Visit to Hell', *Washington Post,* Parade Magazine, 7 January, 1990. pp. 16–17. See p. 16.

11.   John T. Gordge 'The Outlook for Madagascar', *African Affairs,* Vol. 48, no. 191 (1949), 133–141. See p. 137. For a condescending Freudian analysis of the Malgache insurgents' chant 'Rano! Rano! (Water! Water!)' see O. Manoni, *Prospero and Calaban: The Psychology of Colonization.* New York: Frederick A. Praeger, 1964, pp. 58–62.

12.   John Lonsdale,'Mau Maus of the Mind: Making Mau Mau and Remaking Kenya', *Journal of African History,* Vol. 31 (1990), 393–421. See p. 421. Maloba, op. cit., p. 73 cites Kenya's colonial governor Sir Philip Mitchell's belief that the Kikuyu were 'particularly given to black and foul mysteries, to ritual murder, to ordeals by oath and poison and cults of terror, in which murder is the central feature.' A related view of the Mau Mau oaths suggested they produced a form of mental illness. See Anthony Clayton, *Counter-Insurgency in Kenya 1952–1960.* Nairobi: Transafrica Publishers 1976, p. 16. In an analysis of Renamo which echoes some of these assessments of Mau Mau, Otto Roesch, 'Renamo and the Peasantry in Southern Mozambique: A view from Gaza Province', *Canadian Journal of African Studies,* Vol. 26, no. 3 (1992), 462–484, asserts that 'It is widely believed throughout southern Mozambique that part of the military preparation of children involves treatment at the hands of traditional healers, who psychologically "alter" the children through the use of medicines and magic, to make them psychologically predisposed and emotionally insensitive to the gratuitous violence they habitually visit upon the civilian population.' See pp. 480–481.

13.   B. Davidson, op. cit., p. 127. Davidson characterizes this view as the 'counterpart' of 'witchcraft explanations' of reality.

14.   See Terence Ranger, 'Bandits and Guerrillas: the case of Zimbabwe', in *Banditry, Rebellion and Social Protest in Africa,* edited by Donald Crummey. London: James Currey, 198, pp. 373–396 for a thorough discussion of the relationship between legitimacy and the concept of 'social banditry' in Zimbabwe and elsewhere in Southern Africa. See also E. J. Hobsbawm, 'Social Banditry', in *Rural Protest: Peasant Movements and*

Social Change, edited by Henry A. Landsberger. London: Macmillan, 1974, pp. 142–157. Hobsbawm listed several additional analytic considerations inherent in the concept of 'social banditry' and provided the useful caution that '... the study of social banditry throws little light on the great majority of agrarian social movements likely to occur in the last third of the twentieth century.' See p. 142. Colin Darch, 'Are there Warlords in Provincial Mozambique? Questions of the Social Base of MNR Banditry', Review of African Political Economy, no. 45/46 (1989), 34–49. On pp. 36–38 Darch assesses the relevance of the 'warlord' label in the Mozambican context. Roesch, op. cit., p. 480 favors the use of 'predatory bandit band' and a 'tendency to degenerate into warlordism' to characterize Renamo. Anders Nilsson, 'From Pseudo-Terrorists to Pseudo Guerrillas: The MNR in Mozambique (Part I)', *Review of African Political Economy,* no. 57, (1993), pp. 60–71. See pp. 60–63 for an attempt to define Renamo as a movement which began as a pseudo-gang, resembling those employed by the British in Kenya, and eventually became what Nilsson considers a pseudo-guerrilla movement. In Nilsson (Part II), op. cit., p. 41 Renamo is described as the manifestation of a 'socio-economic and psycho-political process' leading to various forms of violent behavior.

15. A. S. Cleary, 'The Myth of Mau Mau in its International Context', *African Affairs,* Vol. 89, no. 355, (1990), 227–245. This article provides an interesting discussion of the way in which London used its portrayal of Mau Mau to minimize external actors' interest and involvement in the insurgency.

16. For a more extensive discussion of the context out of which the LLA emerged, see David Johnson and Phyllis Martin, (eds), *Frontline Southern Africa.* New York: Four Walls Eight Windows, 1988, pp. 200–208, and also Paul L. Moorcraft, *African Nemesis; War and Revolution in Southern Africa (1945–2010).* London: Brassey's, 1990, pp. 315–317. For one of the earliest academic assessments providing a balanced view of the South African factor in the Mozambican war, see Tom Young, 'The MNR/Renamo External and Internal Dynamics', *African Affairs,* Vol. 89, no. 357 (1990), pp. 491–509.

17. Johnson and Martin, op. cit., pp. 66–81, and Moorcraft, *African Nemesis,* op. cit., pp. 303–304. For details on the Zimbabwean National Army's counterinsurgency campaign against Super-ZAPU, see Annette Seegers, 'Revolutionary Armies of Africa': Mozambique and Zimbabwe', in *Military Power and Politics in Black Africa,* edited by Simon Baynham. New York: St. Martin's Press, 1986, pp. 152–154.

18. William Finnegan, *A Complicated War: The Harrowing of Mozambique.* Berkeley and Los Angeles: University of California Press, 1992, pp. 188–189.

19. David Ottaway, 'ANC vs. Inkatha: Anatomy of a Slaughter', *Washington Post,* 2 May 1991, pp. 21, 28. See p. 28. Insurgencies such as the Holy Spirit Movement in Uganda, whose members also charged into battle believing they were bulletproof, underscore the difficulties inherent in attempting to define a 'typical peasant movement'. This problem is highlighted in 'Understanding Alice: Uganda's Holy Spirit Movement in Context', by Tim Allen, *Africa,* Vol. 61, no. 3 (1991), pp. 370–399. In 1986, members of the Holy Spirit Movement were reportedly coating their upper

torsos with a special oil, evidently intended to make them bulletproof, prior to attacking Ugandan government troops. Allen rightly points out that more than class struggle is involved in accounting for why participants in movements inspired by magico-religious traditions resort to violence. See pp. 372, 395. An equally complex set of forces and principles undoubtedly motivates the National Patriotic Front of Liberia (NPFL) whose members were described, in 1990, as relying '... on juju rather than military skills to protect themselves from enemy bullets. Some daub a magic white powder known as *leh* on their faces. This is supposed to throw up a false image next to the wearer which attracts the enemy's fire.' See 'Liberia: Taylor's one-man band', *Africa Confidential*, Vol. 31, no. 15 (1990), p. 5.

20.   Finnegan, op. cit., pp. 125–126. The government official was Luis Bernardo Honwana, Mozambiques' Minister of Culture.

21.   For a recent discussion, see Patrick Chabal, 'Some Reflections on the post-colonial state in Portuguese speaking Africa', *Africa Insight*, vol. 23, no. 3 (1993), 129–135.

22.   Max Gluckman, *Order and Rebellion in Tribal Africa*. New York: Free Press, 1963, pp. 139–145. See Frank Furedi, *The Mau Mau War in Perspective*. London: James Currey, 1989, p. 109 for a further discussion of the 'anti-modern-anti-nationalist' distinction. For an implicitly evolutionary explanation which envisages the increasing irrelevance and ultimate disappearance of traditional African religion, see Basil Davidson, *The African Genius*. Boston: Little Brown, 1969, pp. 303, 310–311. A more subtle explanation of the complex relationship between 'prophets and preachers' and the 'organizers of mass nationalism' appears in T. O. Ranger, 'Connexions between "Primary Resistance" Movements and Modern Mass Nationalism in East and Central Africa. Part I', *Journal of African History*, Vol. IX, no.3 (1968), 437–453. According to Ranger, mass emotional enthusiasm and involvement are critical components shared by both traditional and modern movements. Moreover, traditionally inspired movements often struggled for a modern, albeit utopian, set of goals which also contained points of congruence with contemporary anti-colonial independence movements. This observation is developed further in T. O. Ranger 'Connexions between "Primary Resistance" Movements in East and Central Africa. Part II', *Journal of African History*, Vol. IX, no. 4 (1968), 631–641. See pp. 632–635.

23.   'L'Insurrection malgache', *Bulletin des Missions* (Abbaye de Saint-Andrés-les Bruges), Vol. XXIV (1950–1951), 157–171 and 255–276. See p. 168. The recent campaigns of the Ugandan Holy Spirit Movement also have been described by participants as a 'holy war'. Given the millennial features of the HSM, however, this is not surprising. Future studies might need to distinguish between revivalist movements which emphasize apocalyptic outcomes and those seeking more worldly revivals. For further details on the HSM, see Heike Behrend, 'Is Alice Lakwena a witch? The Holy Spirit Movement and its fight against evil in the north', in Holger Bernt Hansen and Michael Twaddle (eds), *Changing Uganda; The Dilemmas of Structural Adjustment and Revolutionary Change*. London: James Currey, 1991, pp. 162–177.

24. For a detailed definition and discussion of the terms 'attitude', 'conduct', and 'motives', underlying what he has called the 'religious symbolism of war', see James A. Aho, *Religious Mythology and the Art of War.* Westport, Connecticut: Greenwood Press, 1981, p. 12 .

Bibliography

BOOKS

Africa Watch. *Conspicuous Destruction; War, Famine and the Reform Process in Mozambique.* New York: Human Rights Watch, 1992.

Aho, James A. *Religious Mythology and the Art of War; Comparative Religious Symbolisms of Military Violence.* Westport, Connecticut: Greenwood Press, 1981.

Arlinghaus, Bruce E. and Pauline Baker (eds). *African Armies: Evolution and Capabilities.* Boulder: Westview Press, 1986.

Barnett, Donald J. and Kariri Njama. *Mau Mau From Within.* New York: Monthly Review Press, 1966.

Baynham, Simon (ed.). *Military Power and Politics in Black Africa.* New York: St. Martin's Press, 1986.

Beckett, Ian F. W. and John Pimlott (eds). *Armed Forces and Modern Counterinsurgency.* New York: St. Martin's Press, 1985.

Boiteau, Pierre. *Contribution à l'Histoire de la Nation Malgache.* Paris: Editions Sociales, 1958.

Bridgeland, Fred. *Jonas Savimbi: A Key to Africa.* New York: Paragon House, 1986.

Brown, Mervyn. *Madagascar Rediscovered.* Hamden, Conn.: Archon Books, 1979.

Brzezinski, Zbigniew (ed.). *Africa and the Communist World.* California: Stanford University Press, 1963.

Buijtenhuijs, Robert. *Mau Mau Twenty Years After – The Myth and the Survivors.* The Hague, Netherlands: Mouton, 1973.

Cahen, Michel. *Mozambique. La Révolution Implosée.* Paris: Editions L'Harmattan, 1987.

Campbell, Guy. *The Charging Buffalo; A History of the Kenya Regiment, 1937–1963.* London: Leo Cooper in association with Secker & Warburg, 1986.

Casseville, Henry. *L'île ensanglantée (Madagascar 1946–1947).* Paris: Fasquelle Editeurs, 1948.

Centre de Recherche et d'Information Socio-Politiques (CRISP). *Congo, 1964, 1965; Political Documents of a Developing Nation.* Princeton, New Jersey: Princeton University Press, 1966, 1967.

Chabal, Patrick. *Amilcar Cabral; Revolutionary Leadership and Peoples War.* London: Cambridge University Press, 1983.

Chaliand, Gerard. *Armed Struggle in Africa: With the Guerrillas in Portuguese Guinea.* New York: Monthly Review Press, 1969.

Clayton, Anthony. *Counter-Insurgency in Kenya 1952–1960.* Nairobi: Transafrica Publishers, 1976.

Coquery-Vidrovitch, Catherine, Alain Forest and Herbert Weiss. *Rébellion-Révolution au Zaire: 1963–1965 (Tome 1) .* Paris: Harmattan Editions, 1987.

Covell, Maureen. *Madagascar: Politics, Economics, and Society.* London: Frances Pinter, 1987.

Crummey, Donald (ed.). *Banditry, Rebellion and Social Protest in Africa.* London: James Currey, 1986.

Davidson, Basil. *The People's Cause; A History of Guerrillas in Africa*. Harlow, Essex: Longman 1981.

Davidson, Basil. *Africa in Modern History*. London: Allen Lane, 1978.

Davidson, Basil. *The African Genius*. Boston: Little Brown, 1969.

Deschamps, Hubert. *Histoire de Madagascar*. Paris: Editions Berger-Levrault, 1961.

Edgerton, Robert B. *Mau Mau: An African Crucible*. New York: Free Press, 1989.

Ellis, Stephen. *The Rising of the Red Shawls; A Revolt in Madagascar 1895–1899*. Cambridge: Cambridge University Press, 1985.

Faligot, Roger and Pascal Krop; translated by W. D. Halls. *La Piscine; The French Secret Service since 1944*. New York: Basil Blackwell, 1989.

Finnegan, William. *A Complicated War: The Harrowing of Mozambique*. Berkeley and Los Angeles: University of California Press, 1992.

First, Ruth. *Power in Africa; Political Power in Africa and the Coup d'Etat*. Harmondsworth, England: Penguin Books, 1972.

Flower, Ken. *Serving Secretly: An Intelligence Chief on Record; Rhodesia into Zimbabwe, 1964–1981*. London: John Murray, 1987.

Furedi, Frank. *The Mau Mau War in Perspective*. London: James Currey, 1989.

Gardinier, David E. *Cameroon – United Nations Challenge to French Policy*. London: Oxford University Press, 1963.

Geffray, Christian. *La cause des armes au Mozambique; Anthropologie d'une guerre civile*. Paris: Editions Karthala, 1990.

Gibson, Richard. *African Liberation Movements: Contemporary Struggles Against White Minority Rule*. New York: Oxford University Press, 1972.

Gluckman, Max. *Order and Rebellion in Tribal Africa*. New York: Free Press, 1963.

Grimal, Henri. *Decolonization*. Boulder, Colorado: Westview Press, 1978.

Grundy, Kenneth W. *Guerrilla Struggle in Africa*. New York: Grossman Publishers, 1971.

Hanlon, Joseph. *Apartheid's Second Front: South Africa's War Against Its Neighbors*. New York: Viking Penguin, 1986.

Hanlon, Joseph. *Mozambique: The Revolution Under Fire*. London: Zed Books, 1984.

Hansen, Holger Bernt and Michael Twaddle (eds). *Changing Uganda; The Dilemmas of Structural Adjustment and Revolutionary Change*. London: James Currey, 1991.

Hardeyman, J.T. *Madagascar on the Move*. London: Livingstone Press, 1950.

Hempstone, Smith. *Africa – Angry Young Giant*. New York: Frederick A. Praeger, 1961.

Henriksen, Thomas H. *Revolution and Counterrevolution; Mozambique's War of Independence, 1964–1974*. Westport, Connecticut: Greenwood Press, 1983.

Heseltine, Nigel. *Madagascar*. New York: Praeger, 1971.

Hodgkin, Thomas. *Nationalism in Colonial Africa*. London: Muller, 1956.

Isaacman, Allen and Barbara. *Mozambique: From Colonialism to Revolution, 1900–1982*. Boulder, Colorado: Westview Press, 1983.

Johnson, David and Martin, Phyllis (eds). *Frontline Southern Africa*. New York: Four Walls Eight Windows, 1988.

Johnson, Willard R. *The Cameroon Federation: Political Integration in a Fragmentary Society*. Princeton, NJ: Princeton University Press, 1970.

Joseph, Richard. *Radical Nationalism in Cameroun.* Oxford: Clarendon Press, 1977.

Kanogo, Tabitha. *Squatters and the Roots of Mau Mau, 1905–1963.* London: James Currey, 1987.

Kanza, Thomas. *The Rise and Fall of Patrice Lumumba.* London: Rex Collings, 1978.

Keller, Edmond J. and Donald Rothchild (eds). *Afro-Marxist Regimes: Ideology and Public Policy.* London: Lynne Rienner, 1987.

Kenyatta, Jomo. *Facing Mount Kenya.* London: Martin Secker & Warburg, 1953.

Kofele-Kale, Ndiva (ed.). *An African Experiment in Nation Building: The Bilingual Cameroon Republic Since Reunification.* Boulder, Colorado: Westview Press, 1980.

Lan, David. *Guns and Rain; Guerrillas and Spirit Mediums in Zimbabwe.* London: James Currey, 1985.

Landsberger, Henry A. *Rural Protest: Peasant Movements and Social Change.* London: Macmillan, 1974.

Levine, Victor T. *The Cameroons: From Mandate to Independence.* Berkeley and Los Angeles: University of California Press, 1964.

Maloba, Wunyabari O. *Mau Mau and Kenya; An Analysis of a Peasant Revolt.* Bloomington and Indianapolis: Indiana University Press. 1993.

Manoni, O. *Prospero and Caliban; The Psychology of Colonization.* New York: Frederick A. Praeger, 1964.

Martens, Ludo. *Pierre Mulele; ou la seconde vie de Patrice Lumumba.* Berchem, Belgium: Editions EPO, 1985.

Mazrui, Ali A. and Michael Tidy. *Nationalism and New States in Africa.* London: Heinemann Educational, 1984.

Moorcraft, Paul L. *African Nemesis; War and Revolution in Southern Africa (1945–2010).* London: Brassey's, 1990.

Munslow, Barry. *Mozambique: The Revolution and its Origins.* New York: Longman, 1983.

Odinga, Oginga. *Not Yet Uhuru.* New York: Hill & Wang, 1967.

Olorunsola, Victor A. *The Politics of Cultural Sub-Nationalism.* Garden City, NY: Doubleday, 1972.

Paget, Julian. *Counter-Insurgency Operations: Techniques of Guerrilla Warfare.* New York: Walker, 1967.

Presley, Cora Ann. *Kikuyu Women, the Mau Mau Rebellion, and Social Change in Kenya.* Boulder, Colorado: Westview Press, 1992.

Ranger, Terence O. *Peasant Consciousness and Guerrilla War in Zimbabwe.* London: James Currey, 1985.

Rosberg, Jr., Carl G. and John Nottingham. *The Myth of Mau Mau: Nationalism in Kenya.* New York: Frederick A. Praeger, 1966.

Rotberg, Robert I. and Ali A. Mazrui. *Protest and Power in Black Africa.* New York: Oxford University Press, 1970.

Rubin, Neville N. *Cameroon: An African Federation.* New York: Praeger, 1971.

Special Operations Research Office. *Casebook on Insurgency and Revolutionary Warfare.* Washington, DC: The American University, 1962.

Stratton, Arthur. *The Great Red Island.* New York: Charles Scribner's Sons, 1964.

Thompson, Robert. *Defeating Communist Insurgency; Experiences from Malaya and Vietnam.* London: Chatto & Windus, 1966.

Throup, David. *Economic and Social Origins of Mau Mau, 1945–1953*. London; James Currey, 1988.

Tronchon, Jacques. *L'insurrection malgache de 1947; Essai d'interprétation historique*. Paris: Editions diffusion Karthala, 1986.

Verhaegen, Benoit. *Rébellions au Congo*. Brussels: Centre de Recherche et d'Information Socio-Politique, 1965.

Vines, Alex. *Renamo: Terrorism in Mozambique*. Centre for Southern African Studies, University of York, 1991.

Walton, John. *Reluctant Rebels; Comparative Studies of Revolution and Underdevelopment*. New York: Columbia University Press, 1984.

Weiss, Herbert. *Political Protest in the Congo: The Parti Solidaire Africaine during the Independence Struggle*. Princeton: Princeton University Press, 1967.

Welch, Jr., Claude E. *Anatomy of Rebellion*. Albany: State University Press of New York, 1980.

Welch, Jr., Claude E. (ed.). *Soldier and State in Africa*. Evanston, Illinois: Northwestern University Press, 1970.

Wolf, Eric R. *Peasant Wars of the Twentieth Century*. New York: Harper & Row, 1969.

Young, Crawford. *Politics in the Congo*. Princeton: Princeton University Press, 1965.

ARTICLES AND MONOGRAPHS

Abreu, Paradela de. 'Interview with Evo Fernandes', *Jornal de O Dia* (Lisbon), 24, 27 December 1984, 2, 13–14.

Alexiev, Alexander R. *Marxism and Resistance in the Third World*. Santa Monica, California: The Rand Corporation, April 1988.

Allen, Tim. 'Understanding Alice: Uganda's Holy Spirit Movement in Context', *Africa*, Vol. 61, no. 3 (1991), 370–399.

Almeida, M. Martins de. 'Interview with Manuel Frank', *Jornal de O Dia* (Lisbon), 15 July 1989, 4–5.

Anonymous. 'Liberia: Taylor's one-man band', *Africa Confidential* (London), Vol. 31, no. 15, 27 July 1990, p. 5

Anonymous. 'Fumo declares support for Renamo; U.S. Policy Criticized', *O Diabo* (Lisbon), 30 December 1986, p. 17.

Anonymous. 'Captured MNR bandit describes Camp in Zomba Malawi', *Sunday Mail* (Harare), 21 December 1986, p. 2.

Anonymous. 'Interview with Prime Minister Mario Machungo', *Financial Mail*, (Johannesburg), 12 December 1986, pp. 34–35.

Anonymous. 'War Aid for Mozambique: British Spit and Polish', *New York Times*, 12 May 1986, p. 18.

Anonymous. 'Interview with Evo Fernandes', *Journal of Defense and Diplomacy*, Vol. 3, no. 9 (1985), 46–49.

Anonymous. 'Interview with Afonso Dhlakama', *International Herald Tribune*, 14 September 1983.

Anonymous. Several articles on the war in Mozambique were published in *Africa Confidential* (London) including Vol. 24, 21 June 1982, pp. 1–5, Vol. 27, 30 January 1985, pp. 4–7, Vol. 30, 23 June 1989, pp. 1–3.

Anonymous. 'L'Insurrection malgache', *Bulletin des Missions* (Abbaye des Saint Andrés-les Bruges), Vol. XXIV (1950–1951), 157–171, 255–276.

Arms Control and Disarmament Agency. *World Military Expenditures and Arms Transfers, 1990.* Washington, DC: US Government Printing Office, 1991.

Atieno-Odhiambo, E.S. 'The Production of History in Kenya: The Mau Mau Debate', *Canadian Journal of African Studies*, Vol. 25, no. 2 (1991), 300–307.

Beckett, Ian F. W. 'The Portuguese Army: the Campaign in Mozambique, 1964–1974', in *Armed Forces in Modern Counter-Insurgency*, edited by Ian F. W. Beckett and John Pimlott. New York: St. Martin's Press, 1985, 136–162.

Behn, Sharon. 'The Unknown Side', *Africa Events*, May 1987, pp. 24–26.

Behrend, Heike. 'Is Alice Lakwena a Witch? The Holy Spirit Movement and its fight against evil in the north', in *Changing Uganda; The Dilemmas of Social Adjustment and Revolutionary Change*, edited by Holger Bernt Hansen and Michael Twaddle. London: James Currey, 1991, pp. 162–177.

Berman, Bruce J. 'Nationalism, Ethnicity, and Modernity: The Paradox of Mau Mau', *Canadian Journal of African Studies*, Vol. 25, no. 2 (1991), 181–206.

Bridgeland, Fred. 'Savimbi's Respect for Indigenous Customs "Secret of Success", *Diamond Fields Advertiser* (Kimberley, South Africa), 2 October 1984, p. A2.

Brooke, James. 'Guinea-Bissau Tries to Deprogram a Popular Cult', *New York Times*, 3 January 1988, p. 10.

C., J. M. 'Renamo Discredited in the West', *Expresso* (International), 8 November 1986, p. VII.

Cammack, Diana. 'The 'Human Face' of Destabilization: The War in Mozambique', *Review of African Poltical Economy*, no. 40 (1987), 65–75.

Campbell, Kurt M. 'Southern Africa in Soviet Foreign Policy', *Adelphi Papers*, no. 227. London: International Institute for Strategic Studies, 1987/1988.

Cesar, Antonio. 'Interviews with captured Renamo cadre', A series of six articles appearing in *Diario de Mocambique* (Beira), 27–29 December 1984 and 3–5 January 1985.

Chabal, Patrick. 'Some reflections on the post-colonial state in Portuguese-speaking Africa', *Africa Insight*, vol. 23, no. 3 (1993), 129–135.

Chem-Langhee, Bongfen and Martin Z. Njeuma. 'The Pan Kamerun Movement, 1949–1961', in *An African Experiment in Nation Building: The Bilingual Cameroon Republic Since Reunification*, edited by Ndiva Kofele-Kale. Boulder, Colorado: Westview Press, 1980, pp. 25–64.

Claiborne, William. 'West Eyes Arms for Mozambique', *Washington Post*, 24 January 1988, p. A22.

Cleary, A.S. 'The Myth of Mau Mau in its International Context', *African Affairs*, Vol. 89, no. 355 (1990), 227–245.

Cline, Sybil. 'Forgotten Freedom Fighters', *Soldier of Fortune*, January 1990, 30–39, 88.

Clough, Marshall S. and Kennell A. Jackson, Jr. *A Bibliography on Mau Mau.* California: Stanford University, 1975.

Darch, Colin. 'Are there Warlords in Provincial Mozambique? Questions of the Social Base of MNR Banditry', *Review of African Political Economy*, no. 45/46 (1989), 34–49.

Defense, Department of. *Soviet Military Power.* Washington, DC: Department of Defense, 1986.

Erskine, Emmanuel A. Lt. Gen. (Ret.), Brigadier B. L. Kapoor (Ret.), and Lt. Col. Richard Augustus Norton. *Peace, Security, and Humanitarian Relief in Northern Mozambique.* New York: International Peace Academy, 1987.

Fauvet, Paul. 'Roots of Counterrevolution: The Mozambique National Resistance', *Review of African Political Economy*, no. 29 (1984), 108–121.

Finnegan, William. 'A Reporter At Large', *New Yorker*, Part I, 22 May 1990, 43–76 and Part II, 29 May 1990, 69–96.

Fox, Renee C., Willy de Craemer and Jean-Marie Ribeaucourt. 'The "Second Independence": Study of the Kwilu Rebellion in the Congo', *Comparative Studies in Society and History*, Vol. 8, no. 1 (1965), 78–109.

Gersony, Robert. *Summary of Mozambican Refugee Accounts of Principally Conflict-Related Experience in Mozambique.* Washington, DC: Bureau of Refugee Programs, Department of State, 1988.

Gordge, John T. 'The Outlook for Madagascar', *African Affairs*, Vol. 48, no. 191 (1949), 133–141.

Gouws, Piet. 'Renamo's Long Path of Struggle, Strife and More Success', *Beeld* (Johannesburg), 6 and 8 November 1984.

Gravel, Pierre Bettez. 'Of Bandits and Pirates: An Essay on the Vicarious Insurgency of Peasants', *Journal of Political and Military Sociology*, Vol. 13 (1985), 209–217.

Grilz, Almerigo. 'Rebels of Mozambique', *Jane's Defence Weekly*, 12 July 1986, 20–22.

Gunn, Gillian. 'The Chissano Era – Mozambique comes to terms with itself', *Africa Insight*, Vol. 19, no 1 (1989), 16–20.

Hall, Margaret. 'The Mozambican National Resistance Movement (Renamo): A Study in the Destruction of an African Country', *Africa*, Vol. 60, no. 1 (1990), 39–68.

Heather, Randall W. 'Intelligence and Counter-Insurgency in Kenya, 1952–1956', *Intelligence and National Security*, Vol. 5, no. 3 (1990), 57–83.

Hobsbawm, E. J. 'Social Banditry', in *Rural Protest: Peasant Movements and Social Change*, edited by Henry A. Landsberger. London: Macmillan, 1974, pp. 142–157.

Howe, Herbert and Marina Ottaway. 'State Power Consolidation in Mozambique', in *Afro-Marxist Regimes: Ideology and Public Policy*, edited by Edmond J. Keller and Donald Rothchild. London: Lynne Rienner, 1987, pp. 43–65.

Huxley, Elspeth. 'The Cause and Cure of Mau Mau', *New Commonwealth*, Vol. 27, 18 January 1954, 62–64.

Jaster, Robert S. 'The Security Outlook in Mozambique', *Survival*, Vol. XXVII, no. 6 (1985), 258–263.

Jenson, Holger. 'Resistance Chief Plans Diplomatic Offensive', *Washington Times*, 17 December 1986, pp. 1A, 6A.

Job, Roger. 'Mozambique: The War without a Name', *Le Soir* (Brussels), 30 and 31 January and 1 February 1990.

Johnson, Willard. 'The Union des Population du Cameroun in Rebellion: The Integrative Backlash of Insurgency', in *Protest and Power in Black Africa*, edited by Robert I. Rotberg and Ali A. Mazrui. New York: Oxford University Press, 1970, pp. 671–692.

Joseph, Richard A. 'Ruben Um Nyobe and the "Kamerun" Rebellion', *African Affairs*, Vol. 73, no. 293 (1974), 428–448.

Jowitt, Ken. 'The New World Disorder', *Journal of Democracy*, Vol. 20, no. 1 (1991), 11–20.

Legum, Colin. 'The MNR', *CSIS Africa Notes*, no. 16, 15 July 1983.

Legum, Colin and John Drysdale. 'Congo Democratic Republic (Kinshasa)', *Africa Contemporary Record, Annual Survey and Documents 1968–1969*. London: Africa Research Limited, 1969, pp. 441–445.

Lonsdale, John. 'Mau Maus of the Mind: Making Mau Mau and Remaking Kenya', *Journal of African History*, Vol. 31 (1990), 393–421.

Maier, Karl. 'A Traditional Revival', *Africa Report*, July–August 1991, pp. 64–67.

Maier, Karl. 'Healer in Mozambique Leads Attack on Rebels', *Washington Post*, 4 August 1990, 19.

Maier, Karl. 'The Battle for Zambezia', *Africa Report*, March–April, 1989, 13–16.

Melo, Richardo de. Untitled article about Renamo in *Sunday Times* (Johannesburg), 27 May 1986, p. 18.

Minter, William. *The Mozambican National Resistance as described by ex-participants*. Washington, DC: Georgetown University Press, 1989.

Moorcraft, Paul. 'The Savage, Silent Civil War', *Army*, April 1987, 42–52.

Moorcraft, Paul. Untitled article about Renamo in *Sunday Times* (Johannesburg), 30 November 1986, pp. 23 and 25.

Morgan, Glenda. 'Violence in Mozambique: Towards an Understanding of Renamo', *Journal of Modern African Studies*, Vol. 28, no. 4 (1990), 603–619.

Nesbitt, Prexy. 'Terminators, Crusaders, and Gladiators: Western (private & public) Support for Renamo and Unita', *Review of African Political Economy*, no. 43 (1988), 111–124.

Newsinger, John. 'A counter-insurgency tale: Kitson in Kenya', *Race and Class*, Vol. 31, no. 4 (1990), 61–72.

Nilsson, Anders. 'From Pseudo-Terrorists to Pseudo-Guerrillas: the MNR in Mozambique (Part I)', *Review of African Political Economy*, no. 57 (1993), 60–71.

Nilsson, Anders. 'From Pseudo-Terrorists to Pseudo-Guerrillas: the MNR in Mozambique (Part II)', *Review of African Political Economy*, no. 58 (1993), 34–42.

Ofcansky, Thomas P. 'The Mau Mau Revolt in Kenya, 1952–1960; A Preliminary Bibliography', *Africana Journal*, Vol. 15 (1990), 97–126.

Ottaway, David. 'Mozambican Describes Detention by Rebels', *Washington Post*, 25 May 1992, p. A21.

Ottoway, David. 'ANC vs. Inkatha: Anatomy of a Slaughter', *Washington Post*, 2 May 1991, pp. 21 and 28.

Pear, Robert with James Brook. 'Rightists in U.S. Aid Mozambique Rebels', *New York Times*, 22 May 1988, pp. 1 and 14.

Perinbam, B. Marie. 'Fanon and the Revolutionary Peasantry – The Algerian Case', *Journal of Modern African Studies*, Vol. 11, no. 3 (1973), 427–445.

Ranger, Terence. 'Bandits and Guerrillas: the case of Zimbabwe', in *Banditry, Rebellion and Social Protest in Africa*, edited by Donald Crummey. London: James Currey, 1986, 373–396.

Ranger, Terence. 'Connexions between "Primary Resistance" Movements and Modern Mass Nationalism in East and Central Africa. Part I', *Journal of African History*, Vol. IX, no. 3 (1968), 437–453.

Ranger, Terence. 'Connexions between "Primary Resistance" Movements and Modern Mass Nationalism in East and Central Africa. Part II', *Journal of African History*, Vol. IX, no. 4 (1968), 631–641.

Renamo. *Newsbulletin*, no. 14, January 1988. Washington, DC: Department of Information, National Resistance of Mozambique.

Renamo. *A Luta Continua* (Lisbon). Occasional publication printed in Portugal throughout the 1980s.

Roberts, Andrew. 'Mozambique Pique', *The American Spectator*, Vol. 25, no. 3, (1992), 48–49.

Roesch, Otto. 'Renamo and the Peasantry in Southern Mozambique: A View from Gaza Province', *Canadian Journal of African Studies*, Vol. 26, no. 3 (1992), 462–484.

Saul, John S. 'Development and Counterdevelopment Strategies in Mozambique', in Keller and Rothchild.

Schneidman, Witney. 'Conflict Resolution in Mozambique: A Status Report', *CSIS Africa Notes*, no. 121, 28 February 1991.

Seegers, Annette. 'From Liberation to Modernization: Transforming Revolutionary Paramilitary Forces into Standing Professional Armies', in *African Armies: Evolution and Capabilities*, edited by Bruce E. Arlinghaus and Pauline Baker. Boulder, Colorado: Westview Press, 1986, 52–83.

Seegers, Annette. 'Revolutionary Armies of Africa: Mozambique and Zimbabwe', in *Military Power and Politics in Black Africa*, edited by Simon Baynham. New York: St. Martins Press, 1986, 129–165.

Turner, Thomas. 'Congo-Kinshasa', in *The Politics of Cultural Sub-Nationalism*, edited by Victor A. Olorunsola. Garden City: Doubleday, 1972, 195–283.

United States Institute of Peace. *Conflict and Conflict Resolution in Mozambique*. Washington, DC: United States Institute of Peace, April 1993.

Verhaegen, Benoit. 'La rébellion muleliste au Kwilu: chronologie des événements et essai d'interprétation (janvier 1962–juillet 1964)', in *Rébellion-Révolution au Zaire, 1963–1965, Tome 1*, edited by Catherine Coquery-Vidrovitch, Alain Forest, and Herbert Weiss. Paris: Harmattan Editions, 1987, pp. 120–167.

Verhaegen, Benoit. 'Le rôle de l'ethnie et de l'individu dans la rébellion du Kwilu et dans son echec', in *Rébellion-Révolution au Zaire, 1963–1965, Tome 1*, edited by Catherine Coquery-Vidrovitch, Alain Forest, and Herbert Weiss. Paris: Harmattan Editions, 1987, 147–167.

Vines, Alex. 'Diary', *Southern African Review of Books*, July–October 1991, pp. 31–32.

Vonnegut, Kurt. 'My Visit to Hell', *Washington Post*, Parade Magazine, 7 January 1990, pp. 16–17

Weiss, Herbert and Adrienne Fulco. 'Les partisans au Kwilu: analyse des origines sociales des membres et cadres des équipes de base', *Rébellion-Révolution au Zaire, 1963–1965, Tome 1*, edited by Catherine Coquery-Vidrovitch, Alain Forest, and Herbert Weiss. Paris: Harmattan Editions, 1987, pp. 168–181.

Welch, Jr., Claude E. 'Ideological Foundations of Revolution in Kwilu', *African Studies Review*, Vol. 18, no. 2 (1975) 116–128.

Welch, Jr. Claude E. 'Obstacles to Peasant Warfare in Africa', *African Studies Review*, Vol. 20, no. 3 (1977), 121–130.

Wheeler, Jack. 'Renamo: Winning One in Africa', *Soldier of Fortune*, February 1986, 64–69, 117–118.

Willame, Jean-Claude. 'Congo-Kinshasa: General Mobutu and Two Political Generations', in *Soldier and State in Africa*, edited by Claude E. Welch, Jr. Evanston, Illinois: Northwestern University Press, 1970, pp. 124–151.

Wilson, K. B. 'Cults of Violence and Counter-Violence in Mozambique', *Journal of Southern African Studies*, Vol. 18, no. 3 (1992), 527–582.

Wren, Christopher S. 'Pretoria Aids Mozambique's Military', *New York Times*, 30 November 1988, A3

Young, Crawford M. 'Rebellion and the Congo', in *Protest and Power in Black Africa*, edited by Robert I. Rotberg and Ali A. Mazrui. New York: Oxford University Press, 1970, 968–1011.

Young, Crawford M. 'Congo-Kinshasa Situation Report', *Africa Report*, Vol. 12, no. 7 (1967), 12–18.

Young, Tom. 'The MNR/RENAMO: External and Internal Dynamics', *African Affairs*, Vol. 89, no. 357 (1990), 491–509.

ARCHIVES

National Archives. Washington, DC *Record Group 59*. General Records of the Department of State. Despatch no. 332, American Consulate Tananarive, Madagascar, 31 March 1947. RG 59, 851 W.00/3-3147.

Despatch no. 349, American Consulate, Tananarive, Madagascar, 22 April 1947. RG 59, 851 W.00/4-2247.

Despatch no. 351, American Consulate, Tananarive, Madagascar, 30 April 1947. RG 851 W.00/4-3047.

Despatch no. 401, American Consulate, Tananarive, Madagascar, 5 July 1947, enclosure no. 1. RG 59, 851 W.00/7-547.

Despatch no. 414, American Consulate, Tananarive, Madagascar, 18 July 1947. RG 59, 851 W.00/7-1847.

Despatch no. 425, American Consulate, Tananarive, Madagascar, 1 August 1947. RG 59, 851 W.00/8-147.

Despatch no. 434, American Consulate, Tananarive, Madagascar, 9 August 1947. RG 59, 851 W.00/8-947.

Despatch no. 439, American Consulate, Tananarive, Madagascar, 16 August 1947. RG 59, 851 W.00/8-1647.

Despatch no. 495, American Consulate, Tananarive, Madagascar, 15 November 1947. RG 59, 851 W.00/11-1547.

Despatch no. 12, American Consulate, Tananarive, Madagascar, 17 January 1948. RG 59, 851 W.00/1-1748.

Despatch no. 74, American Consulate, Tananarive, Madagascar, 8 April 1948. RG 59, 851 W.00/4-848.

Despatch no. 83, American Consulate, Tananarive, Madagascar, 20 April 1948. RG 59, 851 W.00/4-2048.

Despatch no. 164, American Consulate, Tananarive, Madagascar, 7 September 1948. RG 59, 851 W.009-748.

Despatch no. 221, American Consulate, Tananarive, Madagascar, 8 December 1948. RG 59, 851 W.00/12-848.

Index

Aberdare Mountains 28, 31
Abo (Cameroonian secret society)
    46
Abo, Leonie 63
Accra 42
Action Socialiste 49
Adoula, Cyril 52
Afghanistan 4, 8
Africa Livre 71
African National Congress (ANC)
    70, 86, 101, 103
Ahidjou, Ahmadou 42–3, 45–6
Alahamady (month of) 15
aldeamento (strategic hamlet) 83
Algeria 4, 21, 44–5
Alliance des Bakongo (Abako) 51
Andrianampoinimerina, King 14
Angola 4, 47, 65–6, 73, 95, 98,
    102
Antonio, Manuel 93–4
Armée de Liberation Nationale
    Kamerunaise (ALNK) 41–3,
    46–7

BaDinga 60, 63
BaLori 60
BaLuhya 28
Bambala 60, 62
Bambunda 62–3
Bamileke 37–8, 40–3, 45–6, 116 n.8
BaNkutsu 60
Bapende 60, 62, 118 n.12
BashiLele 60
Basotho 101
Bassa 37, 39–41, 43, 45–7, 116 n.8
BaSuku 60
BaWongo 60
BaYanzi 60
Beira 'Corridor' 88, 92
Belgium 49–50, 52, 65
Ben Bella 4
Bene Simon (People of Simon) sect
    52
Betsileo 13

Betsimisaraka 11
Botswana 101
Boxer Rebellion 8
British Cameroons 37, 39–40, 44
Burma 29

Cabora Bassa 82
Cabral, Amilcar 97, 132 n.6
Cairo 40–1, 44, 55, 67
Cameroon 3–4, 36, 40, 42–3, 45–7
Cameroonian Peoples Union (UPC)
    36–48, 99, 122 n.57
Central Intelligence Organization
    (CIO) 70, 73, 92
Chad 40, 95
Chaliand, Gerard 7
China 8, 44–5, 55–6, 66, 70
Christianity 105
Cold War 1, 36
Communism 103
Conakry 41, 44
Congo-Brazzaville 43–5, 50, 63,
    65–6
Congo/Zaire 3–5, 48, 58–9, 63–4,
    79, 104–5
Congolese National Army (ANC)
    57, 60–3, 65
Christina, Orlando 73
Cuba 43, 101
curandeiro (traditional healer) 76,
    80, 93, 131 n.72
Czechoslovakia 44

Dakar 36
Davidson, Basil 7
de Gaulle, General Charles 9
Democratic Movement for the
    Malagasy Renovation (MDRM)
    9–14, 18, 20–1, 23
Dhlakama, Afonso 74, 77, 80, 85–6,
    90, 93–4
Diego Suarez 12
dos Santos, Marcelino 68
Douala 36, 38–43, 46

Egypt 40
Embu 27
England 22–3, 34, 36, 88
Erskine, General Sir George 31
Ethiopia 34
evolués 19
Ewondo Maka 45

fanjakana (territorial unit) 16
Fanon, Franz 97
Farafangana 12, 108 n.10
Fernandes, Evo 73, 75–6, 94–5
feiticeiros (spirit-mediums) 76, 79,
    104, 131 n.72
Fianarantsoa-Manakara rail line 17
flechas (Portuguese trained
    commando force) 79, 126 n.12
Flower, Ken 73, 124 n.12
fokonolona (village council) 15–16,
    19, 104, 109 n.19
Force Publique 58
France 8–10, 12, 14, 17, 21, 36
Frente de Cabo Delgado (FCD) 71
Front for the Liberation of
    Mozambique (FRELIMO) 5–7,
    67–8, 70, 72–6, 78, 83, 94, 98
Fusiliers, Royal Northumberland and
    Inniskilling, Lancashire 31

Garbey, Brigadier General 17
Geneva 43
Germany 14, 37
Gizenga, Antoine 49, 51, 54
Gorongosa 81
Great Britain 20
Guevara, Che 107 n.4
Guinea 41, 44–5, 50
Guinea, Portuguese 47
Gumane, Paulo 67–8
Gungu 60, 63
Gwambe, Adelino 67–8

Harare 91
Hind, Major General 31
Ho Chi Minh 4, 7, 21, 39, 67
Hodgkin, Thomas 6
Holy Spirit Movement (HSM) 103,
    135 n.19
Holy War 1

Idiofa 60–1, 63
Indochina 21
Islam 105
Italy 14

'jeunesse' (Congolese youth
    movement) 54
Jeunesse Nationaliste Malgache (Jina)
    9, 13–15, 99, 104, 109 n.13
Jihad 105
Jonathon, Leabua 101

Kamba 25, 28
Kamitatu, Cleophas 53–5
Kandaka, Damien 62, 120 n.49
Kasai Province 51–2, 65
Kasavubu, President Joseph 51–2, 65
Katanga Province 51–2, 61, 65
Kaunda, Kenneth 68
Kavandame, Lazaro 71
Kenya 3–5, 21, 23, 31, 33–4, 36,
    46–7, 50, 79, 104–5
Kenya African Union (KAU) 23–4,
    26–7
Kenya Defense Council 28–9
Kenya Parliament 32, 113 n.33
Kenya Riigi 32
Kenyatta, Jomo 23, 26, 34
Kikuyu (tribe) 24–5, 27, 35, 99, 112
    n.20
Kikuyu Central Association (KCA)
    22–4, 26–7, 111 n.3
Kikuyu War Council 27
Kikwit 50, 60
Kimathi, Dedan 28–9, 33
Kimbangu, Simon 52–3
Kimpata Eku 60
Kinge 50
Kings African Rifles 31
Kingue, Abel 36, 39
Kipsigis 28
Kumba 39–40, 43
Kumsze (Douala self-help
    association) 37, 45
Kwango 49–50
Kwilu 49–50, 52–66, 72, 93, 99

Lari 28
Lenin 7–8

Lesotho Liberation Army (LLA)
  101
Limpopo 'corridors' 92
Lingala 59
Lisbon 72–3, 79
London 26, 31
Lords Resistance Army 103
Lumumba, Patrice 51, 55, 59, 64,
  72
Luo 28
Lusaka 68–9

Maasai 28
Mabunda, David 67
Machava (barracks revolt) 71
Machel, Samora 68
Macua 93
Madagascar 3, 5, 9–10, 14, 19–21,
  29, 31, 33, 36, 46–7, 50, 79,
  104–5
Magaia, Felipe 71
Mahluza, Fanuel 67–8, 72, 75
'Maji Maji' 17
Majunga 17
Makonde 68
Malawi 69, 89, 91
Mali 45
Manakara 12, 108 n.10
Manende 16
Mao Tse-tung 4, 7–8, 38–9, 67
Maoist-Leninist (precepts of guerrilla
  warfare) 7, 55, 58
Maputo 71–75, 81–3, 89
Maquis 14
Maseru 101
Massaga, Woungli 43
Matip, Theodore Mayi 40, 47
Matsangaisse, André 74, 79–81, 93
Mau Mau 22, 24–5, 27–35, 67, 79,
  96, 99, 104, 111 n.5, 115 n.53
Mbida, André Marie 39–40
menalamba (red shawl) 15
Merina 11, 13, 15
Meru 27
Middle East 1
Mobutu, General 60, 63, 96
Momo, Paul 41–42
Mondlane, Eduardo 68, 72, 81
Moromanga 12

Moumie, Felix 36, 38–41, 43, 116
  n.16
Moungo 40, 42
Mozambican Armed Forces (FAM)
  71, 74, 77, 82–3, 88, 94
Mozambican National Union
  (UNAMO) 93–4
Mozambique 4–5, 67–81, 84–91,
  93, 95, 105
Mozambique African National Union
  (MANU) 68–9
Mpeve (Spirit) sect 52–4, 99, 118
  n.12
Mugabe, Robert 70
mujahedin 8
Mulele, Pierre 49, 54–68, 72, 80, 96,
  102, 119 n.34, n.35
mundo mugo wa ita 29–30

Nacala 88–89
Nairobi 28, 31, 35, 72
Naivasha 24–5, 28
Namibia 47
'Naprama' 93–4, 131 n.72
Nasser, Gamal 44
National Coalition Party (PCN) 69
National Democratic Union of
  Mozambique (UDENAMO)
  67–9, 75
National Liberation Council (CNL)
  59
National Patriotic Front of Liberia
  (NPFL) 103, 136 n.19
National Resistance of Mozambique
  (RENAMO) 4–8, 69–95,
  98–99, 102–3
National Union for the Total
  Independence of Angola
  (UNITA) 98, 102
Ndau 74, 80–1
Ndebele 101–2
nganga (traditional healer) 59
Ngondo (Bamileke association) 37
Nicaragua 4
Nigeria 39
N'komati Accord 86, 88–9
Nkrumah, Kwame 55
North Korea 101
North Vietnam 44

Ofana, Ossande 43
Oliveira, Paulo 73
Oman 89
Operation 'Anvil' 31
Operation 'Dante' 32
Operation 'First Flute' 32
Operation 'Hammer' 31
Ouandie, Ernest 36, 39, 43

Paris 10–11, 17, 20, 40
Parti des Désherités de Madagascar
    (PADESM) 12
Parti Nationaliste Malgache
    (PANAMA) 9–10, 14–15, 99
Parti Solidaire Africain (PSA)
    49–51, 53–5
Partido Africano da Independénçia da
    Guiné e Cabo Verde (PAIGC)
    97
Party of the Restoration of Malgache
    Independence (PRIM) 107–8
    n.1
Pellet, Lt.-General 17
Phiri, Jimo 93
Popular Movement for the Liberation
    of Angola (MPLA) 66, 73, 122
    n.57
Portugal 67, 69
Prague 55
Pretoria 7, 86–7, 102
'pseudo-gangs' 32, 126 n.34

Quelimane 88

Rabemanenjara, Jacques 10–11
Radaoroson, Michel 13, 18
Rakotondrabe, Samuel 13
Raseta, Joseph 10–12, 20, 108 n.7
Ratsimalah 16
Ravoahangy, Joseph 10–11, 108 n.7
Razafindrabe, Victorien 13, 18
regulo 76
Revolutionary Committee of
    Mozambique (COREMO)
    68–9, 72
Revolutionary Party of Mozambique
    (PRM) 69, 71
Rhodesia 4–5, 49, 69–70, 73–4, 79,
    85, 97, 99–100

Rome (Mozambican peace accord)
    92, 98
Rumbezi African National Union
    (UNAR) 69, 71
Russia 4

Salazar, Antonio 65
Sanaga Maritime Region 37, 40, 42
Saudi Arabia 89
Savimbi, Jonas 133 n.7
Savoir Vivre (Art of Living) 52–4,
    56, 59, 99
Shangaan 68
Shona 81, 101–2
Simango, Uria T. 67–9, 123 n.11
Singap, Martin 41–2
Smith, Ian 97
Stanleyville 51
Sorbonne 11
South Africa 71, 74, 77, 79, 82,
    85–9, 91–2, 100–2
South African Defense Force (SADF)
    5, 85, 87–8
Southern Africa 4, 5–7, 69, 86, 101–2
Southeast Asia 21
Soviet Bloc 4, 51
Soviet Union 8, 44, 51, 91, 101
Soweto 103
Sudan 66, 95
Sumane, Amos 68–9
'Super Zanu' 101–2
Swaziland 91

'talking serpent' sect 58
Tamatave 13, 17
Tananarive 11–12, 17–18
Tanganyika 16
Tanzania 66, 70, 91
Tanzania Peoples Defense Force
    (TPDF) 88, 91
Tete Province 81
Tiraileurs (Algerian, Moroccan,
    Senegalese and Somali) 17
Touré, Sékou 41, 44
Tronchon, Jacques 19

Uganda 66, 95
Um Nkoda Nton (Cameroonian secret
    society) 47

Um Nyobe, Ruben 36, 38–41, 44–7, 80

Union Camerounaise 46

Union des Population du Cameroun, *see* Cameroonian Peoples Union (UPC)

United Democratic Front of Mozambique (FUMO) 72

United Nations 36, 44

United States 20, 65

USSR 44

Vendée 8

Vichy 9

Vietnam 4

Vilankulu, Artur 72

Voz da Africa Livre 84–5, 87

Vy Vato Sakelika (VVS – Iron and Stone) 108 n.7

Yaounde 38–9, 41–2, 46

Zaire 96

Zambezia Province 71, 80, 94

Zambezi River 82, 88, 94

Zambia 66, 70, 88

Zimbabwe 47, 49, 85, 88, 91, 101–2

Zimbabwean African National Union (ZANU) 70, 97

Zimbabwean African Peoples Union (ZAPU) 101

Zimbabwean National Army (ZNA) 88, 91–2

Zulu (spirits) 81